Finance, Technology, and Sustainability for Sustainable Innovation

Parvez Alam Khan
https://orcid.org/0000-0001-8200-2461
Universiti Teknologi PETRONAS, Malaysia

Satirenjit Kaur Johl
Universiti Teknologi PETRONAS, Malaysia

Lawrence Arokiasamy
Universiti Teknologi PETRONAS, Malaysia

Nasir Abdul Jalil
Universiti Teknologi PETRONAS, Malaysia

Mohd Salim
https://orcid.org/0000-0003-0162-8433
Aligrah Muslim University, India

IGI Global
Scientific Publishing
Publishing Tomorrow's Research Today

Vice President of Editorial Melissa Wagner
Director of Acquisitions Mikaela Felty
Director of Book Development Jocelynn Hessler
Production Manager Mike Brehm
Cover Design Jose Rosado

Published in the United States of America by
IGI Global Scientific Publishing
701 East Chocolate Avenue
Hershey, PA, 17033, USA
Tel: 717-533-8845 | Fax: 717-533-7115
Website: https://www.igi-global.com E-mail: cust@igi-global.com

Library of Congress Cataloging-in-Publication Data

(CIP Data Pending)
ISBN13: 979-8-3693-6195-5
Isbn13Softcover: 979-8-3693-6196-2
EISBN13: 979-8-3693-6197-9

British Cataloguing in Publication Data
A Cataloguing in Publication record for this book is available from the British Library.

Table of Contents

Detailed Table of Contents

With investors' interest in environmental sustainability growing, sustainability practices and development have taken on significant importance within organizations. This chapter describes how using green investments can help businesses adopt sustainable business practices. The chapter is based on descriptive study and primarily used the secondary sources of data. The data is primarily supported by credible, previously published works, such as journal articles and working papers. The primary focus is placed on the importance of green investment in sustainable business practices. The findings demonstrated that green investment plays an integral role while doing the sustainable business. It has also been found that many companies in India are engaged in sustainable business activities through numerous large-scale projects. The study looks at the green and sustainable business and its involvement to sustainable development. All the green and sustainable measures have specific application areas identified by the study, particularly in the banking and finance industries.

Financial inclusion is vital for the prosperity of any economy. Technology has paved the way for a new system of banking, known as Fintech. Mobile banking and mobile payments are the new normal. Keeping in mind this wide usage of fintech mobile payment systems in India, this research paper analyzes the growth of mobile payments for financial inclusion. This study examines and assesses the role of Government Initiatives India stack in financial inclusion. The growth of mobile payments in India is examined by using secondary data. This paper also examines the future Strategies of Fintech mobile payment companies.

This study investigates the perceived readiness for technological change among rural entrepreneurs operating in the traditional food sector. A total of 14 entrepreneurs were selected as respondents for interviews to gather critical data. The sample selection considered various demographic factors such as business type, business experience, and the unique traditional food products offered by each entrepreneur. The study results reveal a range of opinions and readiness levels among respondents. Some entrepreneurs demonstrate a positive and open attitude towards technology use, seeing it as a tool to enhance operational efficiency and reach a wider market. Conversely, some respondent's express doubts about technology's ability to integrate the values and uniqueness of their traditional food products. The findings of this study offer valuable insights for stakeholders in the traditional food industry to design interventions or programs suitable for enhancing the readiness and capabilities of rural entrepreneurs in technology adoption.

Preface

INTRODUCTION

The growing urgency of environmental degradation, social inequality, and economic uncertainty has intensified scholarly and policy interest in the interconnected roles of finance, technology, and sustainability in shaping pathways toward sustainable innovation. Financial systems today are no longer assessed solely by efficiency or profitability; they are increasingly evaluated by their capacity to promote inclusive growth, support technological transformation, and address environmental and social challenges. In parallel, rapid advances in digital technologies, including fintech, blockchain, artificial intelligence, and data-driven platforms, are transforming the design and implementation of financial services, business models, and sustainability initiatives. This edited volume, *Finance, Technology, and Sustainability for Sustainable Innovation*, brings together contemporary research that critically examines these intersections across diverse contexts.

The volume begins by establishing the conceptual and theoretical foundations of sustainable finance and financial inclusion. Early contributions explore the concept of green finance, its definitions, scope, and benefits, positioning it as a critical mechanism for supporting environmentally responsible economic activities. This foundation is strengthened through examinations of corporate social responsibility and firm performance, with particular attention given to mediating and moderating mechanisms that shape organizational outcomes. Theoretical perspectives on financial inclusion as a public good further underscore its broader societal and developmental significance.

Building on these foundations, the book proceeds to analyze green investment and digital financial innovation as enablers of sustainable business practices. Several chapters investigate how green investments, fintech solutions, mobile payments, and digital finance ecosystems enhance financial inclusion, align business strategies with sustainability objectives, and promote ethical financial behavior. These contributions demonstrate how technology-driven financial innovations can reduce access barriers, improve transparency, and support sustainable development, particularly within emerging and developing economies.

The volume further explores the transformative potential of blockchain and decentralized financial technologies. Contributions examine blockchain-driven efficiency in banking systems, the role of artificial intelligence in decentralized finance, and the application of smart contracts in enabling secure and transparent transactions. Attention is also given to future system resilience through discussions on quantum-resistant blockchain frameworks, highlighting the importance of technological preparedness for sustainable financial infrastructures.

Recognizing that sustainable innovation extends beyond financial and technological systems, the book also emphasizes organizational, human, and knowledge-based dimensions. Chapters addressing organizational green technology innovation, self-leadership and creativity in information technology, and the role of tacit knowledge among technopreneurs illustrate how leadership, human capital, and institutional capabilities influence sustainability outcomes. Issues of governance, inclusivity, and technological readiness are further examined through analyses of women's representation on corporate boards and the preparedness of rural micro and small enterprises for technological change.

The scope of the volume is broadened through applied and sector-specific sustainability perspectives. Industry-focused research illustrates how waste can be transformed into a competitive advantage through recycled materials, demonstrating the commercial viability of sustainability-oriented innovation. Environmental assessments offer empirical insights into forest carbon measurement and natural resource stewardship, underscoring the importance of scientific evaluation in addressing climate-related challenges. Complementing these supply-side and institutional perspectives, the book also incorporates a consumer-oriented sustainability lens. A dedicated chapter examines sustainable purchase intentions toward organic food among Generation Z consumers, offering demand-side insights into sustainable consumption behavior and highlighting the influence of values, awareness, and attitudes on environmentally responsible markets.

Collectively, the chapters in this volume reflect a multidisciplinary and international scholarly effort, with contributions from researchers across Asia, Africa, Europe, and North America. The diversity of perspectives, methodological approaches, and sectoral contexts underscores the complexity of sustainable innovation and the necessity of integrated solutions that bridge finance, technology, organizational behavior, environmental management, and consumer studies.

This book is intended to serve as a comprehensive resource for academics, graduate students, practitioners, and policymakers interested in sustainable finance, technological innovation, and sustainability-driven development. By bringing together conceptual insights, empirical evidence, and applied perspectives, the volume aims to advance scholarly discourse, inform policy formulation, and support the development of resilient, inclusive, and sustainable economic systems.

ORGANIZATION OF THE BOOK

Chapter 1: Green Finance: Definitions and Benefits

In recent years, green finance has garnered considerable international interest, establishing itself as a pivotal element in advancing towards a sustainable future and facilitating the shift to an eco-friendly economy. It is instrumental in fostering sustainable development and addressing global warming by mitigating its adverse impacts and enhancing environmental sustainability. This article explores the diverse aspects of green finance, concentrating on its definitions and benefits. It delves into key concepts and principles, emphasizing both the practical and theoretical benefits for companies and investors in a sustainability-focused economy. This analysis aims to offer a thorough understanding of green finance, highlighting its essential role in promoting environmentally sustainable economic growth.

Chapter 2: Public Good Theory of Financial Inclusion

Financial inclusion as a public good can be funded by the state and private firms to ensure that everyone has affordable access to formal financial services. Historically, an economic solution for financial inclusion has been to create public banks and issue banking license to private banks. Today, the solution for financial inclusion lies in offering different types of public and private support to financial service providers to ensure that formal financial services is available and affordable so that everyone can access and use financial services to meet their needs. This paper discusses the necessity of financial inclusion to be considered a public good because financial inclusion is central to successful economic and social development. This article presents a detailed understanding of the public good theory of financial inclusion. It explains the sense in which financial inclusion is a public good and it explores the implications for development policy.

Chapter 3: Relevance of Green Investment to Facilitate the Sustainable Business Practices and Development

This chapter describes how using green investments can help businesses adopt sustainable business practices. The chapter is based on descriptive study and primarily used the secondary sources of data. The data is primarily supported by credible, previously published works, such as journal articles and working papers. The primary focus is placed on the importance of green investment in sustainable business practices. The findings demonstrated that green investment plays an integral role while doing the sustainable business. It has also been found that many companies in India are engaged in sustainable business activities through numerous large-scale projects. The study looks at the green and sustainable business and its involvement to sustainable development. All the green and sustainable measures have specific application areas identified by the study, particularly in the banking and finance industries.

Chapter 4: Technological Innovation: Fintech and Mobile Payments' Role in Financial Inclusion

Financial inclusion is vital for the prosperity of any economy. Technology has paved the way for a new system of banking, known as Fintech. Mobile banking and mobile payments are the new normal. Keeping in mind this wide usage of fintech mobile payment systems in India, this research paper analyzes the growth of mobile payments for financial inclusion. This study examines and assesses the role of Government Initiatives India stack in financial inclusion. The growth of mobile payments in India is examined by using secondary data. This paper also examines the future Strategies of Fintech mobile payment companies.

Chapter 5: Blockchain-Driven Transformation: A Transaction Cost Economics Approach to Banking Efficiency

Chapter 5 uses Transaction Cost Economics (TCE) to examine whether blockchain will lower banking transaction costs. The study's conceptual exploration begins with early institutional economics research. This article will address Blockchain Technology (BcT) and its potential use in the banking industry to reduce information asymmetry and transaction costs. Based on a theoretical model, transaction costs are environmental unpredictability, opportunism, restricted rationality, and contract asset specificity. An example showed how BcT saves money through efficiency and trust. This study proposes a model that captures blockchain's potential influence and the revolution below. Due to scalability, regulatory, and uncertainty issues, the study shows hopeful signs but also constraints. Finally, empirical investigations, comparative evaluations, and futuristic blockchain exploration helps to blockchain banking research by providing a basic explanation and encouraging more study.

Chapter 6: The Critical Role of Tacit Knowledge of Technopreneurs Towards Sustainable Success in the ICT SMEs in Malaysia: A Thematic Survey

This chapter aims to examine the important role of tacit knowledge among ICT technopreneurs in facing the ever-fierce and challenging business and economic situation, especially after the world just came out of Covid-19. A semi-structured interview method was used to collect data from 15 ICT technopreneurs from SMEs in ICT-related industries in Malaysia. This study uses word cloud analysis to get an initial idea of the role of tacit knowledge and employs thematic analysis to extract and visualize data patterns and themes to gain a more informed understanding of the interviews that have been conducted. The findings of the study show that among the important roles of tacit knowledge of technopreneurs are to facilitate the negotiation process, risk taking, decision making, leadership, and strategy development to help ICT technopreneurs to face current business challenges. This study confirms that tacit knowledge is very significant in helping ICT technopreneurs to deal with challenging business situations and in achieving success in the ICT business.

Chapter 7: Sustainable Purchase Intentions Toward Organic Food Evidence from Generation Z Consumers

Organic food industry is an industry that contributes and supports the competitive edge in the framework of the agriculture sector of most of the nations, including Malaysia. The market for organic food is expanding which coupled with the rise of the awareness of consumers for health particularly in the post Covid-19. This can be observed with the earlier research that consumer awareness towards purchasing the eco-friendly and healthy food products is increasing. Research has also shown that the consumers belonging to the Generation Z segment in Malaysia will pay for green products. In order to better understand the sustainable organic food purchase intentions of Generation Z, the present research has two goals. Firstly, it measures the sustainable purchase intentions of Generation Z for organic food, and then it examines the indirect effect of attitude on how health consciousness, environmental concern, and trust for organic labels drive organic food purchase intentions.

Chapter 8: The Influence of Women on Boards on the Nexus between Environmental Performance and Firm Value in Malaysia

This chapter examines the association between environmental performance and firm value in the presence of female directors based on Malaysian context. The present study utilises 74 listed firms on Bursa Malaysia covering 2012-2020. Results obtained from Pool-OLS panel regression analysis reveal that the presence of female directors positively influences the nexus between environmental performance and firm value in Malaysia. This paper contributes not only to academic discourse but also offers practical implications for businesses aiming to enhance their environmental performance, particularly in developing countries like Malaysia. The utilization of Malaysian data provides novel empirical evidence within an emerging market, enhancing our understanding of the intricate relationships between gender diversity, environmental performance, and firm value.

Chapter 9: Perceived Readiness for Technological Change in Rural Micro and Small Enterprises (MSEs) in Peninsular Malaysia's Traditional Food Sector: A Thematic Survey

The final chapter investigates the perceived readiness for technological change among rural entrepreneurs operating in the traditional food sector. A total of 14 entrepreneurs were selected as respondents for interviews to gather critical data. The sample selection considered various demographic factors such as business type, business experience, and the unique traditional food products offered by each entrepreneur. The study results reveal a range of opinions and readiness levels among respondents. Some entrepreneurs demonstrate a positive and open attitude towards technology use, seeing it as a tool to enhance operational efficiency and reach a wider market. Conversely, some respondent's express doubts about technology's ability to integrate the values and uniqueness of their traditional food products. The findings of this study offer valuable insights for stakeholders in the traditional food industry to design interventions or programs suitable for enhancing the readiness and capabilities of rural entrepreneurs in technology adoption.

May this book inspire thoughtful consideration, informed action, and a shared commitment to building a world where technological progress harmonizes with ecological responsibility

Parvez Alam Khan

University Technology Petronas, Malaysia

Satirenjit Kaur Johl

University Technology Petronas, Malaysia

Mohd Salim

Woxsen University, India

Lawrence Arokiasamy

University Technology Petronas, Malaysia

Nasir Abdul Jalil

University Technology Petronas, Malaysia

Chapter 1
Green Finance: Definitions and Benefits

Yassine Ech-Chatty
https://orcid.org/0009-0007-4920-3457
Ibn Tofail University, Kenitra, Morocco

Azzouz Elhamma
Ibn Tofail University, Kenitra, Morocco

ABSTRACT

In recent years, green finance has garnered considerable international interest, establishing itself as a pivotal element in advancing towards a sustainable future and facilitating the shift to an eco-friendly economy. It is instrumental in fostering sustainable development and addressing global warming by mitigating its adverse impacts and enhancing environmental sustainability. This article explores the diverse aspects of green finance, concentrating on its definitions and benefits. It delves into key concepts and principles, emphasizing both the practical and theoretical benefits for companies and investors in a sustainability-focused economy. This analysis aims to offer a thorough understanding of green finance, highlighting its essential role in promoting environmentally sustainable economic growth.

DOI: 10.4018/979-8-3693-6195-5.ch001

INTRODUCTION

The formal endorsement of the Paris Agreement at the 21st Conference of the Parties (COP21) of the United Nations Framework Convention on Climate Change (UNFCCC) on December 12 signifies the growing importance of financial issues in global climate negotiations (Economy-climate, D.E.S.M., 2021). In this context, a primary challenge for nations worldwide is to efficiently direct capital flows towards a green and sustainable economy, while integrating sustainability into investment decisions, financing, and financial risk assessments (Deschryver, 2020).

Green finance plays a crucial role in fostering a thriving green economy (Han, J., & Gao, H. Y., 2024), making significant contributions to climate change mitigation and adaptation efforts (Déséglise & Freijido, 2019). It actively supports the achievement of carbon neutrality and becomes a key component of strategies aimed at reducing greenhouse gas emissions. Furthermore, it represents a pathway towards sustainable development and innovation (Falcon, 2019). Increasingly, financial institutions, corporations, and investors are adopting more sustainable practices by incorporating Environmental, Social, and Governance (ESG) criteria into their strategies, recognizing their growing significance for investors and society at large (Eccles et al., 2020).

Aligning financial flows with low-carbon, climate-resilient development trajectories is now an essential commitment. This alignment is necessary to facilitate the transition to a green economy, promote sustainable development, and mitigate the effects of climate change (Frimousse & Peretti, 2021). In a context where time is of the essence, delaying action is no longer a viable option.

This article aims to explore the core principles of green finance, underscoring its wide-ranging benefits for corporations, investors, and the global economy in achieving sustainable, low-carbon, and climate-resilient development. Through a review of prior research, four analytical dimensions will be examined. The first dimension will address the definitions and fundamental principles of green finance and its role as an essential driver in promoting sustainable development and climate change mitigation. The second will elucidate the benefits of green finance. The third will analyze the challenges and opportunities, while the fourth will consider future prospects and likely developments.

I. DEFINITIONS AND FUNDAMENTAL PRINCIPLES OF GREEN FINANCE

1. Exploring Various Definitions of Green Finance

Green finance is gaining significant attention in national and international debates across political, economic, and civic spheres, serving as a crucial pillar for steering the economy toward environmental sustainability. Notably, during the United Nations Conference on Sustainable Development, commonly referred to as Rio+20, green finance was acknowledged as a critical component of European economic strategies. It plays a central role in implementing environmental policies and achieving the “20-20-20” goals, which aim for a 20% improvement in energy efficiency, a 20% reduction in greenhouse gas emissions, and a 20% share of renewable energy in the total energy mix (Trends and Projections in Europe, 2021).

Green finance refers to the mechanisms that direct capital to finance investment projects in green industries and sustainable development (Chane, 2018). According to the OECD, green finance involves channeling capital towards environmentally sustainable projects that facilitate the transition to a low-carbon economy and enhance climate resilience, thereby promoting environmental stewardship and sustainable development. This multi-faceted transition aims to achieve sustainable development goals, transform the economy into one that is low-carbon and resource-efficient, and combat climate change (Lahouel et al., 2021). Similarly, the People's Bank of China defines green finance as economic activities that promote environmental improvement, address climate change challenges, and contribute to poverty reduction (PBC, 2016).

In essence, the definition of green finance is flexible and encompasses various initiatives, processes, financial products or services, and associated financial and fiscal regulations designed to protect the natural environment and mitigate the impacts of climate change on markets and investments (Deschryver, 2020).

In conclusion, these definitions and other widely accepted elements help clarify the concept of green finance. It is viewed as a financial innovation aimed at promoting sustainability in economic, environmental, and social terms, serving as a vital tool in combating climate change. Furthermore, green finance signifies a shift in economic discourse, where the environment is now perceived as a driver of innovation and growth, rather than an obstacle to competitiveness. It is essential to direct financial flows towards sustainable development goals, stimulating investment and financing projects aligned with climate objectives. This also includes the imperative to redirect financing away from initiatives detrimental to these objectives.

2. Clarifying Definitions: Towards Consistency in Green Finance

Various concepts proliferate in literature, debates, and the business world to denote a new direction in finance, awakened with a fresh approach to combating climate change. This direction has invigorated these concepts, leading to their significant development. Distinguishing between green finance, climate finance, and sustainable finance remains crucial, despite the diversity of initiatives sometimes being confusing. The United Nations Environment Programme provides clear descriptions:

- ✓ Sustainable finance involves financial practices that incorporate environmental, social, and governance (ESG) factors, in addition to economic considerations ;
- ✓ Green finance includes climate finance but excludes social and economic aspects ;
- ✓ Climate finance is considered a specific category within environmental (green) finance.

To clarify, sustainable finance is the broadest term, encompassing all financial activities that foster sustainable development by integrating economic, environmental, and social dimensions (Ryszawska, 2016). It is often used to denote socially responsible investment (SRI) (Jeffers, 2015). Green finance, a key component of sustainable finance, is expected to provide necessary capital through innovative development strategies (World Bank, 2017). Furthermore, green finance is defined as the targeted allocation of financial capital to projects, businesses, and technologies that support the energy transition to low-carbon systems, promote resource efficiency, and encourage sustainable agricultural practices, water management, recycling, eco-innovation, and clean technology development (Scholtens, 2017).

Climate finance, a crucial component of green finance, is characterized by the strategic allocation of funds from public, private, and alternative sources at local, national, or transnational levels. Its fundamental aim is to support projects and initiatives focused on mitigation and adaptation to address and neutralize the consequences of climate change (Buchner et al., 2014).

Overall, the growing popularity and evolution of the concepts of green finance, sustainable finance, and climate finance reflect the increasing awareness of the importance of financial actions in addressing the challenges of climate change and promoting sustainable development.

3. Underlying Principles of Green Finance as a Lever for Mitigating Environmental Risks

Green finance, like any financial discipline, is founded on principles that serve as guidelines and standards in investments and financial decisions to support projects and businesses contributing to environmental sustainability (Dikau & Volz, 2021). These principles, which can vary among organizations and institutions according to contingency theory, generally include elements such as:

- ✓ Integration of Environmental Criteria: Considering environmental impacts in investment and financing decisions (Plihon & Rigot, 2022) ;
- ✓ Management of Environmental Risks: Assessing and managing environmental risks in financial activities. With increasing climate risks, understanding the extent of these risks on the financial sector is crucial (European Investment Bank, 2023) ;

- ✓ Promotion of Green Investments: Facilitating environmentally sustainable projects, diminishing dependency on fossil fuels, and enhancing the ecological growth of nations (Han & Gao, 2024) ;
- ✓ Transparency and Disclosure: Providing transparent information about the environmental performance of investments and financial instruments or products. The Financial Stability Board advocates for compulsory disclosure norms for all financial institutions within their public financial records to enhance the transparency of risks associated with climate change. Such measures are anticipated to establish a foundation for green macro-prudential regulation and stress testing related to climate (Financial Stability Board, 2017) ;
- ✓ Stakeholder Engagement: Involving stakeholders, including investors, businesses, governments, and civil society, in promoting sustainable financial practices. The participation of private sector stakeholders and non-governmental organizations ensures greater transparency in the governance and management of environmental finance (Han & Gao, 2024) ;
- ✓ Financial Innovation: Encouraging the development of innovative financial products that support environmental sustainability, such as green bonds, socially responsible investment funds, and impact loans. Fintech is a primary driver of financial innovations that will achieve the Sustainable Development Goals (SDGs) (Arner et al., 2020).

These principles aim to align financial activities with sustainable development goals and foster the transition towards a more environmentally friendly economy. They are often utilized by financial institutions, institutional investors, governments, and international organizations to guide their financial policies and practices towards environmental sustainability.

4. The Role of Standards and Regulations in Defining Green Finance

Over the past two decades, nations have committed at both local and international levels to concerted efforts for environmental protection and the judicious use of natural resources. This approach aims to foster sustainable economic growth and facilitate the enduring eradication of poverty (World Bank, n.d.). To fulfill their commitments and align with the Sustainable Development Goals, various countries worldwide have implemented the principles of green finance, facing challenges such as the consolidation of sustainable development governance, the greening of the financial sector, successful green transition, low carbon development, and the valorization of natural resources. However, without a regulatory framework and standards, progress cannot be made further (Lehmann, 2020).

In this context, the European Union's strategy for sustainable finance is long-term, aiming to adopt as holistic a view of financial regulation as possible, thereby fully redirecting capital flows toward the transition (Deschryver, 2020). Furthermore, the main elements of green finance regulation have been established, and emerging and developing economies are increasingly adopting international standards (Lehmann, 2020).

Building upon this progress, Akomea-Frimpong and colleagues (2022) developed a theoretical model to clarify the ways in which green finance can bolster eco-friendly initiatives. Their research substantiated that well-defined regulations, transparency in financial markets, and heightened public awareness constitute the essential foundations for the effectiveness of green finance programs (Han & Gao, 2024).

Regulations and standards play a central role in defining and promoting green finance. They set the criteria and standards that qualify a financial product or investment as “green,” incorporating specific requirements related to environmental impact, sustainability, and contributions to climate objectives (UNEP, 2016). Regulation often requires transparent disclosure of environmental and social information, thus improving data availability and facilitating the assessment of the environmental performance of investments for stakeholders (European Investment Bank, 2023; Christensen et al., 2021).

The regulatory framework also appears conducive to encouraging companies of all sizes to move towards sustainability. This is achieved through the implementation of fiscal or financial incentives to foster investments in environmentally friendly green projects (tax reductions, subsidies, other financial benefits) (Han, J., & Gao, H. Y., 2024). Moreover, financial standards and regulations ensure the monitoring and oversight of financial activities to comply with established environmental sustainability norms, which may include control mechanisms, surveillance, auditing, and the imposition of sanctions for non-compliance (Richardson, 2009).

In terms of innovation, standards and the regulatory framework play a crucial role in encouraging and promoting innovation in green finance. By setting ambitious goals, these standards motivate financial actors to invest in the research and development of new technologies and sustainable financial products and can serve as benchmarks for guiding innovation efforts towards more sustainable solutions (UNEP FI, 2021). Additionally, a clear regulatory framework can facilitate the emergence of new green financial products, providing a conducive environment for investment and experimentation. By fostering innovation, standards and regulatory frameworks thus help to accelerate the transition to a greener and more sustainable economy (European Commission, 2018).

Finally, standards and regulations provide a foundational framework for defining and promoting green finance by establishing norms, enhancing transparency, offering incentives, and ensuring the monitoring and control of financial activities in the realm of environmental sustainability.

II. THE ADVANTAGES OF GREEN FINANCE

1. Economic Benefits

Green finance represents an innovative financial phenomenon that combines economic gains with environmental protection (Wang and Zhi, 2016). Investments in green projects stimulate the economy and foster local development. This is achieved through funding renewable energy, green buildings, and the sustainable management of natural resources, creating job opportunities in burgeoning sectors aimed at building a more inclusive, sustainable, and climate-resilient economy (International Renewable Energy Agency, 2019).

Additionally, green finance, facilitated by green funds and green banks, can drive innovation within the green economy. By supporting research and development of green technologies, it can help bring about novel environmental solutions. Scholars have underscored the significance of reducing costs in economic markets to promote sustainable growth, noting the pivotal role that digitalization and internet-based technologies play in cost reduction (Wu, 2024).

Corporate involvement in sustainability initiatives will lead to a higher demand for environmentally friendly products, allowing businesses to access new markets and broaden their customer base by fulfilling this increasing demand. If the market mechanisms of green finance are efficiently structured, they can guide capital flows, manage environmental risks effectively, and ensure the optimal allocation of environmental and social resources (Wang & Zhi, 2016).

2. Environmental and Social Benefits

Regarding environmental and social aspects, green finance provides a plethora of environmental and social benefits. It is regarded as the optimal alternative for financing environmentally friendly projects and organizations (Zakari & Khan, 2022). Green finance takes into account positive and effective environmental outcomes, even in funding tasks related to various environmental activities such as renewable electricity, the creation of green industries, the production of green bricks, clean energy, pollution management, water management, climate change mitigation and adaptation strategies, and biodiversity (Mfelam et al., 2023).

Investments in clean energy and efficient waste management have beneficial impacts on air and water quality, significantly contributing to the improvement of public health and the environment. Simultaneously, the shift towards a green economy promotes job creation in expanding areas, such as renewable energies and waste management, thereby reducing unemployment rates and fostering sustainable and inclusive economic growth (EMF, 2015).

Finally, green finance bolsters the ability of communities and ecosystems to withstand climate change, equipping them with improved preparedness for severe meteorological phenomena. This underscores the critical role of green finance in forging a sustainable future for the planet.

III. GREEN FINANCE AS MITIGATION OF ENVIRONMENTAL RISKS

1. Analysis of Major Environmental Risks

According to the United States Environmental Protection Agency (EPA), "environmental risk analysis is a systematic process that evaluates the risks to human health and the environment associated with exposure to chemical, physical, or biological agents." Therefore, environmental risk assessment is crucial in the decision-making process related to investments and financing, providing a measure of potential threats to the environment and society (Busch & Lewandowski, 2018).

The European Banking Authority (EBA) develops guidelines to help investors understand the risks projects may pose to sustainable development goals and to identify ways for investment managers to control risk reduction and mitigation measures. Assessments must be comprehensive, covering physical, legal, financial, and technological risks associated with an activity and holding the project manager accountable for risk analysis throughout supply chains and within value chains (Anthony et al., 2021).

This analysis involves several key steps, such as identifying potential hazards, assessing probabilities and consequences, evaluating the vulnerability of populations and ecosystems, and proposing mitigation measures. As the EPA emphasizes, "a comprehensive assessment of environmental risks allows for informed decisions to protect human health and the environment."

Consequently, the analysis of major environmental risks is of paramount importance in the current context of climate change and increasing pressure on natural resources (United Nations Environment Programme Finance Initiative, n.d.). This approach helps identify risks related to extreme weather events, ecosystem degradation, air and water pollution, among others. By integrating the results of this analysis into investment and financing decision-making, companies and investors can better manage environmental risks and contribute to sustainable and resilient development. This approach is essential for ensuring the long-term viability of economic and financial activities, taking into account environmental and social issues (World Economic Forum, 2020). Moreover, it enables the anticipation of potential impacts on activities and the implementation of appropriate mitigation measures to reduce risks and enhance the resilience of businesses and investors to environmental changes (IPCC, 2014). Thus, environmental risk analysis is a crucial tool in financial decision-making to promote sustainable and resilient development. A key element of this approach is to better manage environmental and social risks, seize opportunities that offer both a decent rate of return and environmental benefits, and ensure greater accountability.

2. How Green Finance Can Mitigate These Risks

Climate-related risks could severely impact business operations and financial institutions (Development, S., & Network, S., 2022). However, leaders of financial institutions have recently become aware of the economic and financial risks posed by uncontrolled global warming and have started to take action across all sectors, especially finance, viewing it as the primary tool for promoting a more sustainable economy (Kempf, 2020). Wang and Fan (2023) concentrate their study on the Chinese market to discern the attributes of green finance affecting investor choices. Their findings suggest that green financial instruments can lessen investment risks and secure satisfactory returns, thus enhancing the appeal of sustainable projects to investors (Han, J., & Gao, H. Y., 2024).

Anupam Dutta, Elie Bouri, Timo Rothovius, and Gazi Salah Uddin conducted a study on how climate risk affects the stock prices of clean energy firms. They found that heightened climate risk encourages investors and policymakers to pivot to alternative energy sectors, resulting in an increased demand for renewable energy sources (Dutta, Bouri, Rothovius, & Uddin, 2023). In summary, green finance stimulates investment in renewable energy and energy efficiency initiatives, leading to a reduction in greenhouse gas emissions. According to the International Energy Agency (IEA), "renewable energies play a crucial role in reducing CO2 emissions and transitioning to a low-carbon economy."

Additionally, green finance is designed to facilitate initiatives that advance the ecological shift towards a low-carbon economy. Such initiatives may include projects related to renewable energy, energy efficiency, sustainable management of waste and water, and the conservation of biodiversity (Kaminker et al., 2013).

In conclusion, green finance can mitigate social and environmental risks by directing investments towards sustainable projects that facilitate the transition to a greener economy. This can also encourage investors to adopt more responsible environmental and social practices. Consequently, green finance seeks to align the interests of investors and society.

IV. THE ROLE OF FINANCIAL ACTORS IN BUILDING RESILIENT STRATEGIES

The Sustainable Development Goals (SDGs) outline a clear and tangible vision for a desirable future, prompting investors to assess and report on the social and environmental performance of their investments (Dutta, 2023). Amidst an urgent environmental crisis, it is essential for the international community to intensify efforts and mobilize resources to address environmental issues and climate change effectively, aiming to achieve these ambitious goals (United Nations, 2015).

Public authorities have implemented regulatory, economic, and financial measures to redirect investments toward projects that preserve biodiversity. Financial structures have recently committed to transitioning towards a green economy. Financial actors are crucial in tackling significant global challenges, which have severe consequences (Galaz et al., 2018). Experts argue that financial players are central to advancing sustainable environmental strategies. By facilitating capital flow and supporting innovation, they can significantly drive extensive changes in environmental governance (Falcone & Sica, 2019).

Furthermore, financial actors help investors better integrate and consider environmental, social, and governance (ESG) risks in investment decisions, particularly in seeking sustainable returns over time. This approach enhances their resilience to various challenges (Dutta, 2023). Their commitment to sustainable development and social responsibility also promotes transparency in ESG reporting and fosters innovation by creating financial products that support resilience, such as green bonds or climate risk insurance (Flammer, 2020). As a result, this bolsters the resilience of businesses and communities to future challenges.

Developing the green financial system should enhance the capital market's role in optimally allocating resources. The financial sector is vital in directing green investments, achievable through financial funding and social capital, primarily via financial channels (Zahan & Chuanmin, 2021). Therefore, increasing the engagement of banks, financial regulators, and community-based organizations in incorporating environmental and social factors into the conventional financial system is imperative to facilitate the transition towards a low-carbon economy (Falcone & Sica, 2019).

V. CHALLENGES AND OPPORTUNITIES

At the 7th OECD Forum on green finance and investment, discussions focused on priority strategies to stimulate economic recovery while bolstering momentum for green finance and investments. The key findings highlighted the importance of an economic recovery that is both inclusive and environmentally friendly, underscoring the pivotal role of the public sector in directing private investments towards economic prosperity, in harmony with biodiversity preservation and combating climate change. They also call for enhanced market integrity and transparency, notably through the harmonization of green finance definitions and improved data communication. Additionally, they spotlight the risks associated with underinvestment in crucial green infrastructure while identifying the opportunities presented by transitioning to a sustainable and equitable economic model (OECD, 2020).

The recent transformation in finance aligns with the new trend of greening finance or greening the financial sector (Ryszawska, 2016). However, the widespread adoption of green finance faces several major challenges. It is crucial to measure and make transparent the ESG criteria to avoid greenwashing, a practice criticized by several companies. Furthermore, there is a need for greater awareness among investors and businesses, some of whom may still be hesitant about these issues. Additionally, effective implementation of sustainable policies and practices across the entire sector is necessary. Integrating non-financial investment risks into asset valuation poses an additional challenge. Lastly, strengthening and harmonizing legislation at both national and international levels is essential to facilitate the widespread adoption of green finance.

VI. FUTURE OUTLOOK AND PROBABLE EVOLUTION

The future outlook for green finance is promising, with likely developments expected to enhance its role in the increasing integration of environmental, social, and governance (ESG) considerations into investment decisions. Additionally, both national and international scientific communities anticipate an expansion of sustainable financial markets and increased regulation to support sustainable development goals, advancing the transition to a greener and more sustainable economy (Busch et al., 2016). A key aspect of this progress involves better management of environmental and social risks, seizing opportunities that offer both a decent rate of return and environmental benefits, and ensuring greater accountability.

In summary, green finance is expected to continue its rapid growth, driven by an increasing awareness of environmental issues and potential economic benefits (Environmental Science & Policy). New regulations and standards are also likely to promote its expansion (Journal of Sustainable Finance & Investment). Furthermore, financial innovation is expected to play a crucial role, with the development of more sophisticated and accessible green financial products and instruments (World Bank, n.d). Lastly, enhanced collaboration between public and private sector actors is deemed essential to support the growth of green finance (Organisation for Economic Co-operation and Development report, n.d).

VII. CONCLUSION

In conclusion, this article has highlighted the strategic importance of green finance in the emergence of a sustainable economy. By detailing its fundamental principles and exploring the benefits it offers, we have seen how it serves as a critical lever for businesses and investors eager to actively engage in the ecological transition. Green finance, with its innovative approach and significant contributions, plays a leading role in mitigating environmental impacts and promoting economic development that respects planetary boundaries. This in-depth exploration reveals not only the viability of green finance as a driver of sustainable economic growth but also emphasizes the urgency and necessity for economic actors to align with its principles to ensure a prosperous and ecologically stable future.

REFERENCES

Anthony, I. A. N., Yuan, J., & Xia, S. U. N. (2021). Promoting China – European Union Cooperation on Green. SIPRI Policy Brief, 2021, 0–8. https://www.jstor.org/stable/resrep29591

Buchner, B., Stadelmann, M., Wilkinson, J., Mazza, F., Rosenberg, A., & Abramskiehn, D. (2014). The Global Landscape of Climate Finance 2014. Climate Policy Initiative Report

Busch, T., Bauer, R., & Orlitzky, M. (2016). Sustainable Development and Financial Markets: Old Paths and New Avenues. *Business & Society*, *55*(3), 303–329. DOI: 10.1177/0007650315570701

Busch, T., & Lewandowski, S. (2018). Corporate carbon and financial performance a meta-analysis. *Journal of Industrial Ecology*, *22*(4), 745–759. DOI: 10.1111/jiec.12591

Chane, A. (2018). La finance verte en Chine, une composante essentielle de la transition vers une économie bas-carbone. Idées Économiques et Sociales, N° 192(2), 42–45.).DOI: 10.3917/idee.192.0042

Christensen, H. B., Hail, L., & Leuz, C. (2021). Mandatory CSR and sustainability reporting: Economic analysis and literature review. *Review of Accounting Studies*, *26*(3), 1176–1248. DOI: 10.1007/s11142-021-09609-5

Deschryver, P. (2020). Accélérer la transition énergétique: le rôle de la finance verte et ses enjeux pour l'Europe. In Ifri. https://www.ifri.org/fr/publications/etudes-de-lifri/accelerer-transition-energetique-role-de-finance-verte-enjeux-leurope

Déséglise, C., & Freijido, D. L. (2019). Financing sustainable infrastructure at scale. *Journal of International Affairs*, *73*(1), 33–48.

Dikau, S., & Volz, U. (2021). "Central Banking, Climate Change, and Green Finance." Asian Development Bank Institute.https://www.adb.org/sites/default/files/publication/908751/climate-change-climate-finance-experience-directions.pdf

Dutta, A., Bouri, E., Rothovius, T., & Uddin, G. S. (2023). Climate risk and green investments: New evidence. Energy, 265(February 2022), 126376. DOI: 10.1016/j.energy.2022.126376

EMF. (2015). Towards a circular economy: Business rationale for an accelerated transition. Ellen MacArthur Foundation (EMF), 20. https://www.ellenmacarthurfoundation.org/circular-economy-articles

Falcone, P. M., & Sica, E. (2019). Assessing the opportunities and challenges of green finance in Italy: An analysis of the biomass production sector. *Sustainability (Basel), 11*(2), 517. Advance online publication. DOI: 10.3390/su11020517

Financial Stability Board. (2017). Final Report: Recommendations of the Task Force on Climate-Related Financial Disclosure. https://www.fsb-tcfd.org/wp content/uploads/2017/06/FINAL-2017-TCFD-Report-11052018.pdf

Flammer, C. (2020). Green Bonds: Effectiveness and Implications for Public Policy. In Environmental and Energy Policy and the Economy (Vol. 1). DOI: 10.1086/706794

Frimousse, S., & Peretti, J. M. (2021). La contribution de la finance verte et durable à la performance extra-financière. *Question (s) de management, 36*(6), 141-166.

Galaz, V., Crona, B., Dauriach, A., Scholtens, B., & Steffen, W. (2018). Finance and the Earth system – Exploring the links between financial actors and non-linear changes in the climate system. *Global Environmental Change, 53*(January), 296–302. DOI: 10.1016/j.gloenvcha.2018.09.008

Han, J., & Gao, H. Y. (2024). Green finance, social inclusion, and sustainable economic growth in OECD member countries. *Humanities & Social Sciences Communications, 11*(1), 1–8. DOI: 10.1057/s41599-024-02662-w

International Renewable Energy Agency. (2019). "Renewable Energy and Jobs – Annual Review 2019

Jeffers, E. (2015). Pourquoi faut-il une finance durable et soutenable ? Revue d'économie Financière, N° 117(1), 225–236. .DOI: 10.3917/ecofi.117.0225

Kaminker, C., et al. (2013), « L'investissement institutionnel dans les infrastructures vertes: Études de cas », OECD Working Papers on Finance, Insurance and Private Pensions, n° 35, Éditions OCDE, Paris, DOI: 10.1787/20797117

Kempf, H. (2020). Verdir la politique monétaire. *Revue d'Économie Politique*, *130*(3), 311–343. DOI: 10.3917/redp.303.0311

Lahouel, B. B., Zaied, Y. B., & Taleb, L. (2021). Éditorial. La finance s' éveille au réchauffement climatique. *Question (s) de management, 36*(6), 31-35.

Mfelam, J. R., Nasser, O. A., & Kadouamai, S. (2023). Coûts induits à la pratique de la finance verte dans les banques. *Revista del Instituto Internacional de Costos*, (22), 72–91.

Plihon, D., & Rigot, S. (2022). Les intermédiaires financiers publics face au changement climatique. *Revue Économique (Paris)*, *73*(2), 243–266. DOI: 10.3917/reco.732.0243

Richardson, B. J. (2009). Keeping ethical investment ethical: Regulatory issues for investing for sustainability. *Journal of Business Ethics*, *87*(4), 555–572. DOI: 10.1007/s10551-008-9958-y

Ryszawska, B. (2016). Sustainability transition needs sustainable finance. *Copernican Journal of Finance & Accounting*, *5*(1), 185. DOI: 10.12775/CJFA.2016.011

Scholtens, B. (2017). Finance as a Driver of Corporate Social Responsibility. *Journal of Business Ethics*, *68*(1), 19–33. DOI: 10.1007/s10551-006-9037-1

United Nations. (2015). "Transforming Our World: The 2030 Agenda for Sustainable Development." Assemblée Générale des Nations Unies. https://sdgs.un.org/2030agenda

Wang, Y., & Zhi, Q. (2016). The Role of Green Finance in Environmental Protection: Two Aspects of Market Mechanism and Policies. *Energy Procedia*, *104*, 311–316. DOI: 10.1016/j.egypro.2016.12.053

Wu, J. (2024). Role of green finance and carbon accounting in achieving sustainability. *Humanities & Social Sciences Communications*, *11*(1), 1–7. DOI: 10.1057/s41599-023-02492-2

Zahan, I., & Chuanmin, S. (2021). Towards a green economic policy framework in China: Role of green investment in fostering clean energy consumption and environmental sustainability. *Environmental Science and Pollution Research International*, *28*(32), 43618–43628. DOI: 10.1007/s11356-021-13041-2

Zakari, A., & Khan, I. (2022). The Introduction of Green Finance: A Curse or a Benefit to Environmental Sustainability? *Energy RESEARCH LETTERS*, *3*(3). Advance online publication. DOI: 10.46557/001c.29977

Chapter 2
Public Good Theory of Financial Inclusion

Peterson K. Ozili
https://orcid.org/0000-0001-6292-1161
Central Bank of Nigeria, Nigeria

ABSTRACT

Financial inclusion as a public good can be funded by the state and private firms to ensure that everyone has affordable access to formal financial services. Historically, an economic solution for financial inclusion has been to create public banks and issue banking license to private banks. Today, the solution for financial inclusion lies in offering different types of public and private support to financial service providers to ensure that formal financial services is available and affordable so that everyone can access and use financial services to meet their needs. This paper discusses the necessity of financial inclusion to be considered a public good because financial inclusion is important for successful economic and social development. This article presents a detailed understanding of the public good theory of financial inclusion. It explains the sense in which financial inclusion is a public good and it explores the implications for development policy.

DOI: 10.4018/979-8-3693-6195-5.ch002

1. INTRODUCTION

This article explores the public good theory of financial inclusion. It attempts to explain financial inclusion in light of the characteristics of public goods. It explains the sense in which financial inclusion is a public good and the implications for development policy.

Financial inclusion is an important development policy agenda for many countries around the world. The digital financial services (DFS) revolution, especially the growth of Fintech, BigTech, and cryptocurrency, has increased the avenues through which financial inclusion can be achieved (Ouma et al, 2017; Donovan, 2012; Ozili, 2024). It has made financial services become abundant in supply such that the use of financial services by one individual does not prevent usage of the same financial services by another individual, and this is a characteristic of a public good. Treating financial inclusion as a public good not only improves people's welfare through public policies, but it also introduces a whole new dimension to on-going debates in the finance and welfare literature about how access to finance affects welfare outcomes.

Turning to the economic literature, a public good is a physical good or a service that is provided without profit to all members of the population either by the government or a private individual or an organization (Stiglitz, 1999; Samuelson, 1954). A public good has two main properties that distinguish it from a private good. The first property is "nonrivalrous consumption" which means that the consumption of the good by one individual does not prevent others from consumption of the good, while the second property of a public good is "nonexcludability" which means that it is difficult or impossible to exclude an individual from enjoying the good (Stiglitz, 1999; Samuelson, 1954). In contrast, non-public goods can be rivalrous and non-excludable. Other non-public goods may be non-rival and excludable. Only private goods are both rivalrous and excludable (Varian, 1992).

In this study, financial inclusion is considered to be a public good because both the state and the private sector can play a significant role in promoting financial inclusion since financial inclusion is essential for the smooth functioning of society —economically, politically, and culturally.

Without financial inclusion, people cannot access insurance products to protect their wealth, they cannot access loans to acquire new assets, they cannot safekeep their money in a bank, and it would be harder for them to participate meaningfully in the formal economy. Therefore, it is important to explore the sense in which financial inclusion is a public good.

This study contributes to the economic literature that explore the various types of public goods. This study argues that financial inclusion can be considered a public good due to its non-rivalry and non-excludability characteristics and due to government investment in financial inclusion and its effect on the public. The study further contributes to the theoretical financial inclusion literature that develop frameworks to understand financial inclusion. It adds to the literature by proposing that financial inclusion can be viewed as public good because its benefits extend beyond an individual or a firm.

The rest of the article is structured as follows. Section 2 presents the theoretical underpinning. Section 3 explains the non-rivalry and non-excludability attributes of financial inclusion as a public good. Section 4 discusses financial inclusion as a local and global public good. Section 5 explores the role of the individual, firm and the state. Section 6 explores the implication for development policy. Section 7 presents the conclusion of the article.

2. THEORETICAL UNDERPINNING

The public good theory of financial inclusion was first postulated by Peterson Ozili in his work "*Theories of financial inclusion*". The theory states that financial inclusion should be treated as a public good because the provision of financial services to everyone has public benefits to users and society (Ozili, 2020). The theory argues that formal financial services should be extended to the whole population and without discrimination. I expand the public good theory of financial inclusion by proposing that the "public" nature of financial inclusion as a public good is also linked to government investment in financial inclusion, and the effect of its provision to the public.

Regarding government investment in financial inclusion, if the government invests in financial inclusion by creating an enabling policy and legal environment for financial inclusion to take place and by issuing licenses to financial service providers such as commercial banks, fintech companies, microfinance banks and bigtech players, then such government investment in financial inclusion makes financial inclusion a public good rather than a private good. If financial inclusion is enabled by government policies, financial service providers have no reason to introduce barriers that prevent non-paying individuals from owning a formal account, a bank account or a mobile money account. This explains the sense in which financial inclusion is a public good and it explains why ownership of a bank account, or a mobile money account, is usually free for users. Regarding the effect of its provision to the public, financial inclusion has a positive effect on the public because financial inclusion gives people access to formal savings, payment, loans, insurance products which they can use to earn income, acquire wealth, save for emergencies, and spend on education and healthcare to live a fulfilled life (Ouma et al, 2017; Donovan, 2012).

Furthermore, the main proposition of the public good theory of financial inclusion is that financial inclusion is a public good because (i) financial inclusion is of interest to more than one individual or firm, (meaning that it is beneficial to many people and firms); (ii) formal financial services are not completely used up in the act of consumption; (iii) the marginal cost of offering financial services to additional users is zero; (iv) the provision of formal financial services to one individual does not reduce its availability to others; (v) financial inclusion benefits everyone including those who free ride on it (i.e. those who own a formal account but do not make any financial transaction); and (v) financial services can be enjoyed over and over again by anyone without diminishing the benefit it delivers to others. The implication of the public good theory of financial inclusion is that, as a public good, access to formal financial services should be granted to everyone without restriction or discrimination and for the benefit of all. When this occurs, it will lead to the financial inclusion of all members of society (Ozili, 2020).

3. NON-RIVALRY AND NON-EXCLUDABILITY OF FINANCIAL INCLUSION AS A PUBLIC GOOD

The sense in which financial inclusion is a public good can be explained in terms of the characteristics of a public good. If a financially included individual brings unbanked adults into the formal financial system so that they can use formal banking services or a digital payment service, the financially included individual will continue to access and use formal financial services at the same time as the unbanked adult who has now become "banked". As more people join the financial system, everyone will be able to use formal financial services at the same time without anyone being excluded.

Financial inclusion as a public good has a "nonrival access and usage" characteristic. This means that all users of formal financial services are not in competition (rivalry) with each other to access and use existing formal financial services. In other words, all individuals that use formal financial services benefit equally from it. It means that financial inclusion is relatively unaffected by demand because formal financial services can be accessed and used by many people at the same time. If formal financial services is available to one person, it can be available to everyone else at no additional cost because its use by one person does not reduce its availability to others.

Financial inclusion as a public good also has a "nonexcludability" characteristic. This means that, in an ideal world, no one can be excluded from accessing and using formal financial services. It means that formal financial services cannot be kept secret and must be immediately available to all customers to access and use. In a nutshell, the "nonexcludability" characteristic of financial inclusion as a public good suggests that nobody can be excluded from accessing and using formal financial services of any type.

4. FINANCIAL INCLUSION AS A LOCAL AND GLOBAL PUBLIC GOOD

Financial inclusion as a public good may be local to a community, city or a country. This can occur if local laws and regulations require that access and usage of certain financial services is allowed only within a limited geographical area such as a community, city or country. Examples include a housing loan offered by microfinance banks in a small community, or life insurance products which are available only in cities that are prone to natural disasters. The most important feature of financial inclusion as a local public good is that customers can reveal their preferences and demand for tailored financial services that meet their needs in the city or community where they reside. People living near the city or community may or may not be excluded from benefiting from the tailored financial services, but people living far away from the city or community will certainly not benefit from the tailored financial services offered in the city or community. People can also move from one location to another location to access a preferred financial service that is available elsewhere. The implication of financial inclusion as a local public good is that people will move to cities or communities that offer financial services that fit their preferences, and over time, the community or city will be inhabited by people that have similar financial services preferences.

Financial inclusion can also be viewed as a global public good because financial inclusion benefits everybody in the world, and it is crucial for global development. Financial inclusion as a global public good entail public decision-making, public distribution of financial services, and public usage of financial services around the world and the benefits depend on the cost of access for people in different jurisdictions. Financial inclusion as a global public good can be promoted through international cooperation with individuals, communities, countries, international non-governmental organisations (NGOs) and the collective efforts of developed and developing countries.

5. THE ROLE OF THE INDIVIDUAL, FIRM AND THE STATE

The role of individuals in financial inclusion as a public good is to access and use available and affordable financial services that meet their needs. Individuals should be able to visit financial service providers, or use their digital platforms, to learn about available financial products and services, how they can meet their needs, the cost of available financial products and services, and reach a decision as to whether it is appropriate to meet their needs.

Regarding the role of firms, ideally, private firms will not produce public goods because there is no profit or reward in producing public goods (Vasudeva & Teegen, 2011). Despite this, private firms, such as financial service providers, still have a role to play in promoting financial inclusion as a public good. The role of financial service providers is to continue to produce enough financial services to meet the demand of the growing population. This is important because when financial service providers fail to offer financial services at the level society wants, or doesn't produce it at all, a market failure will occur. This situation must be avoided at all cost. Also, it is possible that the financial service providers that are seeking sustainable competitive advantage and long-term profitability will have incentives to promote financial inclusion as a public good without expecting significant profit in the short term.

Regarding the role of the state, a fundamental implication of the public good theory of financial inclusion is that the state will play some role in the provision of formal financial services. Without the state playing some role, formal financial services will be under-supplied, and it can lead to market failure which should be avoided. If financial service providers cannot make a decent profit from offering formal financial services, then they will have limited incentives to continue to offer formal financial services to customers. It will lead them to focus on their profit margin and they will not give high importance to the benefits that accrue to users of formal financial services. The State can adopt two strategies to address the profitability problem facing financial service providers when financial inclusion is viewed as a public good. The first strategy is to increase the profit that financial service providers make from offering financial services to customers. This can be achieved by increasing the interest rate on loan products or increasing the fees and transaction costs on payment services or other formal financial services. The second strategy for addressing the profitability problem is to provide direct government support to financial service providers by subsidizing the cost of basic formal financial services so that financial service providers can continue to offer financial services at low-cost to users.

6. IMPLICATION FOR DEVELOPMENT POLICY

The effective provision of financial services as a public good can improve the financial wellbeing of people, especially poor people. Historical approaches to financial inclusion view financial inclusion as a private good which do not require government support, but this approach is too narrow. A new approach is needed – one that view financial inclusion as a public good which requires government support. Without making financial inclusion a public good, the rich (i.e., bank shareholders, owners and high-net worth clients/customers) can influence financial service providers to exclude the poor because the rich can lobby for exclusive financial services, better financial services that favour them, or if need be, the rich can lobby financial service providers to relocate away from rural and sub-urban areas where the poor live to urban areas where the rich reside. This can lead to financial exclusion which is detrimental to the development agenda of financial inclusion.

To make financial inclusion a public good, the government should introduce interventions that enable unbanked, underserved and poor people to participate in the formal financial system so that they can benefit from using existing formal financial services. There is also a need to introduce regulations that correct structural imbalances, remove bias, and address other issues that prevent the people at the bottom of the pyramid from accessing and using formal financial services in the financial system. Governance institutions also have a collective responsibility to create conditions that enable financial inclusion to take place, and they have to deal with any under-provision of financial services that may arise if private financial service providers do not have sufficient incentives to provide more financial services for unbanked and underserved customers. When financial inclusion is made a public good, it can increase access and use of formal financial services and improve the financial wellbeing of people, especially in developing countries.

7. CONCLUSION

This study discussed and extended the public good theory of financial inclusion. The earlier version of the theory argued that financial inclusion is a public good because access to formal financial services should be guaranteed for everyone because access to formal financial services to one individual does not reduce its availability to others. For this reason, the provision of formal financial services, which is what financial inclusion is about, should be a public good. In the extended theory, proposed in this article, it was argued that financial inclusion should be a public good due to (i) its nonrivalry characteristic, (ii) its non-excludability characteristic, (iii) government investment in financial inclusion, and (iv) the positive effect of financial inclusion on people. The implication is that, as a public good, there should be unrestricted access to formal financial services for every member of the population. Society and the economy need to attain a high level of financial inclusion to function properly. This can be achieved if policymakers consider financial inclusion to be a public good. However, it should be acknowledged that financial service providers are in the financial inclusion business to make profit from the provision of financial services, but the free rider problem can prevent financial service providers from providing financial services in abundant supply. Therefore, the government should intervene to reduce the free rider problem by collecting taxes from users of financial services and use the collected taxes to increase government investment in financial inclusion in the form of financial support to financial service providers or through other forms of government support. The government should also intervene to ensure that there are sufficient incentives to induce financial service providers to provide adequate level of financial services to meet the demand of a growing population.

REFERENCES

Donovan, K. (2012). Mobile money for financial inclusion. *Information and Communications for development, 61*(1), 61-73.

Ouma, S. A., Odongo, T. M., & Were, M. (2017). Mobile financial services and financial inclusion: Is it a boon for savings mobilization?. *Review of development finance, 7*(1), 29-35.

Ozili, P. K. (2020). Theories of financial inclusion. In *Uncertainty and challenges in contemporary economic behaviour* (pp. 89–115). Emerald Publishing Limited. DOI: 10.1108/978-1-80043-095-220201008

Ozili, P. K. (2024). Digital Innovations for Increasing Financial Inclusion: CBDC, Cryptocurrency, Embedded finance, Artificial Intelligence, WaaS, Fintech, Bigtech, and DeFi. In *Impact of Artificial Intelligence on Society* (pp. 174-184). Chapman and Hall/CRC.

Samuelson, P. A. (1954). The pure theory of public expenditure. *The Review of Economics and Statistics, 36*(4), 387–389. DOI: 10.2307/1925895

Stiglitz, J. E. (1999). Knowledge as a global public good. *Global public goods: International cooperation in the 21st century, 308*, 308-325.

Varian, H. R. (1992). *Microeconomic Analysis* (3rd ed.). Norton.

Vasudeva, G., & Teegen, H. (2011). Why do private firms invest in public goods? In *Cross-Sector Leadership for the Green Economy: Integrating Research and Practice on Sustainable Enterprise* (pp. 263–276). Palgrave Macmillan US. DOI: 10.1057/9781137015891_14

Chapter 3
Relevance of Green Investment to Facilitate the Sustainable Business Practices and Development

Rajinder Kaur
https://orcid.org/0000-0002-7049-0434
Chandigarh University, India

Swati Sharma
https://orcid.org/0000-0002-2029-5251
Chandigarh University, India

ABSTRACT

With investors' interest in environmental sustainability growing, sustainability practices and development have taken on significant importance within organizations. This chapter describes how using green investments can help businesses adopt sustainable business practices. The chapter is based on descriptive study and primarily used the secondary sources of data. The data is primarily supported by credible, previously published works, such as journal articles and working papers. The primary focus is placed on the importance of green investment in sustainable business

DOI: 10.4018/979-8-3693-6195-5.ch003

practices. The findings demonstrated that green investment plays an integral role while doing the sustainable business. It has also been found that many companies in India are engaged in sustainable business activities through numerous large-scale projects. The study looks at the green and sustainable business and its involvement to sustainable development. All the green and sustainable measures have specific application areas identified by the study, particularly in the banking and finance industries.

INTRODUCTION

On the political and economic level, there are certain environmental concerned debates are going on from the last decade (Fareed et al., 2021; Wen et al., 2022). The agenda of all these discussions always remains the same i.e., sustainable development. The achievement of sustainable development, which calls for the effective implementation of policies and methods that can minimise greenhouse gas (GHG) secretion, is essential for the survival of humanity. The greatest barrier to achieving sustainable development, according to GHG emissions, particularly CO2 emissions, is thought to be this one (IPCC, 2014). The most difficult threat that humanity is currently confronting has arisen in recent years as global climate change. Although putting environmental regulations into place has helped to reduce environmental problems to a certain limit, they have also raised the prices of goods and services. Government and researchers are motivated by these discussions to examine the connections among environmental legislation, industry competitiveness, and the responsibilities of businesses towards society (Kitzmueller & Shimshack, 2012). Most countries have adopted the process of industrialisation since the industrial revolution, but they have also borne the environmental penalty. People's awareness of environmental issues grows as industrialisation intensifies (Lu & Sohail, 2022; Sohail et al., 2022). Similar to this, when environmental concerns grew, businesses interest grows in the area of making stronger the environment efficiency (Wei et al., 2022). As a result, there is increasing pressure on businesses and organisations from all sectors of society, in particular, public and environment concerned people, to carry out their obligations with regard to environmental safety and protection (Khan et al., 2022). On the line of this concept, social accountability of organisations has gained in popularity and has recently been the standard approach for modern firms to operate business (Benabou & Tirole, 2010; Yasara et al., 2019). In other words, environmentally responsible business practises have gained popularity as a tool for attaining sustainable business growth.

CONCEPTUAL FRAMEWORK

Sustainable Business

Organisations should prioritise sustainability practises and development since they improve business performance. Because investors prefer to invest in sustainable organisations, which then have an impact on the success of the organisation, sustainability practises and development have become crucial. The requirement for sustainability has grown as market competition has increased because consumers are more interested in businesses that are environmentally conscious, which tends to raise organisational profitability over the long term (Liu et al., 2022). To effectively adapt to the shifting market needs, this entire process necessitates strategic decision-making (Burhan and Rahmanti, 2012). Any company that engages in environmentally conscious or "green" operations to make sure that all procedures, units, and producing activities appropriately handle ongoing environmental problems while the retention of profit is considered to be a sustainable business (Arif & Sohail, 2020). It is a company that "meets the needs of the present world without compromising the ability of future generations to meet their own needs," to use the expression of the statement (Greenstone et al., 2012). It involves figuring out how to create items that will benefit from the state of the environment right now and on what degree a company's goods work with eco-friendly resources (Rai & Jambhulkar, 2018). A sustainable business, often known as a green business, is an organisation that works to achieve the triple bottom line and has little to no negative impact, or even the potential for positive impact, on the local or global scenerio, region, a certain group of people, or economy. Any company that engages in environmentally harmless or green operations to make sure that all manufacturing, processing, and product development activities appropriately handle contemporary environmental problems with the retention of profit is considered a sustainable business (Ullah et al., 2022). It is a company that, in other words, "meets the needs of the present world without compromising the ability of future generations to meet their own needs." It involves figuring out how to create items that will benefit from the state of the environment right now and how accurately a company's goods work with renewable resources (Devi, 2022). The sustainability agenda considers the triple bottom line of sustainable development, which accounts for the economy, the environment, and society through business methods used by the company across all of its operations (Gujar, 2020). Green investment promotes innovation by sponsoring research and development for sustainable technology and practices. According to Horbach, Rammer, and Rennings (2012), green technologies are frequently the product of R&D efforts, which lead to new solutions that increase corporate competitiveness. Furthermore, these technologies can open up new markets and opportunities for organizations committed to sustainability. According to research, green investment is critical for developing and deploying renewable energy and low-carbon technology. The International Renewable Energy Agency (IRENA) believes that investments in renewable energy must expand dramatically in order to satisfy global climate commitments. According to Kaminker and Stewart (2012), green investment accelerates the transition to renewable energy, lowering greenhouse gas emissions and fossil fuel dependency. Green investment promotes innovation by sponsoring research and development for sustainable technology and practices. According to Horbach et al. (2012), green technologies are frequently the product of R&D efforts, which lead to new solutions that increase corporate competitiveness. Furthermore, these technologies can open up new markets and opportunities for organizations committed to sustainability. Compliance with environmental standards is a major driver of green investment. Flammer (2013) found that organizations who invest in green practices are better positioned to comply with rules and avoid legal penalties. These investments also assist organizations in managing risks related to environmental liability and operational disruptions caused by environmental challenges. Green investments are critical to fulfilling the United Nations Sustainable Development Goals (SDGs). Sachs et al. (2019) contend that major investment in environmentally friendly buildings, clean energy, and sustainable practices is required to achieve the SDGs. Businesses that align their plans with the SDGs can promote sustainable development while also capitalizing on new growth prospects. There is increasing confirmation that green investments improve long-term financial performance. Eccles, Ioannou, and Serafeim (2014) discovered that companies that prioritize sustainability outperform their rivals in terms of financial and accounting performance. Green investments help to save money by increasing energy efficiency and reducing waste, which improves financial stability. Several studies show that incorporating ESG criteria into investment choices has become a major driver of green investments. Firms with high ESG performance are more likely to attract investors interested in sustainable development and risk management. Studies show that companies with strong sustainability practices often enjoy higher valuations and better market performance. This is attributed to the growing investor demand for responsible investment opportunities and the perceived lower risk of such companies (Clark et al., 2015). A meta-analysis of more than 2,000 empirical research revealed a favorable relationship between Environmental, Social, and Governance (ESG) performance and financial success. This shows that green investments can provide long-term financial returns (Friede et al., 2015).

Green Investment

A crucial element in the growth of firms is financial management. It only refers to the action of managing investments or financial resources (Shahab et al., 2016; Sohail et al., 2021). Frameworks for managing finances are essential for promoting monetary development, which includes manageable financial growth, sex equity, human rights, environmental adaptability, increased natural responsibility, and low carbon emissions (Al Muhairi & Nobanee, 2019). Green and the acquisition of environmental advantages. Thus, low-carbon and climate-surviving investments such as green energy technologies, green financial products, green buildings, green supply chains, green logistics models, carbon capture and storage, reforestation, hybrid vehicles, smart grid systems, waste management, less energy-consuming initiatives, as well as green research and development, are all examples of green investment practises (Eyraud et al., 2013).

Previous research has also demonstrated several business green investing practises. The contribution that green financing made on the formulation of China's sustainable development goals (SDGs) was examined by Lee (2020). The study noted a number of recent trends in green finance, such as the switch from green to sustainable bonds, where investors are utilising the SDGs as a road map to spur demand for environmentally friendly securities (Alameri et.al, 2021).

Figure 1. Green investment pyramid

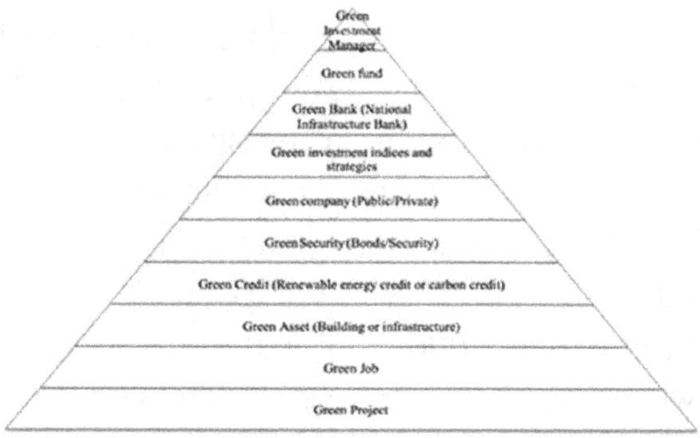

(Inderst et al., 2012)

Rationale of Green Business Practices

Although going green may seem to be the newest fad, company owners may benefit from this movement in a number of ways. By implementing green practises, businesses may foster a healthy work environment for their staff, cut down on waste, and acknowledge their important role in paving the road for social change. There are many reasons for the company considering becoming green to make the switch.

Reduced Waste: Going green can boost a company's general effectiveness. Cutting excessive waste can lower a company's operational expenses.

Greener Options: Offering green options within a firm can improve the workplace environment overall. Because green products include less chemicals, they can benefit workers who have respiratory and other health-related disorders substances that have been linked to internal issues, such as nitrobenzene and sodium hypochlorite.

Public Reaction: While the public's reaction by itself may not be the best incentive to become green, it could be a positive side effect. Economic studies have revealed that businesses using green technology and marketing green products are witnessing a rise in earnings as green efforts gain in popularity.

Table 1. Green investment category structure from IMF perspective

Component		**Item and sub-Item**
Supply factors	Low-emission energy supply	• Low-emission electricity supply
		¬ Nuclear
		¬ Renewable sources of electricity
		♣ Hydro power
		♣ Wind
		♣ Solar
		♣ Biomass
		• Other low-emission/renewable energy supply
		¬ Biofuels
		¬ Biomass
		¬ Solar and geothermal for heating
		• R&D in clean energy
	Carbon sequestration	• Agriculture
		• Deforestation
		• carbon capture and storage technologies
Demand factors	Energy efficiency in energy-consuming sectors	• Households
		• Industry
		• Transport
		• Services
		• Agriculture
Mixed Factors	Energy efficiency in the electricity sector (generation, transmission, distribution)	

Source: IMF (2011)

Determinants of Green Investment

According to a World Bank report, the following are the key obstacles to green investment:

1. The cost of carbon Investors won't be drawn to green investments until carbon pricing are more stable, predictable, and reliable. According to the High-Level Advisory Group on Climate Exchange Financing of the United Nations Secretary-General (AGF 2010), a price of 25 USD per tonne for carbon emissions is sufficient to expand investment to US$100 billion annually and meet the demands of developing nations.
2. Subsidies for fossil fuels: Green investments are undesirable because fossil fuel costs are underpriced and incumbent technologies' prices and resource allocation are distorted.
3. High upfront expenditures and protracted return periods: Although some green investments can be justified financially in some situations, this is not the case for the bulk of them. Because of this, green investments require greater rates of return and produce much larger returns than conventional investments. Therefore, countries should promote the level of profitability of green investments through pricing mechanisms or terms like green certificates.
4. Technological dangers: New technologies come with dangers, including viability and characteristics. If new technology development and financing are not supported by public funding or venture capital, they often become more difficult. Financial investors won't often support projects until the risk-return connection is more secure.
5. Revenue concerns: Investors and banks will carefully examine funding new technologies because of their unpredictable revenue and other hazards. In reality, new technologies have a low credit rating and must offer collateral to cover risks and meet financial obligations.

INDIAN GREEN INVESTMENT COMPANIES

Adani Green

The top green energy business in the world, Adani Green Energy Limited, is listed on a stock exchange. The business conglomerate Adani Group, founded in India, includes Adani Green. The company formulates utility-scale grid-linked wind and solar farm projects and then builds, owns, runs, and maintains them. The National Thermal Power Corporation (NTPC), Solar Energy Corporation of India (SECI), and several State Discoms are some of AGEL's most important clients. The company started its operations in 2015 at the location of Gujarat's Ahmedabad.

Suzlon Energy

One of the first companies in India to offer renewable energy solutions, Suzlon Energy specialises in the wind energy market. The business has built some of the biggest onshore wind farms that are currently in operation in states like Gujarat, Rajasthan, Maharashtra, and Tamil Nadu. The company just entered the solar energy market and has intentions to enter the wind- solar hybrid solutions market. Despite the company's more than 25 years of experience in the Indian industry, financial issues, a substantial amount of debt, and a strong focus on wind energy Energy will continue to be a problem for the business. The company was established in 1995 with the headquarters located in Pune, Maharashtra

Praj Industries

A market leader in process solutions, Praj Industries specialises in integrated systems for bioenergy, high purity water solutions, and engineering-driven enterprises. The Indian government has increased initiatives that will improve energy security while redoubling its focus on biofuels. This has increased demand for Praj's range of bio-energy products, including compressed biogas and ethanol. Additionally, Praj's biogas solution will support the nation's gas economy while assisting in the fight against air pollution and environmental threats brought on by stubble burning. The business was commenced in 1983 and the headquarters are located in Pune, Maharashtra.

Gravita

Modern manufacturing facilities for lead metal and lead products, aluminium alloys, plastic granules, and PET flakes are located at the Indian multinational corporation Gravita India. The business has expertise in recycling materials such as cable scrap, lead scrap, aluminium scrap, plastic scrap, and used lead-acid batteries. Pure lead, lead alloy, aluminium alloy, and PET flakes are just a few of the recycled items the company produces and sells. Over 50 nations in Europe, America, Asia, and Africa have Gravita customers, and more than half of the company's revenue comes from international markets. Manufacturing facilities for the corporation are dispersed across numerous Indian towns, Sri Lanka, and African nations like Ghana, Mozambique, Tanzania, as well as in Nicaragua & Jamaica. In 1992, Gravita has started the business of recycling with the headquarters situated in Jaipur, Rajasthan.

VaTech Wabag

Water treatment for municipal and industrial users is the primary emphasis of the Indian multinational corporation VA Tech Wabag. America, Africa, and Europe are all major markets for the company. Max Reder founded the business in Breslau, Germany, in 1924. After a string of mergers and acquisitions, VA Technologies acquired the company's water business. Va Tech Wabag joined the National Stock Exchange (NSE) and Bombay Stock Exchange (BSE) list of green Indian firms in 2010, and since then the company's stock price has experienced significant fluctuations. It was established in 1924 with the headquarters located in Chennai, Tamil Nadu

ION Exchange

Ion Exchange is involved in a number of environmental solutions, including waste energy production, solid & hazardous waste management, water treatment & recycling, and air pollution prevention. The business serves comprehensive water management services for businesses, residences, and communities, including supply, quantity, quality, discharge, and environmental water management. The business was established in 1964 and the headquarters are located in Mumbai, Maharashtra.

SEVERAL EXAMPLES OF OUTSTANDING EFFORTS IN SUSTAINABLE BUSINESS PRACTICES THROUGH GREEN INVESTMENTS COME FROM WBCSD MEMBER COMPANIES IN INDIA.

All of the enterprises are steadfastly committed to restructuring their operations and implementing environmentally friendly procedures all throughout their supply chains. Here are a few illustrations:

The in-depth research done by the Aditya Birla Group on "2 C Futures" and how companies need to fundamentally restructure their operations to ensure resilience in a hotter environment.

The "Greener India" project of the Godrej Group ensures that environmental sustainability is a crucial component of the entire value chain. They were successful in cutting back on specific GHG emissions by 51%, and they now get more than half of their energy from renewable sources.

ITC's groundbreaking "e-Choupal" has successfully improved the efficiency of the supply chain and addresses problems including dispersed farms, shoddy infrastructure, and the use of several middlemen.

Mahindra Group has played a significant role in revolutionising mobility by producing electric vehicles (EVs) and supporting India's goal of widespread EV use in the personal and commercial sectors by 2030.

Through the food supply chain, UPL's technology advancements—which also incorporate locally available solutions—have addressed a range of concerns, from raising yield to reducing food waste.

By 'closing the loop' initiatives for resource efficiency including sustainable packaging, fertiliser production from waste, and maximising the value of their industrial by-products like fly ash and road building, Tata Group has been actively adopting the ideas of the circular economy.

Reliance Industries recently began an initiative to combat plastic waste in India by providing used plastic for road building. To help with this procedure, they have created their own and contracted out rubbish collection and sorting.

GREEN INVESTMENT'S CONTRIBUTION TO SUSTAINABLE BUSINESS PRACTICES

By giving financial resources to assist environmentally friendly projects and businesses, green investments help to promote sustainability. These investments aid in lowering greenhouse gas emissions, promoting resource conservation, and fostering the growth of a more sustainable and resilient economy by directing capital towards renewable energy, energy efficiency, waste management, and other sustainable practices.

- The companies inviting money by the sources of green investment including the fact that the corporation can receive funds from the public through these means, which is greatly required for sustainability-related ventures since sustainability departments frequently operate with the less budgets in the organisation and the company's participation for the cleaner future might require the real investments of a substantial amount. Therefore, green investment is particularly beneficial to businesses for this purpose.
- Since the public is now conscious of the need to protect the environment, when someone allots a green bond, it inclines to garner a lot of public attention, that makes it simpler for the businesses to raise money. Additionally, the businesses gain public attention for their creative approaches to sustainability, which benefits the business alone.
- From the standpoint of the investor, green investments are advantageous because many of them, including green bonds, are tax-exempt.

- Along with the various advantages, these investments also give investors a sense of personal fulfilment since they know that their money is being used responsibly and for good.
- A lot of green investment instruments must abide by certain defined sets of disclosure rules, which aids investors in determining whether or not the individual who obtained cash is using their money appropriately.
- When there is a significant demand for green bonds, the borrowing costs will be low, which will lower the company's overall spending. The benefits of this decrease in spending will then solely parts in the form of dividends to the investors.

Figure 2. Green bonds issued worldwide from 2014 to 2022 (in billion us dollars)

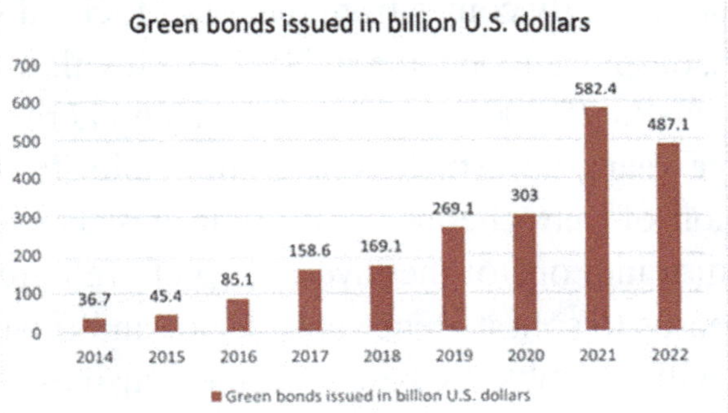

CONCLUSION

With investors' interest in environmental sustainability growing, sustainability practises and development have taken on a significant role in organisations. In this study, sustainability practises and development were taken into account, but from the standpoint of green investments. According to the research, there are several ways in which green investment is crucial for the adoption of sustainable practises and development. To meet the demands of the society, financial management must be effective. The financial decision-making component of financial management aids in the development and application of sustainable practises. India is poised to seize numerous opportunities, particularly in the fields of solar and renewable energy.

With 300 days of sunlight, a long coastline, and several rivers and tributaries, India has all the resources needed to significantly lessen its reliance on coal-based energy sources. India set a lofty goal at the Glasgow Summit 2021 to generate 500 GW of non-fossil fuel energy by 2030 and achieve a net-zero economy by 2070. The government has been creating regulations that will help this happen, including initiatives to encourage private players to take part in making this vision a reality. Tata Power, Reliance, NTPC, and Torrent Power are just a few examples of large, publicly traded Indian companies that have already recognised the opportunity and entered the sustainable business race. However, these firms cannot be referred to as green businesses in India as their primary source of income currently comes from the fossil fuel industry. Consider Reliance, which, despite announcing in 2021 that it will invest more than $10 billion (about Rs 75,000 crores) in the green energy industry over the ensuing three years, nevertheless bases the majority of its activities on the production of petrochemicals, oil, and gas. However, Reliance may very well turn into one of the investors' preferred green companies in India if it chooses to split its renewable sector and float on the Indian bourses. There will undoubtedly be more green businesses in India that raise public capital and are listed on the country's stock exchanges as the country works to achieve its climate goals.

REFRENCES

Al Muhairi, M., & Nobanee, H. (2019). Sustainable Financial Management. SSRN Electronic Journal. DOI: 10.2139/ssrn.3472417

Alameri, M., Alshamsi, F., Alsaedi, S., Alkaabi, A., Alamri, R., Alshamsi, M., & Nobanee, H. (2021). Financial Analysis of Hilton Holdings. doi:-DOI: 10.2139/ssrn.3930493

Arif, U., & Sohail, M. T. (2020). Asset pricing with higher co-moments and CVaR: Evidence from pakistan stock exchange. *International Journal of Economics and Financial Issues*, *10*(5), 243–255. DOI: 10.32479/ijefi.10351

Benabou, R., & Tirole, J. (2010). Individual and corporate social responsibility. *Economica*, *77*(305), 1–19. DOI: 10.1111/j.1468-0335.2009.00843.x

Burhan, A. H. N., & Rahmanti, W. (2012). The impact of sustainability reporting on company performance. Journal of Economics, Business, &. *Accountancy Ventura*, *15*(2), 257–272. DOI: 10.14414/jebav.v15i2.79

Clark, G. L., Feiner, A., & Viehs, M. (2015). *From the Stockholder to the Stakeholder: How Sustainability Can Drive Financial Outperformance*. University of Oxford and Arabesque Partners.

Devi, N. (2022). Green Business Developments in India- A Study on the Eco-Friendly Initiatives Towards Sustainable Developments. *International Journal of Innovative Research in Technology*, *9*(3), 385–388.

Eccles, R. G., Ioannou, I., & Serafeim, G. (2014). The Impact of Corporate Sustainability on Organizational Processes and Performance. *Management Science*, *60*(11), 2835–2857. DOI: 10.1287/mnsc.2014.1984

Eccles, R. G., Ioannou, I., & Serafeim, G. (2014). The Impact of Corporate Sustainability on Organizational Processes and Performance. *Management Science*, *60*(11), 2835–2857. DOI: 10.1287/mnsc.2014.1984

Eyraud, L., Clements, B., & Wane, A. (2013). Green investment: Trends and determinants. *Energy Policy*, *60*, 852–865. DOI: 10.1016/j.enpol.2013.04.039

Fareed, Z., Salem, S., Adebayo, T. S., Pata, U. K., & Shahzad, F. (2021). Role of Export Diversification and Renewable Energy on the Load Capacity Factor in Indonesia: A Fourier Quantile Causality Approach. *Frontiers in Environmental Science*, *9*, 1–9. DOI: 10.3389/fenvs.2021.770152

Flammer, C. (2013). Corporate Social Responsibility and Shareholder Reaction: The Environmental Awareness of Investors. *Academy of Management Journal*, *56*(3), 758–781. DOI: 10.5465/amj.2011.0744

Friede, G., Busch, T., & Bassen, A. (2015). ESG and Financial Performance: Aggregated Evidence from More than 2000 Empirical Studies. *Journal of Sustainable Finance & Investment*, *5*(4), 210–233. DOI: 10.1080/20430795.2015.1118917

Greenstone, M., List, J. A., & Syverson, C. (2012). *The effects of environmental regulation on the competitiveness of US manufacturing (No. w18392)*. National Bureau of Economic Research. DOI: 10.3386/w18392

Gujar (2020). A Study of Sustainable Business Practices in the Indian Pharmaceutical Industry. (Doctoral Thesis). Pacific University, Udaipur, India.

Horbach, J., Rammer, C., & Rennings, K. (2012). Determinants of Eco-innovations by Type of Environmental Impact—The Role of Regulatory Push/Pull, Technology Push and Market Pull. *Ecological Economics*, *78*, 112–122. DOI: 10.1016/j.ecolecon.2012.04.005

Inderst, G., Kaminker, Ch., & Stewart, F. (2012). Defining and Measuring Green Investments: Implications for Institutional Investors Asset Allocations. OECD Working Papers on Finance, Insurance and Private Pensions, No.24, OECD Publishing.

International Renewable Energy Agency (IRENA). (2019). Global Energy Transformation: A Roadmap to 2050.

IPCC. (2014). Climate change 2014, synthesis report. IPCC, Geneva, Switzerland. Retrieved 17 June,2019,fromhttp://www.ipcc.ch/pdf/assessmentreport/ar5/syr/SYR_AR5_FINAL_full_ wcover.pdf

Kaminker, C., & Stewart, F. (2012). The Role of Institutional Investors in Financing Clean Energy. *OECD Working Papers on Finance, Insurance and Private Pensions*, No. 23.

Khan, H. H., Malik, M. N., Konecna, Z., Chofreh, A. G., Goni, F. A., & Klemes, J. J. (2022). Blockchain technology for agricultural supply chains during the COVID-19 pandemic: Benefits and cleaner solutions. *Journal of Cleaner Production, 347*, 131268. DOI: 10.1016/j.jclepro.2022.131268

Kitzmueller, M., & Shimshack, J. (2012). Economic perspectives on corporate social responsibility. *Journal of Economic Literature, 50*(1), 51–84. DOI: 10.1257/jel.50.1.51

Lee, J. W. (2020). Green finance and sustainable development goals: The case of China. Lee, Jung Wan (2020). Green Finance and Sustainable Development Goals: The Case of China. *The Journal of Asian Finance, Economics and Business*, *7*(7), 577–586. DOI: 10.13106/jafeb.2020.vol7.no7.577

Liu, N., Qi, L., Huang, M., Chen, D., Yin, C., Zhang, Y., Wang, X., Yuan, G., Wang, R.-J., Yang, J., Peng, Y.-L., & Lu, X. (2022). Comparative secretome analysis of Magnaporthe oryzae identified proteins involved in virulence and cell wall integrity. *Genomics, Proteomics & Bioinformatics*, *20*(4), 728–746. DOI: 10.1016/j.gpb.2021.02.007

Lu, F., & Sohail, M. T. (2022). Exploring the effects of natural capital depletion and natural disasters on happiness and human wellbeing: A study in China. *Frontiers in Psychology, 13*, 870623. DOI: 10.3389/fpsyg.2022.870623

OECD. (2017). *Investing in Climate, Investing in Growth.* OECD Publishing.

Rai, S., & Jambhulkar, S. (2018). An analytical study of green business practices in india with specific reference to selected indian companies. *International Journal of Management and Social Sciences*, *6*(09), 1–15.

Sachs, J. D., Schmidt-Traub, G., Kroll, C., Lafortune, G., Fuller, G., & Woelm, F. (2019). *Sustainable Development Report 2019.* Bertelsmann Stiftung and Sustainable Development Solutions Network.

Shahab, A., Shihua, Q., Rashid, A., Hasan, F. U., & Sohail, M. T. (2016). Evaluation of water quality for drinking and agricultural suitability in the lower indus plain in sindh province. Pakistan. *Polish Journal of Environmental Studies*, *25*(6), 2563–2574. DOI: 10.15244/pjoes/63777

Sohail, M. T., Xiuyuan, Y., Usman, A., Majeed, M. T., & Ullah, S. (2021). Renewable energy and non-renewable energy consumption: Assessing the asymmetric role of monetary policy uncertainty in energy consumption. *Environmental Science and Pollution Research International*, *28*(24), 31575–31584. DOI: 10.1007/s11356-021-12867-0

Ullah, H., Wang, Z., Mohsin, M., Jiang, W., & Abbas, H. (2022). Multidimensional perspective of green financial innovation between green intellectual capital on sustainable business: The case of Pakistan. *Environmental Science and Pollution Research International*, *29*(4), 5552–5568. DOI: 10.1007/s11356-021-15919-7

Wei, H., Zhang, Y., Xiu, P., Zhang, H., & Zhu, S. (2022). Index-based analysis of industrial structure and environmental efficiency based on sewage discharge assessment in China. *Alexandria Engineering Journal*, *61*(1), 493–500. DOI: 10.1016/j.aej.2021.06.006

Wen, C., Akram, R., Irfan, M., Iqbal, W., Dagar, V., Acevedo-Duqued, Á., & Saydaliev, H. B. (2022). The Asymmetric Nexus between Air Pollution and COVID-19: Evidence from a Non-linear Autoregressive Distributed Lag Model. *Environmental Research*, *209*, 112848. DOI: 10.1016/j.envres.2022.112848

Yasara, A., Farooqa, T., Tabindaa, A. B., Sohailb, M. T., Mahfooza, Y., & Malika, A. (2019). Macrophytes as potential indicator of heavy metals in river water. *Desalination and Water Treatment*, *142*, 272–278. DOI: 10.5004/dwt.2019.23433

Chapter 4
Technological Innovation:
Fintech and Mobile Payments' Role in Financial Inclusion

Veenu Madan
https://orcid.org/0000-0001-7014-1106
Chandigarh University, Mohali, India

Manjit Kour
https://orcid.org/0000-0003-1043-3187
Chandigarh University, Mohali, India

ABSTRACT

Financial inclusion is vital for the prosperity of any economy. Technology has paved the way for a new system of banking, known as Fintech. Mobile banking and mobile payments are the new normal. Keeping in mind this wide usage of fintech mobile payment systems in India, this research paper analyzes the growth of mobile payments for financial inclusion. This study examines and assesses the role of Government Initiatives India stack in financial inclusion. The growth of mobile payments in India is examined by using secondary data. This paper also examines the future Strategies of Fintech mobile payment companies.

DOI: 10.4018/979-8-3693-6195-5.ch004

I. INTRODUCTION

Including the public in the formal financial system is known as financial inclusion. With the availability of internet-based banking, a sizable portion of the population, especially those living in remote regions, are now able to utilize official financial services swiftly and effortlessly which improves the possibility of creating an additional Financial transactions method beyond the bank's physical location and ATM network (Madan & Kour, 2023; Nur et al., 2014). The evolutionary path of information technology leads to redesigning the financial services value chain, which opens up a new business model known as Fintech. Fintech is regarded as one of the technologies that disrupt the banking system and can enable businesses to compete better with new and cutting-edge technologies in the industrial revolution 4.0 (Putritama, 2019). Mobile payments use cellular and other forms of communication networks to pay for goods, services, or bills through the help of portable electronic devices like a cell phone, smartphone, handheld P.C., mobile telecommunications networks, or near-field communication technology (Madan & Kour, 2024; Dahlberg et al., 2006). When the Indian Government declared demonetization in 2016 and prohibited the 500 and 1000 notes in use at the time, 86% of notes in circulation in India became invalid. During that period, mobile payments received considerable attention and provided massive support to the unorganized sector and small vendors to maintain business and manage their finance through mobile payment applications. In Kenya, M-Pesa, and the Philippines, m-cash received considerable acceptance after the financial crises, and in India, mobile payments soared after demonetization with very few and zero investments. In India, people already have smartphones and internet connections, so small vendors don't have difficulty installing smartphone applications (Pal et al., 2020). After demonetization, mobile payment penetration has increased, although use and retention have remained low (S et al., 2018). Most households use mobile phones for payments and transfers in addition to saving (Ouma et al., 2017). Digital financial services now have additional chances to accelerate and widen financial inclusion as a result of the COVID-19 epidemic (Sahay et al., 2020). For financial inclusion, it is necessary to participate the user in designing the applications and impart digital training among the masses.

But we need an adequate regulatory and supervisory framework to support the sector's growth and guarantee that FinTech continues to aid India's financial inclusion efforts (Raj, 2020).

II. BRIEF LITERATURE REVIEW

The new technologies bring radical changes in developing economies, and business organizations are forced to change their structure according to information and communication technology development. Mobile banking in Kenya delivers financial services to unbanked areas and presents substantial regulatory and competition policy challenges. It provides essential conceptual insights into the nature of financial services by unbundling and disaggregating financial services(Klein, 2011).

According to the world bank report, 38% of adults and 73% of poor people are unbanked and have no access to formal financial services. The study further stressed that in developing economies, more than half of the adults had no bank account, and it is necessary to bring them under the umbrella of a formal financial system to make people live better. Recent World Bank Global Findex data indicates improved trends, yet an overwhelming 1.4 billion unbanked worldwide remain, wherein digital exclusion, trust issues, and risks remain major impediments in developing countries. (World Bank, 2023). Mobile technologies provide a better solution to extend legal and financial services. To achieve financial inclusion, it is imperative to comprehend why people are excluded from the financial system.

Government expenditures, time, effort, and resources are reduced due to mobile payments, which may be channelled into other social initiatives to benefit the economy and society. It is more convenient for both the payee and the payer (Sapovadia, 2018). Supporting these notions, the International Monetary Fund (2024) claims that digital financial services can effectively reduce transactional costs and payment efficiency, especially for low-income economies where banks are less present (IMF, 2024).

68 per cent of Indians prefer cash and 48 per cent consider mobile transactions to lack a strong value proposition. The study also found that

about 55% had no idea how the system operated and believed it was too complicated. Privacy is the main factor that affects the adoption of mobile payments. With the use of mobile payment technologies, financial inclusion, corruption, and tax evasion are all social and economic issues in India that may be resolved (Sinha et al., 2019). Supporting these claims, International Monetary Fund (2024) argues that digital financial services have an efficient way to reduce costs, which are usually high, as regards low-income economies, specifically in countries where bank penetration is less pronounced.

It investigated that technology is transforming the finance system, allowing unprecedented access to financial services. They constructed a comprehensive financial inclusion index by combining traditional and digital financial inclusion indices (Sahay et al., 2020). The key to FinTech success is to maximize the advantages while minimizing the dangers. The study also concluded that an inclusive, cost-effective, and robust financial system in the Indian market needs to balance technology and risk through the collaboration of bank and fintech firms (Raj, 2020). More recent empirical studies confirm that collaboration between banks and fintech increases trust among customers as it takes advantage of the trustworthiness of banks (BIS, 2023; World Economic Forum, 2024).

Customers would be less inclined to accept new technology if they have faith in the existing banking system. In India, various factors affect the adoption of fintech mobile payments, i.e., low internet penetration, lack of correct information and hardware, and lack of funds for new fintech startups. These factors must be addressed to create customer confidence (Vinay & Mehrotra, 2019). Despite an internet penetration base of over 55% being achieved in India, the digital skills gap and associated perceived financial risks remaining holding back internet adoption, especially in rural areas, indicate that infrastructural development is not sufficient, suggesting that trust development is equally an essential factor (GSMA, 2023; World Bank, 2024).

III. METHODS

This study is based on secondary data. Data is collected from various government sites NPCI, RBI, and use reports of FCCI, PWC, and India fintech report 2020 Medici. Extensive literature is done to understand the role of Mobile payments in financial inclusion clearly.

IV. GROWTH OF MOBILE PAYMENT

Mobile proximity transactions are the way of the future as we move closer to a cashless world. Although some places no longer utilize cash, many nations still deploy digital technology relatively slowly for a variety of reasons. China is the undisputed master, with 87.3 per cent of the population using cashless forms of payment. In the last two years, adoption in the United States increased the most, from 29 per cent (2019) to 43.2 per cent (2021), surpassing India. Adoption of mobile payments in India was 37.6% in 2019 and increased to 40.1% in 2021according to Emarketer. Com. The adoption rate is meagre in India compared to China. In India, people prefer to keep cash in their pockets for safety instead of digital transactions. There is a great need to study the factors which affect the adoption of mobile payments.

A. Mobile Payment Adoption by Country

China is the global leader in mobile payment adoption. In 2019 81.1% of consumers used proximity mobile payment; in 2021, this rate increased to 87.3%. The most popular provider of mobile payment services in China is Alipay and Tenpay.In India, the denominate player in proximity mobile payment is Phone pay and adoption in 2019 was 37.6% and increased to 40% in 2021.

Figure 1. Mobile payment adoption by country

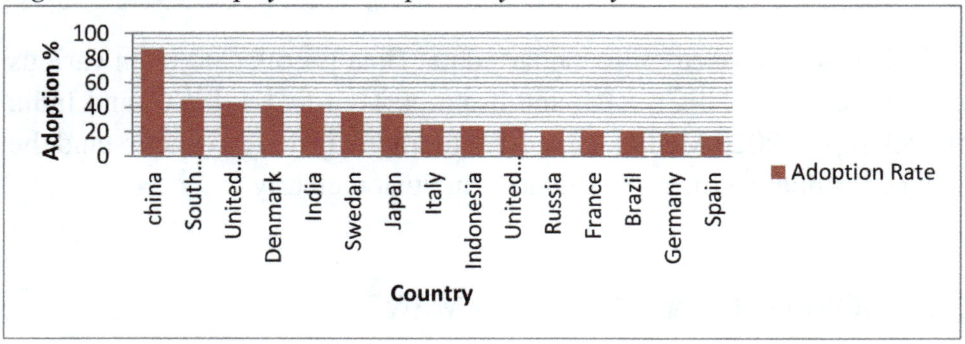

Figure 1 shows the adoption of mobile payment applications by different countries. We can see that India ranks in the 5th position in the adoption of mobile payments with a 40.1% adoption rate. France, Brazil, and Germany still do not prefer to pay through the mobile application they trust when dealing with banks. India's adoption rate of mobile payment still needs to increase because it is far less than in China. Mobile payment application services must be improved to bring Indians into the financial inclusion umbrella.

B. Market Share of UPI Mobile Payment Applications in India

UPI-based transactions launched by the Indian Government in 2016 are a great initiative to make the cash-based economy a cashless economy. UPI is a distinctive platform that aggregates various banking features and services in one location. The Unified Payments Interface was introduced by the Indian Banks Association, the Reserve Bank of India, and the National Payments Corporation of India (NPCI), making it safe and secure.

Table 1. Market share of UPI-based applications

Application	Phone Pe	Google pay	Paytm	Cred	BHIM
Market share %	46.3	36.4	10.2	1.6	5.5

Table 1 shows that NPCI launched BHIM UPI-based application. After that, other companies, phone pay, google pay, and Paytm also launched their application and captured a high market share by offering cashback and other incentives deflating the BHIM application.

Figure 2. Market share of UPI-based applications

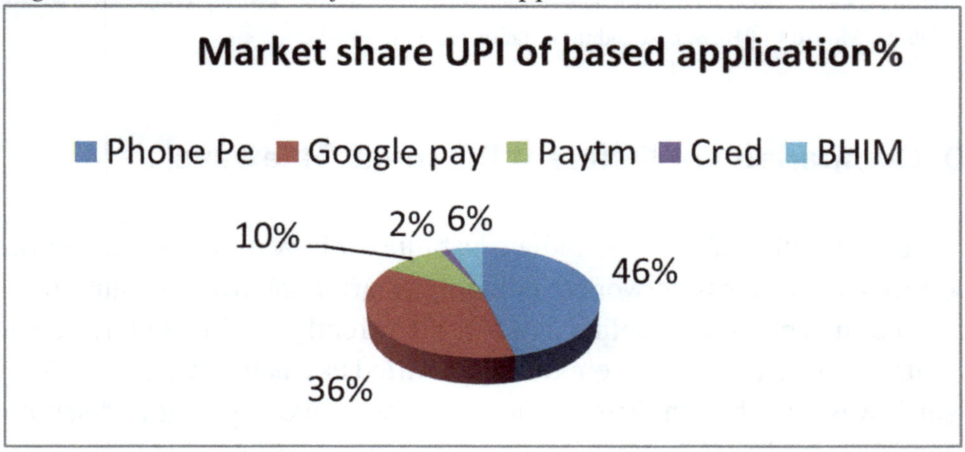

Figure 2 shows that the NPCI has developed into a powerful platform for collaboration that helps not just banks, but also other corporations and FinTech firms participate in a real-time payments system. UPI system created a national open standard for all banks and fintech players. The phone's Pe UPI-based application's market share is the largest at 46%, compared to google pay at 36%. New fintech players capture the entire UPI market.

C. Growth in UPI Transactions

UPI is considerably advanced over existing payment systems and has seen widespread acceptance. At the time of demonetization, the Indian economy depended on cash, and 16,415 billion currency was in circulation, accounting for 12.04% of GDP. The National Payment Corporation of India (NPCI) was established by the Reserve Bank of India (RBI) to operate as an umbrella organization for the creation of affordable retail virtual payment solutions (Gochhwal, 2017)

Table 2. Growth in UPI transactions

	F.Y 2017-18		F.Y 2018-19		F.Y 2019-20		F.Y 2020-21	
Platform	**Volume (in lakh)**	**Value (Cr.)**	**Volume (in lakh)**	**Value (Cr.)**	**Volume (in lakh)**	**Value (Cr.)**	**Volume (in lakh)**	**Value (Cr.)**
UPI	9152	109832	53,534	876970	125186	223307	2131730	4103653

Source: Ministry of Broadcast and information technology

D. Comparison of Different Payment Gateways

For more than 20 years, Indian institutions have offered a range of services via wireless networks, including smartphone banking, automated teller machines, and online payments. Currently, 47% of India's retail clearing and settlement systems use the Unified Payments Interface (UPI), which was launched in 2016 as an instant real-time payment and settlement system [14]. A system known as the "Unified Payments Interface (UPI) is a system that powers multiple bank accounts into a single mobile application (of any participating bank), merging various banking features, seamless fund routing, and merchant payments into one hood." (NPCI). The National Payment Corporation of India (NCPI) developed a unified Payment Interface (UPI) as a potential game-changing cash transfer method via a virtual payment address to support the nation's contactless and paperless economy. Demonetization policies by the government pushed for the wider use of contactless payments(Gupta & Kumar, 2020)

Table 3. Comparison of different payment gateways

Year	AEPS		IMPS		NEFT		UPI		BHIM Aadhaar Pay		Card Payments	
	Volume In lakh	Value In cr.	Volume In lakh	Value In cr.	Volume In lakh	Value In cr.	Volume In lakh	Value In cr.	Volume In lakh	Value In cr.	Volume In lakh	Value In cr.
2015-16	-	-	2208	162226	12529	8327311	-	-	-	-	19593	399588
2016-17	1	51	5067	411106	16221	12003968	180	6961	-	-	34864	658289
2017-18	6	300	10098	892498	19464	17222852	9152	109832	20	78	47486	919035
2018-19	11	501	17529	1590257	23189	22793608	53915	876971	68	815	61769	1196888
2019-20	10	469	25792	2337541	27445	22945580	125186	2131730	91	1303	72384	1434813
2020-21	11	623	32783	2941500	30928	25130910	223307	4103658	161	2580	57787	1291799

Source: RBI Database

Table 3 depicts that before UPI, people's preferred mode of payment was card, NEFT, and IMPS. In 2016 with the introduction of UPI, we can see that there is a massive increase in the volume and value of payment through UPI with the help of smartphone devices.

V. INDIA STACK MODEL

The India Stack, a collection of web APIs constructed on top of the Aadhaar database, allows private firms access to digital infrastructure for identity authentication and the provision of new "services," such as "financial services," leveraging Aadhaar data. The U.N. Sustainable Development Goals specified a global strategic objective of legal identification for all by 2030. Legal identity is critical in boosting people's engagement in society and providing access to resources that can help them live better. Aadhaar, India's digital identity program, is the world's biggest identity project to give basic identification and access to government services throughout the country. Aadhaar cards had been registered by 1.2 billion persons by 2019. Adhar provides an identity not only for citizens but also a resident of the country and helps them to open an account and get the benefits directly in versions (Adam, 2021). Aadar provides digital identity to marginal and minor workers and cab drivers in south India and helps them get online and offline jobs (Krishna, 2021). The Government is focusing on the financial inclusion of the informal sector, which comprises 81 per cent of India's working population. Most of this informality is concentrated in rural and agricultural sectors, using the Aadhar. This governmental use of Aadhaar increased in tandem with and sparked even more interest in commercial Aadhaar verification. Developers like iSPIRIT, a "private" think tank that has facilitated the accessibility of cloud-based digital services known as "India Stack" to be used across public and private sector services and as a basis for digitally-driven financial inclusion, have advocated for an "open" architecture of digitalization for Aadhaar. Many of India's population did not have access to formal banking services and relied heavily on cash for financial transactions. The main motto of the India stack model is to boost financial inclusion by increasing financial services, improving the delivery of public services and benefits, and strengthening competition in the Indian financial industry. This has created a framework for the economy to operationalize user-authorized data portability and interoperability (Carriere-Swallow et al., 2021). India stack model plays an essential role in the pandemic time to directly transfer money to people's accounts under relief packages given by the Government in Jan Dhan accounts and farmers' accounts. India stack uses a unique digital infrastructure to solve problems of businesses, governments, and startups with a set of APIs. It is based on four layers. Presenseless, paperless, cashless, and consent.

Figure 3. India stack model acts as a driver for financial inclusion

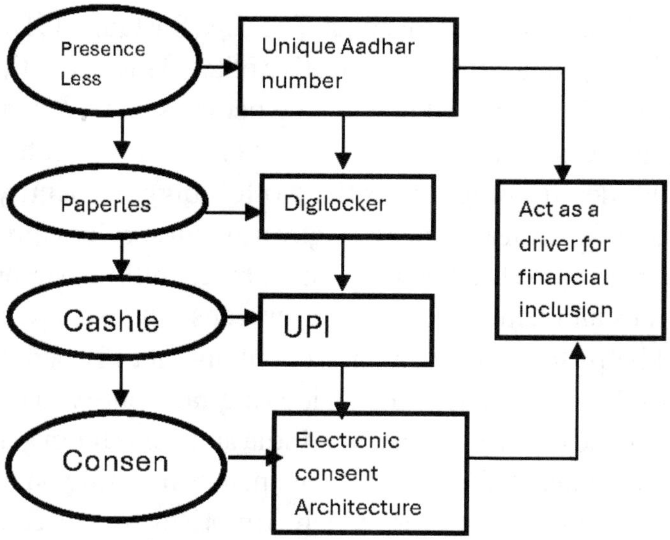

Source: NPCI (Author creation)

VI. FUTURE STRATEGIES OF FINTECH MOBILE PAYMENT COMPANIES

Due to the rapid advancement of I.T. technology and the growing need for easy payment, mobile payment services that were previously only available through financial institutions have evolved into various mobile Fintech payment services. The mobile payment market is becoming active in developing countries, so the masses must provide a secure economic infrastructure (Kang, 2018). China has risen as the world's leading champion of mobile payments due to its demographic dividend, high consumer acceptance, and robust technological infrastructure. The People's Bank of China provides a stable and conducive environment for the growth of mobile payments, and Alipay and chat pay dominate the mobile payment market. Compared to Japan and China, the mobile payment market in India is highly competitive and invested by foreign players. Reserve Bank of India introduced Vision 2021 with 36 action points moving India toward a cashless economy. To capture the rural market USSD based mobile payments were introduced. Mobile payment service providers in India are reinventing their business model. MPSPs in India must expand their product offerings to include new services and payment methods. In India, PhonePe has developed comprehensive access to many payment methods and worked with wallet providers to integrate them into the PhonePe payment container. The growth and innovation in the utilities and bill payment service line may usher in a new era of digital inclusion, and applications become super applications with their holistic view. Incumbents also create their own digital space or make partnerships with fintech companies. Paytm has collaborated with a renowned bank to book a fixed deposit on behalf of customers who have more than INR1 lakh in their wallets at the end of the day (Jain, 2019)

Table 4. Future strategies of fintech mobile payment companies

Segment	Innovation	Description	Product or service
Payment	Virtual cards	During the transaction, eliminate physical touch contactless virtual card launch by repaid firms	Product Expansion
Ensure Tech	COVID insurance	Many Fintech in payment, wealth launched a covid insurance product	Product Expansion
Payment	Priority KYC	Help essential SMEs online in less than 5 minutes	Value-added service

Segment	Innovation	Description	Product or service
Payment	Rental office furniture	Bengaluru Payment Gateway makes a partnership with a furniture rental platform to provide rented furniture for offices and same-day settlement for cash flows	Value-added service
Lending	Credit Product	To pay monthly rent through a credit card new product launched by the credit card payment app Bengaluru firm	Product
Payment	Electronic POS	This new product allows the merchant to download the app on their android phone and accept payment through it	Product
Payment	Free website in a built-in payment gateway	SME merchants can create a free website with a payment gateway	Value-added service
Lending	Anti-lockdown loan	In an anti-lockdown loan, there is no need to pay EMI for three months up to 75000 by P2P lending fintech	Product
Neo bank	Financial literacy	To educate people about branchless banking	Value-added service
Payment	Home delivery	Groceries and other essential items delivered at home service started by Bengaluru-based Fintech	Value-added service
Enabling Tech	Video conferencing	KYC, through a video call	Product

Source: Report of PWC and FICCI 2020

Globally, mobile payments have emerged as a potent instrument for advancing financial inclusion. Numerous without a bank account people are lured to it because of its ease of use, velocity, and reliability because they typically have little confidence in traditional banking. As a result, it is also plausible to assert that mobile wallets serve as a gateway for these unbanked individuals to access the financial services that are denied to them. Furthermore, the constant backing of the Government and other authorities makes it much easier for mobile wallet service providers and guarantees that their effects are felt broadly, leading to the highest level of financial inclusion possible.

VI. CONCLUSION

Although cash reigns supreme, digital is wonderful. India has created the 'India Stack,' a vast, secure, efficient, and scalable public digital infrastructure preparing the way for a significant global 'Digital Payments Revolution. The entrance of very well and competitive technology-first enterprises (formerly controlled by banks) has made digital payments commonplace in India, laying a solid basis for digitalization and cross-selling other financial services and products. This architecture can foster financial inclusion by bringing together various banks and non-banks under a shared infrastructure, as indicated by the surge in high volume-low value payment transactions. The entire framework of publicly provided digital infrastructures has the potential to support a wide range of financial services, as well as broader financial inclusion and development. Fintech reduces paper-based banking and has comprehensive coverage, positively impacting the environment and financial inclusion. Fintech can go a long way in contributing to sustainable economic development goals. A high-quality action plan designed to motivate users (rather than extolling product features or generic benefits of digital payments) with specific “how to use” knowledge, learning, and problem-solving helplines, as well as safeguard features that help subscribers “stay safe,” can help India accelerate its transition to a cashless economy. Fintech payment gateways provide the energy that propels the nation toward digital financial inclusivity.

REFERENCES

Adam, H. (2021). Fintech and Entrepreneurship Boosting in Developing Countries: A Comparative Study of India and Egypt. *Studies in Computational Intelligence*, *974*, 141–156. DOI: 10.1007/978-3-030-73057-4_12

Bank for International Settlements. (2023). *Sound practices: implications of fintech developments for banks and bank supervisors*. BIS.

Carriere-Swallow, Y., Haksar, V., & Patnam, M. (2021). India's Approach to Open Banking: Some Implications for Financial Inclusion. SSRN *Electronic Journal*. DOI: 10.5089/9781513570686.001

Dahlberg, T., Mallat, N., Ondrus, J., & Zmijewska, A. (2006). Mobile Payment Market and Research - Past, Present, and Future. *Presentation at Helsinki Mobility Roundtable, Helsinki, Finland, June 1-2, 2002*(January 2006), 1–16.

Gochhwal, R. (2017). Unified Payment Interface—An Advancement in Payment Systems. *American Journal of Industrial and Business Management*, *07*(10), 1174–1191. DOI: 10.4236/ajibm.2017.710084

GSMA. (2023). State of mobile internet connectivity 2023.

Gupta, S., & Kumar, D. (2020). Upi - An Innovative Step for Making Digital Payment Effective and Consumer Perception on Unified Payment Interface. *The International Journal of Analytical and Experimental Modal Analysis*, *12*(1), 2482–2491.

International Monetary Fund. (2024). Digital money and financial inclusion in emerging economies.

Jain, M. (2019). Fintech in India- Powering Mobile Payments. *Kpmg*, (August), 1–36.

Kandpal, V., & Mehrotra, R. (2019). Financial inclusion: The role of fintech and digital financial services in India. *Indian Journal of Economics & Business*, *19*(1), 85–93.

Kang, J. (2018). Mobile payment in Fintech environment: Trends, security challenges, and services. *Human-Centric Computing and Information Sciences*, *8*(1), 32. Advance online publication. DOI: 10.1186/s13673-018-0155-4

Klein, M. (2011). *Mobile Banking and Financial Inclusion The Regulatory Lessons. May.*

Krishna, S. (2021). Digital identity, datafication and social justice: Understanding Aadhaar use among informal workers in south India. *Information Technology for Development*, *27*(1), 67–90. DOI: 10.1080/02681102.2020.1818544

Madan, V., & Kour, M. (2023). Mobile Payment Usage: Systematic Literature Review. Emerging Trends and Innovations in Industries of the Developing World, 89-93.

Madan, V., & Kour, M. (2024, March). Fintech and Mobile Payments in Transition: An Analysis of Adoption Challenges. In *2024 IEEE International Conference on Interdisciplinary Approaches in Technology and Management for Social Innovation (IATMSI)* (Vol. 2, pp. 1-6). IEEE. DOI: 10.1109/IATMSI60426.2024.10503040

Nur, M., Siddik, A., Sun, G., Yanjuan, C., & Kabiraj, S. (2014). Financial Inclusion through Mobile Banking: A Case of Bangladesh. *Journal of Applied Finance & Banking*, *4*(6), 1792–6599. www.btrc.gov.bd

Ouma, S. A., Odongo, T. M., & Were, M. (2017). Mobile financial services and financial inclusion: Is it a boon for savings mobilization? *Review of Development Finance*, *7*(1), 29–35. DOI: 10.1016/j.rdf.2017.01.001

Pal, A., De', R., & Herath, T. (2020). The Role of Mobile Payment Technology in Sustainable and Human-Centric Development: Evidence from the Post-Demonetization Period in India. *Information Systems Frontiers*, *22*(3), 607–631. DOI: 10.1007/s10796-020-09982-7

Putritama, A. (2019). The Mobile Payment Fintech Continuance Usage Intention in Indonesia. *Journal of Economics*, *15*(2), 243–258. DOI: 10.21831/economia.v15i2.26403

Raj, B. (2020). *Role of FinTech in Accelerating Financial Inclusion in India Role of FinTech in Accelerating Financial Inclusion in India Paper presented at the 3 rd International Conference on Economics and Finance organised by the Nepal Rastra Bank at Kathmandu, Nepal. February.*

Reserve Bank of India. (2024). Payment and settlement systems in India: Annual report.

Sahay, R., von Allmen, U. E., Lahreche, A., Khera, P., Ogawa, S., Bazarbash, M., & Beaton, K. (2020). *The promise of fintech : financial inclusion in the post COVID-19 era* (Issue 20).

Sapovadia, V. (2018). Financial Inclusion, Digital Currency, and Mobile Technology. In *Handbook of Blockchain, Digital Finance, and Inclusion* (1st ed., Vol. 2). Elsevier Inc. DOI: 10.1016/B978-0-12-812282-2.00014-0

Sinha, M., Majra, H., Hutchins, J., & Saxena, R. (2019). Mobile payments in India: The privacy factor. *International Journal of Bank Marketing*, *37*(1), 192–209. DOI: 10.1108/IJBM-05-2017-0099

World Bank. (2023). Global Findex Database 2023: Financial inclusion and digital payments.

World Economic Forum. (2024). The future of financial services in emerging markets.

Chapter 5
Blockchain-Driven Transformation:
A Transaction Cost Economics Approach to Banking Efficiency

Mohammad Ammar Ahsan
Aligarh Muslim University, Aligarh, India

Shamaela Tabassum
Aligarh Muslim University, Aligarh, India

ABSTRACT

Blockchain's innovative trust, security, and transparency solution is transforming technology. This study uses Transaction Cost Economics (TCE) to examine whether blockchain will lower banking transaction costs. The study's conceptual exploration begins with early institutional economics research. This article will address Blockchain Technology (BcT) and its potential use in the banking industry to reduce information asymmetry and transaction costs. Based on a theoretical model, transaction costs are environmental unpredictability, opportunism, restricted rationality, and contract asset specificity. An example showed how BcT saves money through efficiency and trust. This study proposes a model that captures blockchain's potential influence and the revolution below. Due to scalability, regulatory, and uncertainty issues, the study shows hopeful signs but also

DOI: 10.4018/979-8-3693-6195-5.ch005

constraints. Finally, empirical investigations, comparative evaluations, andfuturistic blockchain exploration helps to blockchain banking research by providing a basic explanation and encouraging more study.

1. INTRODUCTION

In the constantly evolving realm of technology, there is one revolutionary advancement that truly stands out, reforming our perceptions of trust, security, and transparency. Imagine a digital record-keeping structure which is so secure and unalterable that it holds the potential to redefine the very core of our interconnected world. The banking world has, for a substantial period, been offering individuals with the promise of reliability, focusing to elucidate the fascination surrounding this innovative technology. Customers actively pursue and recompense for this trust, looking for a secure and fair management of their transactions. Banks, in turn, manage ledger and accounting systems, charging customers for these services. The operational processes within the banking industry are characterized by repetition, time consumption, and high costs (Salim et al., 2023). To address these challenges, prominent banks, including central banks, are actively investigating the integration of Blockchain Technology (BcT) into their current models (Khadka, 2020). Albeshr & Nobanee, (2020) describe it as a digitalized record-keeping technology that uses a public database for secure and networked data storage. It is a technology, which combines encryption, information technology, and mathematics, offers a revolutionary way to advance the banking industry (Kołodziej, 2021). In the midst of blockchain's financial significance on banks, academic debate emphasises the need for thorough investigation.

For many years, institutional economics scholarly discussions have been greatly influenced by Transaction Cost Economics (TCE) (Ahluwalia et al., 2020). Ronald Coase, (1937), as the first researcher who delves into the effect of transaction cost in market as well as firm structure. He was able to do a big work known as "The Nature of the Firm". Building further on Coase's considerations, Kenneth Arrow, (1988) considers the economy organization discussing intermediates contracts and the role of transaction costs, deficiencies of the markets. Williamson, 1971, 1981 & 2002) added to the debate tying elements of market and organisational economics like vertical integration and governance to TCE as well as establishing the failures and successes of markets. In this paper, we discuss the financial decision made when these financial organisations choose to apply BcT as a database solution in the modern environment. To understand the effects of applying blockchain technologies on organisational choices, the TCE is applied to demonstrate how the technologies decentralise, democratise, and decrease the transaction costs integrated with the economic exchange of value. This, in turn, creates solidarity among various participants (Chen, 2018). Thus, it is proposed that blockchain-based technologies have the potential to transform transaction costs in the meaning of both ease and effectiveness. According to the above said framework, the following objectives are aimed: Our aim to get a deeper understanding of several industries as well as the functional jobs they perform in the economy. This research focuses on the financial institutions domain, where high information asymmetry and high transaction costs are typical of the banking industry. More specifically, we explain how these difficulties in the banking sector might be lessened by the intrinsic decentralised, transaction-based architecture of blockchain technologies.

This study is the first attempt to clarify the transaction costs associated with using BcT in the banking sector. Specifically, it examines how blockchains can decrease transaction-heavy processes and provide alternative solutions. To assess the budding influence of BcT on supply chain management, Treiblmaier (2018) employed the TCE model. Through focusing on the banking sector, we hope to supplement Treiblmaier (2018) research in this undertaking. This research opens up the ways on how BcT functions within the banking industry. This analysis demonstrates, through a TCE lens, how the efficiency of the transaction that blockchain provides is conducive to institutional adoption of blockchain since it possesses built-in inefficiencies that are not present in existing banking systems. It discusses how the fundamental inefficiencies related to these harms can be mitigated with the help of BcT, gives practical examples of how consumer datasets can benefit from blockchain-based decentralisation, tokenisation, and establishing trust.

The layout of our manuscript is as follows: a brief literature review of TCE, an overview and brief history of banking and a literature review of BcT and banking and a theoretical model focusing the arguments on transaction costs and the adaptation of BcT in banking. The discussion part of the paper gives further details on how our proposed model is coherent with existing literature and it concludes by outlining some suggestions for further research studies.

2. THEORY OF TRANSACTION COST ECONOMICS

TCE is the prevailing theoretical framework in the field of management and organisation since the Williamson (1973) conceptual paper "Markets and Hierarchies" (Chiles & Mcmackin, 2016; David & Han, 2004; Williamson, 2002). This is not an accurate representation of the neoclassical economic perspective on structures or behaviours. The neoclassical perspective relates to transactions in a free market or a mixed commodity market, where some measure of dependency characterizes the parties involved in the transactions. Conversely, the theory being discussed aims to elucidate the attributes of a company and provide predictions for why certain actions are taken without taking transaction costs into account (David & Han, 2004). Transaction cost is therefore the backbone of the TCE theory and it's made up of transactions. While the former involves the act of buying and selling, the latter refers to the total cost that may be in the form of cash, stocks, services and even other items. Environmental uncertainty, opportunism, constrained rationality, and asset specificity are the origins of transaction costs. Uncertainty in the environment and limited reasoning lead to incomplete agreements and less-than-perfect choices, making the neoclassical economists' goal of informationally full agreements unachievable. When there aren't detailed contracts, it's easy for one side to take advantage of the situation and extract financial rent from the other (Williamson, 2002). Therefore, in the interactions between the people involved, trust becomes essential. The application of mathematical algorithms and decentralised networks in BcT presents a promising solution to the trust problem.

One important factor influencing transaction costs is asset specificity. Assets with low asset specificity have many applications, whereas assets with high asset specificity are those that are difficult to repurpose. Imagine a situation where a supplier makes significant investments in resources meant to produce a particular good for a specific buyer (Ahluwalia et al., 2020). The supplier's assets become unique to that buyer as a result of this commitment. So, if the buyer's needs aren't met, they might be willing to pay less, which would allow them to avoid losing a lot of money on certain assets. The traditional TCE model is depicted in Figure 1.

Figure 1. Traditional transaction cost model

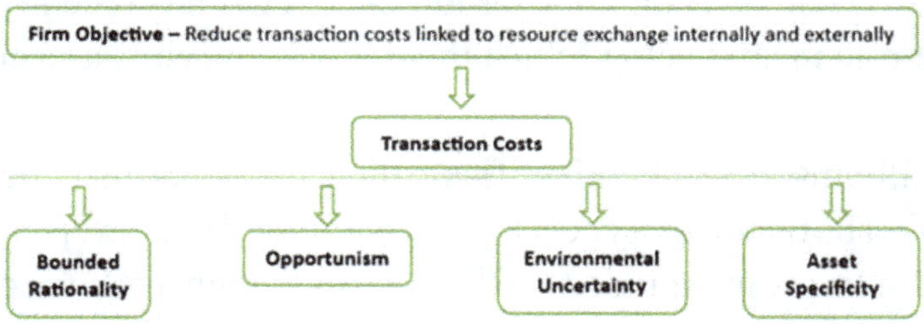

(Ahluwalia et al., 2020)

3. LITERATURE REVIEW

The very first attempt to examine the criticality of transactions and associated costs was Coase's, (1937) groundbreaking study. In the 1960s and 1970s, TCE were formally conceptualised, drawing on ideas expressed in Coase's seminal work (Williamson 1975, 1973; Baumol, 2016). Over the preceding half-century, TCE has become the most influential theory for explaining the fundamental qualities of businesses and has also become a cornerstone theory in the fields of governance and management (Scranton & Chandler, 1991; Conner, 1991; O. Williamson, 1979; Yale et al., 1984). TCE systematically studies multifaceted transactions carried out by economically rational mediators who are prone to opportunistic acts, including assets whose reallocation is difficult in an indefinite environment (Santos & Eisenhardt, 2005; Williamson, 1985).

The theory's ability to make accurate predictions has been supported to different degrees in academic discourse (David & Han, 2004). Upon synthesising data from the study conducted by David & Han, (2004) it was discovered that a mere 47% of the papers published in esteemed business journals provide support for the predictions of TCE. This discovery is consistent with the viewpoints expressed by prominent scholars in the business world regarding TCE (Ghoshal & Moran, 1996; Moran and Ghoshal, 1996; Robins, 1987). Nevertheless, counterarguments and corroborating evidence for TCE exhibit comparable robustness (Mahoney, 1992; Shelanski & Klein, 1995), as researchers attribute inconsistencies in the literature to issues pertaining to sampling or operationalization procedures (David & Han, 2004). Moreover, TCE has recently played a significant role in advancing robust theoretical concepts, as a conceptual framework.

O. E. Williamson, (1985) identifies critical elements influencing transaction costs. The opportunity cost for depositors and borrowers negotiating financial contracts is included in these costs, along with specific costs related to beginning, carrying out, and upholding obligations. For lenders, supplemental costs include costs of obtaining and processing information necessary to evaluate potential borrowers, manage loan procedures, manage collateral tasks, and monitor loans. Costs related to loan collection and collateral seizure are included in the total spectrum. In order to prevent clients from acting in an opportunistic manner, financial intermediaries must proactively manage a variety of transaction costs, including search, screening, training, counselling, credit education, and enforcement (Gray, 1994). By ensuring that borrowers follow loan terms, these expenses—collectively referred to as information costs—have an impact on operational costs and transaction success (Cole, 1998). By eliminating uncreditworthy borrowers from the portfolio, using information costs has the screening effect of improving risk assessment for loan applications and lowering loss rates. Because of the bank's knowledge advantage, there is less need for regulation and surveillance since opportunistic activity is curbed. The significance of transaction cost analysis in financial intermediation theory is emphasised by Benston & Smith, (1976). Financial intermediaries influence the products that customers choose to consume, both in terms of timing and context. The nature and distribution of financial goods are impacted by changes in customer transaction costs and technology. Regulating bodies prevent intermediaries from customising items to match changing consumer demands and technological advancements. To outline the complex interaction among products, financial intermediaries, and transaction costs, a more comprehensive study is suggested, laying the groundwork for additional research in this area. We posit that the utilisation of BcT has the potential to mitigate the challenges that arise in this particular scenario.

This study employs the TCE perspective to elucidate the functioning of BcT. Originally intended to record encrypted transactions involving digital currencies, most notably Bitcoin (Nakamoto, 2022), researchers, including Radziwill, (2018) and Duranti & Rogers, (2016), suggest that the core BcT that powers these currencies should be the main focus. Blockchain, which minimises verification and networking expenses, is acknowledged for its distributed, non-centralized protected record (Duranti & Rogers, 2016), blockchain ensures secure, encrypted, decentralized, verifiable, and cost-effective transaction recording, minimizing verification and networking costs (Catalini & Gans, 2020; Schatsky & Muraskin, 2015). This feature makes transactions based on BcT economically advantageous. To explain the characteristics of the emerging online markets, the following general principles pertaining to higher competition, lower barriers to entry, decreased privacy risks, and dispersed authority have been proffered. Before that, academic literature has explored the use of the blockchain in a few contexts like banking, crowdfunding, supply chain management, and fundraising for startup companies (Belleflamme et al., 2014; Mollick, 2014). This research will look at the feasibility of applying the web of blockchain into the banking sector and examine how the TCE theoretical structure may be utilised to analyse the actual effects of putting into use the BcT within this certain sector.

4. THEORETICAL MODEL

In order to understand how blockchain application A impacts the business model and disrupts Transaction Costs more deeply, Transaction Costs are broken down into the five areas: Search, Verification, Tracking, Replication, and Contractual. The cost of searching and verifying involves identifying a counterparty and checking their credentials to conduct a transaction and exchanging a good or service. Controlling of expenses on the use of items and transactions means close observation of the processes going on here. Ent Corrective costs and replication aid in ensuring the agreement's credibility in future. The technology of the blockchain has a probability of minimizing cost and reducing the much environmental risk by expanding trust in a unique fashion (Ahluwalia et al., 2020).

Figure 2 shows a conceptual framework that explains effectiveness of BcT at critical points in time by demonstrating how it can improve transactional efficiency by creating a stronger trust mechanism inside the system. This is accomplished by providing reliable methods for transaction verification and reducing the expenses related to middlemen. The implementation of BcT fosters confidence among network participants by ensuring transaction security and verifiability. This technology is inherently decentralised, which eliminates the need for dependence on a central authority and adds to the system's integrity. Tokenization combined with a confirmed smart contract helps the system to lessen opportunistic. If the smart requirements are met, the recipient can be allocated to the item. The fundamental processes of BcT offer all the previously listed services, hence eliminating the necessity for a third-party intermediary to serve as an escrow or guarantor for services and transactions.

Figure 2. Modified transaction cost model with blockchain technology

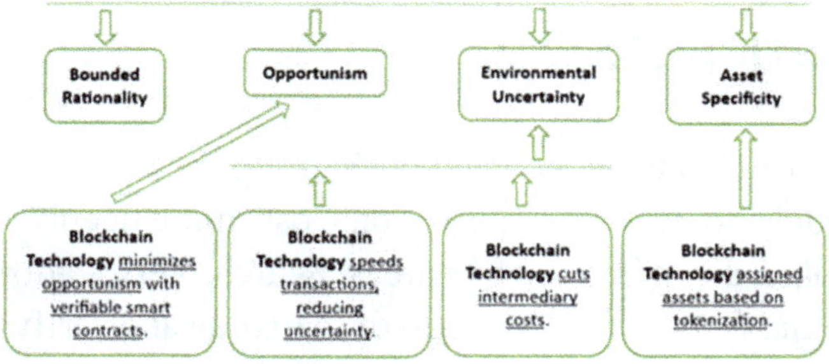

BcT have a revolutionary effect on transaction costs and procedures, as demonstrated by Ahluwalia et al., (2020). They offer, for example, a hypothetical case study of an international money transfer. According to the conventional paradigm, there are several intermediaries involved in the process, including banks and correspondent banks, when a sender located in Country A desires to transfer funds to a recipient in Country B. Every phase has expenses, and there are dangers due to the variable exchange rates; the total costs could be as up to 10%. The completion of such deals might often span many days. Alternatively, a blockchain-based solution. Through an enterprise blockchain system at a bank, funds can be transferred directly and almost instantly from the sender's bank to the recipient's bank, without the involvement of intermediaries or other service providers. By considerably speeding up the transaction completion time, this optimised procedure not only lowers transaction costs but also lessens the uncertainty brought on by exchange rate risks. The IMF, among other institutions and organisations, are actively investigating the application of BcT to improve the effectiveness of international remittances, as the authors point out. Furthermore, with their blockchain-based infrastructure, apps assert to enable international money transfers.

4.1 Smart Contracts Built on Blockchain Technology

Smart contracts represent computer protocols designed to autonomously execute transactions upon the fulfilment of predefined contractual conditions (Shahab & Allam, 2020). Leveraging the capabilities of BcT, these intelligent contracts digitally facilitate contract performance in a credible and transparent manner, obviating the need for intermediary intervention (Iansiti & Lakhani, 2017). In contrast to conventional contractual agreements, smart contracts exhibit superior attributes such as heightened security, credibility, traceability, transparency, and immutability (Lauslahti et al., 2018; Sadiku et al., 2018). Traditional contractual arrangements incur transaction costs associated with the engagement of third-party entities for verification and enforcement. However, the self-implementing nature of smart contracts eliminates the imperative for third-party validation (Allam & Jones, 2019). Furthermore, smart contracts are algorithmically designed to mitigate human error and expedite transactional processes

(Giancaspro, 2017). By enshrining parties' duties and obligations, smart contracts help prevent opportunistic behaviour by removing the necessity for outside enforcement (Vatiero, 2018). This is a significant advantage, especially as transaction costs could rise significantly due to the fear of fraud and insecurity (Karamitsos et al., 2018).

When Nakamoto first unveiled Bitcoin in 2008, it functioned as a cryptocurrency as well as a system. The immutability and transparency of the Bitcoin blockchain have not only facilitated financial transactions but also led to the development of protocols that enable specific types of smart contracts (Bartoletti & Pompianu, 2017). Smart contracts often save their metadata on the blockchain by using the OP_RETURN instruction in the Bitcoin scripting language (Bartoletti & Pompianu, 2017).

4.2 Blockchain Technology and Banking Industry

BcT has the ability to be applied in various domains, but experts in academic research and finance is flexible enough to be used in many different fields, however academic research and financial players (Buitenhek, 2016; Fanning and Centers, 2016; Trautman, 2016; Yermack, 2017) contend that its most significant disruptive impact will be felt in the financial industry. These studies emphasise the significance of distributed ledger technology in blockchain, specifically in private or permissioned blockchain frameworks. They also demonstrate how blockchain can disrupt mainstream business models and technologies that are commonly used in critical financial services transactions.

Studies conducted by Buitenhek, (2016), Guo & Liang, (2016), and Peters & Panayi (2016), have shown that BcT has the potential to completely disrupt existing banking practices, leading to a revolution in the banking industry. With the use of this technology, it is possible to redefine established operational benchmarks, improve transparency, and automate operations between different organisations. Obstacles that traditional banking faces include operational hazards, fraud, transactional delays, and efficiency bottlenecks (Guo & Liang, 2016; Tapscott & Tapscott, 2017). Experts in finance agree that distributed ledger technology on the blockchain can help address these problems by lowering expenses, increasing process effectiveness, and strengthening security. According to

Peters & Panayi (2016), Blockchain has the capacity to revolutionise the banking industry by enabling worldwide money transfers, smart contracts, automated financial records, and digital assets.

As per InnoVentures and Wyman (2015), the fintech investment branch of the Spanish bank, there are currently 20 to 25 identified uses for BcT. It is estimated that by 2022, these applications may potentially help banks save between $15 billion and $20 billion annually in infrastructure costs. These cases encompass several financial areas such as international money transfers, trade financing, syndicated lending, collateral management, and smart contracts. Blockchain is applicable in more areas than these, though. Any industry with long processes, multiple handovers, a lot of paperwork, and a lot of stakeholders stands to gain from blockchain adoption, which can improve operations and boost efficiency, according to research by Buitenhek, (2016), Guo & Liang, (2016), and Peters & Panayi (2016).

Studies by Buitenhek, (2016), Guo & Liang, (2016), and Peters & Panayi (2016) highlight the use of BcT in the streamlining of clearing and settlement services, which have historically been hampered by lengthy lead times, complex procedures, and a wide range of stakeholders. As per the research by Accenture Consulting (2017), bulky investment banks may save $10 billion by executing BcT, which would lower the inadequacies presently handled by multifaceted messaging organizations and tedious reconciliations. Implementation of BcT could be beneficial for securities transactions, which are characterized by slow post-trade clearing and settlement including multiple parties. By mechanizing the clearing and settlement measures, this groundbreaking technology promises safe and transparent securities movement in a matter of seconds or minutes (Buitenhek, (2016). Syndicated loans offer an additional channel via which blockchain can be applied; they expedite transactions by improving workflows and removing the need for intermediaries (Fanning and Centers, 2016). Syndicated loans normally take on average twenty days to settle. From contract commencement to collateral seizure, Rutenberg and Wenner (2017) suggest a fully automated blockchain-based smart contract system for syndicated loans that completely eliminates human participation.

Another area of interest in the banking sector is the payments system, wherein parts of the conventional payment procedures are moved to BcT while also encouraging the adoption of cryptocurrencies. Buitenhek, (2016),

Fanning and Centers, (2016), and Guo & Liang, (2016) have conducted research arguing that the use of blockchain in payments, especially in complex cross-border transactions that depend on intermediary clearing firms, enables direct bank-to-bank transactions and provides benefits like reduce transaction and operating costs as well as faster dispensation. As an illustration, in April 2018, Santander introduced an innovative international money transfer service that use BcT. This service allows users to transmit money across borders and ensures that the transfer is completed either on the same day or the next day.

Blockchain has the potential to significantly lowering compliance costs by automating portions of banks' operating activities. Compliance tasks are frequently marked by labor-intensive procedures that heavily rely on paper and are susceptible to delays, inefficiencies, and heightened risks of fraud and errors (Capgemini Consulting, 2016). BcT's ability to accurately record transactions results in a secure and unchangeable financial audit trail. This eliminates the necessity for regulators to collect, store, reconcile, and organise data. Buitenhek, (2016) contends that BcT, when combined with smart contracts, has the potential to actively ensure adherence to regulations, leading to a substantial decrease in the time, resources, and costs that financial firms allocate to regulatory reporting. This enhancement is anticipated to enhance the overall efficiency, precision, and excellence of the process.

Studies conducted by Buitenhek (2016), Lang (2017), and Parra Moyano and Ross (2017) indicate that BcT has the potential to enhance the efficiency of know your customer (KYC) processes. In the case of blockchain, cryptographic techniques are employed to prevent data duplication so as to reserve disk space and query requests. The purpose of the customer information format is to provide up-to-date information that can be accessed by stakeholders with ease: thus, guaranteeing consistency and reliability of the information recorded. KYC tends to be repeated each time a client has dealings with a different bank, but, if the process is done to the full with one bank, the information can be shared with other banks, thereby saving time.

The research confirms that blockchain is a powerful technological innovation that can provide banks with numerous significant values. On this aspect, some studies by Davidson et al., 2018; MacDonald et al.,

2016 and Yeoh, 2017 have pointed out that BcT, mainly, the reference to public blockchains associated with cryptocurrencies, threatens traditional institutions and may become a serious competitor. The study conducted by MacDonald et al., (2016) has exposed that BcT possesses an implicit potential for revolutionizing banking service governance. Depending on the context, it can go from being a traditionally top-down, bureaucratic organization to a bottom-up, free market model.

The elimination of mediators, particularly in agreements and transactions, is one of the vital features of blockchain since it can be executed directly, which is a threat to traditional banking (Iansiti & Lakhani, 2017; Tapscott & Tapscott, 2017). This revolutionary element raises questions regarding the roles that banks typically play in the negation of trust and system identification, as well as the management of contracts, clearing, settlement, and record keeping (MacDonald et al., 2016; Lindman et al., 2017). Blockchain impacts the financial sector by introducing the innovations in the complex transactions and potentially erasing the exclusive market domination of the banks. Self-sustainability of firms that utilize BcT and offering free financial services pose risks of high financial risks and market share grab from the banking industries. Therefore, the discussion turns to the fact that the blockchain itself might pose a threat to traditional banking and becomes an issue that will negatively affect the banking expenses for carrying out transactions.

5. DISCUSSION

BcT has become an inventive force in the financial world, especially in banking, with the facility to change conventional practices and discourse challenges facing the segment. Studies by Buitenhek, (2016), Guo & Liang, (2016), and Peters & Panayi (2016) showing-off how BcT can reduce transaction costs and rationalize processes. Blockchain has an extensive array of applicability in banking; InnoVentures and Wyman (2015) assessed that by 2022, there may be yearly savings of US $15 billion to US $20 billion across 20 to 25 use cases. This infrastructure cost reduction is applied to trade finance, affiliate lending, intercontinental money transfers, collateral administration, and smart contracts, representing the technology's flexibility. Embracing blockchain is a excessive fit for clearing and settlement services, which are infamous for their complexity and prolonged timeframes. According to Accenture Consulting (2017), eliminating complex messaging systems and manual reconciliations could save big investment banks up to $10 billion in US dollars. The impact of BcT may be seen in securities transactions, where it provides quick and transparent movements in a matter of seconds or minutes (Buitenhek, 2016). Syndicated loans offer a chance for extensive automation using blockchain-based smart contracts, as they typically take 20 days or more to settle (Rutenberg and Wenner (2017). Blockchain lowers costs and speeds up processing times in payment systems by enabling direct bank-to-bank transfers for cross-border transactions (Buitenhek, 2016 and Fanning & Centers, 2016). As demonstrated by Santander's blockchain-based international money transfer service, cryptocurrencies further improve efficiency. Blockchain-based operational process automation also solves regulatory issues. Due to blockchain's secure transaction recording, labour-intensive, paper-centric compliance procedures are no longer necessary, possibly saving a substantial amount of money and time (Buitenhek, 2016). Furthermore, smart contracts have the ability to proactively enforce compliance, which improves the calibre, precision, and promptness of regulatory reporting. Blockchain's cryptographic protections simplify information exchange between various parties involved in Know Your Customer (KYC) procedures, lowering duplication and increasing effectiveness (Lang, 2017; Parra Moyano & Ross, 2017). Notwithstanding these benefits, other research (Davidson et al., 2018; MacDonald et al., 2016; Yeoh, 2017) emphasises how blockchain could provide a challenge to conventional banking. Because of its revolutionary ability to facilitate direct transactions, banks' positions are put in jeopardy, which might hurt their bottom line and reputation.

5.1 Limitations of the Study

There are some backdrops to undertaking theoretical analysis of blockchain and banking based on TCE as the theoretical framework. Therefore, this research mainly draws on theoretical studies and frameworks rather than confirming empirically, focusing on key experiences in applying blockchain within various settings. Admittedly, it is aware that decreasing the value of the intermediate variable–essentially the costs of transactions–may have a number of advantages, but it fails to mention such crucial factors as uncertainty, legal aspects, and scalability problems. The-naïve perspective that globalization of blockchain means that it is applicable to every context does not consider the rise of emergent negatives and instead of urging for a better evaluation. The scarcity of studies with comparative analyses and assessment of the relative performance of the competing technologies hampers our knowledge, leaving us in the dark concerning the dynamic and growing phenomenon that has the potential of producing inconsequential findings since BcT is advancing. However, before elaborating more on how the idea of blockchain fits into the banking sector, it is valuable to remark some of the aforementioned drawbacks that must be solved to achieve this objective in order to achieve a different perspective.

5.2 Future Research Directions

The theoretical issues surrounding BcT and banking, particularly in the context of TCE, have not been largely explored in the existing literature as shown in the previous chapter. Next studies should undertake these questions. Preferential methodology is investigative, relevance to real-life scenarios, potential for expansion, adherence to the law, normative criteria and intelligent, experimental work – these fundamental components are critical for packing thought-provoking ideas into intellectual frameworks. Explaining pros and cons of the BcT approaching financial applications, the conclusion was drawn on specification on a greater understanding concerning future research that will come from an independent line of investigation. The need for comparative assessments of the available technologies is critical in as much as it allows the financial institutions to make proper decisions when it comes to implementing innovations. Thus, to find out new features and the impact of blockchain on the cost of financial transactions, it is also crucial to adopt a futuristic perspective. To comprehend the applicability of the blockchain in the aspect of financial systems and markets additional research should be arranged in the following categories: the experimental paradigm, the fair assessment scheme, the comparative analysis approach, and the topic discussion on the dynamic nature of the technology.

REFERENCES

Ahluwalia, S., Mahto, R. V., & Guerrero, M. (2020). BcT and startup financing: A TCE perspective. *Technological Forecasting and Social Change, 151*(February 2019), 119854. DOI: 10.1016/j.techfore.2019.119854

Albeshr, S., & Nobanee, H. (2020). Blockchain Applications in Banking Industry: A Mini-Review. SSRN *Electronic Journal*. DOI: 10.2139/ssrn.3539152

Allam, Z., & Jones, D. S. (2019). The Potential of Blockchain within Air Rights Development as a Prevention Measure against Urban Sprawl. *Urban Science (Basel, Switzerland), 3*(1), 38. Advance online publication. DOI: 10.3390/urbansci3010038

Arrow, K. J. (1988). The Organization of Economic Activity. *Small Business Economics*, •••, v.

Bartoletti, M., & Pompianu, L. (2017). An analysis of bitcoin OP_RETURN metadata. *Lecture Notes in Computer Science (Including Subseries Lecture Notes in Artificial Intelligence and Lecture Notes in Bioinformatics), 10323 LNCS*, 218–230. DOI: 10.1007/978-3-319-70278-0_14

Baumol, W. J. (2016). *Review : Williamson ' s The Economic Institutions of Capitalism Author (s): William J . Baumol Published by : Wiley on behalf of RAND Corporation Stable URL :* https://www.jstor.org/stable/2555390 *Williamson ' s The Economic Institutions of Capitalism. 17*(2), 279–286.

Belleflamme, P., Lambert, T., & Schwienbacher, A. (2014). Crowdfunding: Tapping the right crowd. *Journal of Business Venturing*, *29*(5), 585–609. DOI: 10.1016/j.jbusvent.2013.07.003

Benston, G. J., & Smith, C. W. (1976). A Transactions Cost Approach to the Theory of Financial Intermediation the Thirty-Fourth Annual Meeting of the American Finance Association Dallas, Texas Published by : Wiley for the American Finance Association Stable URL : https://www.jstor.org/stable/. *The Journal of Finance, 31*(2), 215–231.

Buitenhek, M. (2016). Understanding and applying BcT in banking: Evolution or revolution? *Journal of Digital Banking, 1*(2), 111–119. https://www.henrystewartpublications.com/sites/default/files/02_Buitenhek_JDB_V1.2.pdf. DOI: 10.69554/TXYN8464

Catalini, C., & Gans, J. S. (2020). Some simple economics of the blockchain. *Communications of the ACM, 63*(7), 80–90. DOI: 10.1145/3359552

Chen, Y. (2018). Blockchain tokens and the potential democratization of entrepreneurship and innovation. *Business Horizons, 61*(4), 567–575. DOI: 10.1016/j.bushor.2018.03.006

Chiles, T. H., & Mcmackin, J. F. (2016). Integrating Variable Risk Preferences, Trust, and TCE Author (s): Todd H. Chiles and John F. McMackin Source : The Academy of Management Review, Vol. 21, No. 1 (Jan., 1996), pp. 73-99 Published by. *Academy of Manageme., 21*(1), 73–99.

Coase, R. H. (1937). The Nature of the Firm. *Economica, 4*(16), 386–405. DOI: 10.1111/j.1468-0335.1937.tb00002.x

Cole, R. A. (1998). The importance of relationships to the availability of credit. *Journal of Banking & Finance, 22*(6–8), 959–977. DOI: 10.1016/S0378-4266(98)00007-7

Conner, K. R. (1991). A Historical Comparison of Resource-Based Theory and Five Schools of Thought Within Industrial Organization Economics: Do We Have a New Theory of the Firm? *Journal of Management, 17*(1), 121–154. DOI: 10.1177/014920639101700109

David, R. J., & Han, S. K. (2004). A systematic assessment of the empirical support for TCE. *Strategic Management Journal, 25*(1), 39–58. DOI: 10.1002/smj.359

Davidson, S., De Filippi, P., & Potts, J. (2018). Disrupting Governance: The New Institutional Economics of Distributed Ledger Technology. SSRN *Electronic Journal*, 1–27. DOI: 10.2139/ssrn.2811995

Duranti, L., & Rogers, C. (2016). Trust in Records and Data Online. *Integrity in Government through Records Management: Essays in Honour of Anne Thurston*, 203–214. DOI: 10.4324/9781315589077-21

Fanning, K., & Centers, D. P. (2016). Blockchain and its coming impact on financial services. *Journal of Corporate Accounting & Finance*, *27*(5), 53–57. DOI: 10.1002/jcaf.22179

Ghoshal, S., & Moran, P. (1996). Bad for Practice : A Critique of the Transaction Cost Theory Author (s): Sumantra Ghoshal and Peter Moran Source : The Academy of Management Review, Vol. 21, No. 1 (Jan., 1996), pp. 13-47 Published by : Academy of Management Stable URL : http. *Academy of Management Review*, *21*(1), 13–47. https://www.jstor.org/stable/258627. DOI: 10.2307/258627

Giancaspro, M. (2017). Is a 'smart contract' really a smart idea? Insights from a legal perspective. *Computer Law & Security Review*, *33*(6), 825–835. DOI: 10.1016/j.clsr.2017.05.007

Gray, R. (1994). Transactions Costs and New Institutions: Will CBLTs Have a Role in the Saskatchewan Land Market? *Canadian Journal of Agricultural Economics/Revue Canadienne d'agroeconomie, 42*(4), 501–509. DOI: 10.1111/j.1744-7976.1994.tb00044.x

Guo, Y., & Liang, C. (2016). Blockchain application and outlook in the banking industry. *Financial Innovation*, *2*(1), 24. Advance online publication. DOI: 10.1186/s40854-016-0034-9

Iansiti, M., & Lakhani, K. R. (2017, January). The truth about blockchain: It will take years to transform business, but the journey begins now. *Harvard Business Review*, 117–128.

Innoventures, S., & Wyman, O. (2015). *The Fintech 2.0 Paper: rebooting financial services*. Santander InnoVentures.

Karamitsos, I., Papadaki, M., & Al Barghuthi, N. B. (2018). Design of the Blockchain Smart Contract: A Use Case for Real Estate. *Journal of Information Security*, *09*(03), 177–190. DOI: 10.4236/jis.2018.93013

Khadka, R. (2020). *The impact of BcT in banking: How can blockchain revolutionize the banking industry? October*, 37.

Kołodziej, M. (2021). Development Factors of BcT Within Banking Sector. *Springer Proceedings in Business and Economics*, 125–138. DOI: 10.1007/978-3-030-73667-5_8/COVER

Lauslahti, K., Mattila, J., & Seppala, T. (2018). Smart Contracts How Will BcT Affect Contractual Practices? SSRN *Electronic Journal, 68*. DOI: 10.2139/ssrn.3154043

MacDonald, T. J., Allen, D. W. E., & Potts, J. (2016). Blockchains and the boundaries of self-organized economies: Predictions for the future of banking. *New Economic Windows*, 279–296. DOI: 10.1007/978-3-319-42448-4_14

Mahoney, J. T. (1992). The choice of organizational form: Vertical financial ownership versus other methods of vertical integration. *Strategic Management Journal, 13*(8), 559–584. DOI: 10.1002/smj.4250130802

Mollick, E. (2014). The dynamics of crowdfunding: An exploratory study. *Journal of Business Venturing*, *29*(1), 1–16. DOI: 10.1016/j.jbusvent.2013.06.005

Moran, P., & Ghoshal, S. (1996). Theories of economic organization: The case for realism and balance. *Academy of Management Review*, *21*(1), 58–72.

Nakamoto, S. (2008). Bitcoin: A peer-to-peer electronic cash system.

Parra Moyano, J., & Ross, O. (2017). KYC Optimization Using Distributed Ledger Technology. *Business & Information Systems Engineering*, *59*(6), 411–423. DOI: 10.1007/s12599-017-0504-2

Peters, G. W., & Panayi, E. (2016). Understanding modern banking ledgers through blockchain technologies: Future of transaction processing and smart contracts on the internet of money. *New Economic Windows*, 239–278. DOI: 10.1007/978-3-319-42448-4_13

Radziwill, N. (2018). Blockchain Revolution: How the Technology Behind Bitcoin is Changing Money, Business, and the World. *The Quality Management Journal*, *25*(1), 64–65. DOI: 10.1080/10686967.2018.1404373

Robins, J. A. (1987). Organizational Economics : Notes on the Use of Transaction-Cost Theory in the Study of Organizations Author (s): James A. Robins Published by : Sage Publications, Inc. on behalf of the Johnson Graduate School of Management, Cornell University Stable. *Administrative Science Quarterly*, *32*(1), 68–86. DOI: 10.2307/2392743

Sadiku, M. N. O., Eze, K. G., Musa, S. M., & Perry, R. G. A, P. V., & View, P. (2018). Smart Contracts : A Primer Available online www.jsaer .com Journal of Scientific and Engineering Research, 2018, 5 (5): 538-541 Smart Contracts : A Primer. *Journal of Scientific and Engineering Research, 5*(June), 538–541. file:///C:/Users/USER/Downloads/JSAER2018-05-05-538-541.pdf

Salim, M., Alam Khan, P., Abdul Jalil, N., Kaur Johl, S., Hasan Jafar, S., Irfan, F., & Khan, M. (2023). Fusion of Blockchain and Sustainable Development Goals: A Bibliometric Analysis for Future Trends. *KnE Social Sciences*, *2023*, 633–654. DOI: 10.18502/kss.v8i20.14629

Santos, F. M., & Eisenhardt, K. M. (2005). Organizational boundaries and theories of organization. *Organization Science*, *16*(5), 491–508. DOI: 10.1287/orsc.1050.0152

Schatsky, D., & Muraskin, C. (2015). Beyond bitcoin : Blockchain is coming to disrupt your industry. *Deloitte University Press*, 1–27.

Scranton, P., & Chandler, A. D. (1991). Scale and Scope: The Dynamics of Industrial Capitalism. *Technology and Culture*, *32*(4), 1102. DOI: 10.2307/3106164

Shahab, S., & Allam, Z. (2020). Reducing transaction costs of tradable permit schemes using Blockchain smart contracts. *Growth and Change*, *51*(1), 302–308. DOI: 10.1111/grow.12342

Shelanski, H. A., & Klein, P. G. (1995). Empirical research in TCE: A review and assessment. *Journal of Law Economics and Organization*, *11*(2), 335–361. DOI: 10.1093/oxfordjournals.jleo.a036875

Trautman, L. J. (2016). Is Disruptive BcT the Future of Financial Services? *The Consumer Finance Law Quarterly Report, forthcomin*, 232–242. https://papers.ssrn.com/abstract=2786186

Treiblmaier, H. (2018). The impact of the blockchain on the supply chain: A theory-based research framework and a call for action. *Supply Chain Management*, *23*(6), 545–559. DOI: 10.1108/SCM-01-2018-0029

Vatiero, M. (2018). Smart Contracts and Transaction Costs. SSRN *Electronic Journal*. DOI: 10.2139/ssrn.3259958

Williamson, O. E. (1971). The vertical integration of production: Market failure considerations. *The American Economic Review*, *61*(2), 112–123.

Williamson, O. E. (1973). Markets and hierarchies, some elementary considerations. *The American Economic Review*, *63*(2), 316–325.

Williamson, O.E. (1979). The Journal of Law and Economics-TCE. *The Journal of Law & Economics*, *22*(2), 233–261. DOI: 10.1086/466942

Williamson, O. E. (1985). *The Economic Institutions of Capitalism: Firms, Markets, Relational Contracting*. https://papers.ssrn.com/abstract=1496720

Williamson, O. E. (2002). The theory of the firm as governance structure: From choice to contract. *The Journal of Economic Perspectives*, *16*(3), 171–195. DOI: 10.1257/089533002760278776

Yale, T., Journal, L., & Williamson, O. (1984). Articles Corporate Governance. *Management*, *93*(7), 1197–1230.

Yeoh, P. (2017). Regulatory issues in BcT. *Journal of Financial Regulation and Compliance*, *25*(2), 196–208. DOI: 10.1108/JFRC-08-2016-0068

Yermack, D. (2017). Corporate governance and blockchains. *Review of Finance*, *21*(1), 7–31. DOI: 10.1093/rof/rfw074

Chapter 6

The Critical Role of Tacit Knowledge of Technopreneurs Towards Sustainable Success in the ICT SMEs in Malaysia: A Thematic Survey

Ridzuan Masri
https://orcid.org/0000-0002-3584-9771
MILA University, Malaysia

Siti Haryani Mat Yusoff
https://orcid.org/0000-0002-8073-4148
Nilai University, Malaysia

ABSTRACT

This study aims to examine the important role of tacit knowledge among ICT technopreneurs in facing the ever-fierce and challenging business and economic situation, especially after the world just came out of Covid-19. A semi-structured interview method was used to collect data from 15 ICT

DOI: 10.4018/979-8-3693-6195-5.ch006

technopreneurs from SMEs in ICT-related industries in Malaysia. This study uses word cloud analysis to get an initial idea of the role of tacit knowledge and employs thematic analysis to extract and visualize data patterns and themes to gain a more informed understanding of the interviews that have been conducted. The findings of the study show that among the important roles of tacit knowledge of technopreneurs are to facilitate the negotiation process, risk taking, decision making, leadership, and strategy development to help ICT technopreneurs to face current business challenges. This study confirms that tacit knowledge is very significant in helping ICT technopreneurs to deal with challenging business situations and in achieving success in the ICT business.

1.0 INTRODUCTION

Tacit knowledge is a type of knowledge that is not easily stated explicitly. This knowledge is usually based on personal experience, including an understanding of how to do something, and is difficult to characterize in formal or documented form. Tacit knowledge is also not easily transferred from one individual to another through conventional means such as printed sources or formal training.

According to Polanyi (1966), tacit knowledge is a knowledge that cannot be understood easily in the form of words or visuals and is mostly realized indirectly by individuals. In another study, Nonaka and Takeuchi (1995) identified tacit knowledge as hidden knowledge and highly subjective and abstract in nature that is often related to personal experience and intuitive understanding (Hanif et al, 2020), perspective-dependent (Zhang & Gao, 2022; Abraham & Collins, 2017) and instinctive (Figurny, 2021).

Tacit knowledge plays an important role in shaping entrepreneurial intentions and entrepreneurial capabilities, especially in the context of technopreneurship. Through experience, intuition and informal learning, tacit knowledge enables technopreneurs to identify business opportunities that are not easily detected through formal data alone, thus supporting the opportunity recognition process (Roundy, 2020; Yew, 2021). Studies have also shown that knowledge also influences decision-making in uncertain situations, where technopreneurs need to rely on intuitive judgment and past experience to assess risks and choose appropriate strategic actions (Brockmann & Anthony, 1998; Greiner et al., 2007). From the point of view of skills development, tacit knowledge contributes to the formation of practical skills, problem-solving abilities, and individual adaptability in a dynamic ICT environment (Wuytens et al., 2022; Zahra, 2021). Therefore, understanding the role of tacit knowledge in these three aspects is important to explain how technopreneurs build a competitive advantage and achieve sustainable business success.

The topic of tacit knowledge is widely studied and learned by international organizations as well such as UNESCO when they studied the effectiveness of mentoring programs to develop on-line courses for teachers in India (DeWaard & Chavhan, 2020), whereas, Microsoft Inc and Intel Corp have invested heavily for training their managers in the form of codified and tacit knowledge so that, their employees are always be able to innovate within the framework of the virtual organizational setting (Kippenberger, 1997). These confirmed that tacit knowledge is very important for the development of the organization and the success of any projects. In the business context, tacit knowledge can be a source of excellence for a company when it is used wisely.

1.1 ICT Entrepreneurships Environment in Malaysia

ICT-based entrepreneurships in Malaysia are growing and becoming incessantly important especially in the current era of rapid digitalisation. In 2022, the businesses in Malaysia have increased their ICT budget compared to 2021 and earlier. The global ICT market in Malaysia was valued in 2022 at USD15.86 billion and between 2022-2026, ICT-based revenue opportunities in Malaysia are estimated at USD100.44 billion (GlobalData, 2023), thus making ICT technopreneurs hip in Malaysia a very important field and still relevant to majority technopreneurs involved in this business.

ICT plays an important role in the provision of job opportunities, economic growth, and innovation. In 2021 alone, employment opportunities in the ICT sector in Malaysia accounted for 44% of new job creation and were highest compared to job opportunities in other sectors (BERNAMA, 2023). As reported by NST (2022), studies have also shown that there has been an increase in the number of ICT-based technopreneurs in Malaysia in a short period of time.

However, there are some challenges affecting the development of ICT entrepreneurship in this country. Among the observable challenges are the concerns about the security of users' privacy data, lack of capital, and lack of support from the government in providing infrastructure and funding resulting in disrupting the company's expansion efforts, adverse price wars including long-term sustainability especially when forced to compete with global industry players and the challenges of online shopping platforms that offer low prices of similar items and numerous substitutable goods and services.To overcome these challenges, the government has launched various initiatives and programmes to strengthen the ICT-based entrepreneurial ecosystem in Malaysia, such as the Malaysian Digital Economy Blueprint (MyDigital), National Internet of Things (IoT) Strategic Roadmap, and SME Technology Financing Programme (STFP).

1.2 Problem Statement

In Malaysia, the ICT sector is growing rapidly and contributes significantly to job creation and economic growth in the country (BERNAMA, 2023; GlobalData, 2023). However, ICT technopreneurs face various challenges including resource constraints, global competition, data security issues, rapid technological change as well as the pressure to maintain long-term business viability. Past studies have shown that failure to harness tacit knowledge can lead to weaknesses in innovation, less effective decision-making as well as loss of competitive advantage, especially among technology-based SMEs (Yao et al., 2022; Zahra, 2021). While there are empirical evidences abroad that showing tacit knowledge has a positive impact on innovation and organizational performance (Cuvero et al., 2022; Kucharska & Erickson, 2023), there is still a lack of empirical studies exploring how ICT technopreneurs particularly in Malaysia are using tacit knowledge in practical terms to support the success and sustainability of their businesses. This lack of understanding creates a significant knowledge gap in the existing literature at the domestic level as well as limits the ability of policymakers and industry practitioners to develop more effective support strategies.

Therefore, this study aims to fill the gap by empirically exploring the role of tacit knowledge among ICT technopreneurs in Malaysia, particularly in the context of problem solving, innovation and sustainable business success. The findings of this study are expected to contribute to the academic literature as well as provide practical implications for technopreneurs and stakeholders in strengthening the country's ICT entrepreneurship ecosystem. Table 1 below shows the research question, research objectives and the interview questions as follows:

Table 1. The relationship between Research Questions (RQ), Research Objective (RO) dan Interview Question (IQ)

RQ	RO	IQ
What critical role does tacit knowledge contribute to ICT technopreneurs?	1. To identify the form of tacit knowledge of ICT technopreneurs; 2.	3. IQ 1 - Can you describe an example of a situation where the hidden knowledge (tacit) found in you plays a critical role in resolving the issue?
	4. To identify the critical role that tacit knowledge technopreneurs play to ensure the organizational sustainability	5. IQ 2 - What are the important factors that contribute to your success as a technopreneur?

Source: Researcher (2024)

2.0 LITERATURE REVIEW

The use and transfer of tacit knowledge has become a topic of study that is gaining ground in today's circle of scholars (Yew, 2021; Lovell & Powells, 2020; Ge et al, 2023). Tacit knowledge refers to knowledge that is not formally or explicitly explained and it has a lot to do with the experience, expertise and involvement of the individual in a particular field. The use of tacit knowledge is very important for entrepreneurs in empowering their businesses as it can enhance their ability to manage business more effectively (Roundy, 2020). Such experiential and intuitive knowledge enables entrepreneurs to recognize business opportunities that are not readily identifiable through formal information alone, thereby supporting the process of opportunity recognition.

However, there is still less research on tacit knowledge among today's entrepreneurs. According to some studies, a lack of recognition of the importance and the usage of tacit knowledge among entrepreneurs (Yao et al, 2022), has caused such an important topic like this to receive less attention among entrepreneurs, especially in small and medium ICT firms. This is perhaps due to limited understanding of it concepts as well as limitations in measuring tacit knowledge.

There are also some studies that show that tacit knowledge is important for entrepreneurs and they too agreed that tacit knowledge is a type of knowledge that is difficult to transfer from one person to another (Wuytens et al, 2022; Hirano et al, 2017; Kabir, 2019). In uncertain and dynamic environments, tacit knowledge plays a crucial role in entrepreneurial decision-making, as it allows entrepreneurs to rely on intuition and past experience when evaluating risks and selecting strategic actions. Therefore, there are a number of instances where entrepreneurs experience difficulties in maintaining tacit knowledge in their business related to certain specialties that can drastically affecting business operations (Chukwujioke et al, 2013).

There are also limited research on how best to acquire, store, record and use tacit knowledge to enhance entrepreneurial capability and success. Therefore, there is a need to focus more on the study of tacit knowledge among entrepreneurs as well as to develop the best methods for the storage and utilization of such tacit knowledge.

Tacit knowledge gained from various sources is an important aspect of entrepreneurship and has significantly impacting the success of entrepreneurs (Bidgoli et al., 2022; Stefanidis et al, 2007). Through continuous experiential learning, tacit knowledge also contributes to the development of entrepreneurial skills, including problem-solving ability, adaptability, and practical competence. The recent empirical study by Kucharska & Erickson (2023) that involved employees in the IT industry in the United States revealed that tacit knowledge sharing has a positive effect on innovation activities. In another study conducted by Cuvero et al (2022) on tacit knowledge spillover effects of high-tech entrepreneurs in the United Kingdom are highly possible through innovation and knowledge implementation using virtual and physical entrepreneurial ecosystems. These studies show that tacit knowledge is very important to be nurtured to members of the organization, but the role of entrepreneurs in driving efforts to spread tacit knowledge is still not sufficiently studied in depth including the tacit knowledge needed by entrepreneurs themselves.

The research in New Zealand on ICT firms by Castaneda & Toulson (2021) posits that not all technology-based companies let the tacit knowledge to be shared, except ICT companies that actively carry out bilateral communication in the form of dialogue, rather than the use of IT tools for tacit knowledge transfer. Therefore, although there are studies related to tacit knowledge among technology-based entrepreneurs, there are still research gaps that require further investigation to understand how tacit knowledge can be used at its best by ICT entrepreneurs in retaining the sustainable business success in the long run and possesses high value in terms of its competitive advantage.

The study on the role and use of tacit knowledge in the ICT sectors in Malaysia especially among its technopreneurs is still little, however, very important to be further explored as this sector plays an important role for the country's economic growth.

Findings from the literature highlight show that tacit knowledge serves as a core to entrepreneurial capabilities and technopreneurial success, by being influenced by several key facilitating factors. Tacit knowledge is formed and reinforced through hands-on experience, continuous learning processes and social interactions in professional networks, which enable technopreneurs to develop an intuitive understanding of markets, technologies and customers (Polanyi, 1966; Nonaka & Takeuchi, 1995; Roundy, 2020). These facilitating factors support the use of tacit knowledge in identifying business opportunities, making strategic decisions under uncertainty, as well as developing the practical and innovative skills needed in a dynamic ICT environment (Yew, 2021; Wuytens et al., 2022). Accordingly, the existing literature suggests that the relationship between tacit knowledge, facilitating factors and entrepreneurial capabilities plays an important role in shaping technopreneurial success and business sustainability, but this relationship is still under-explored empirically in the context of ICT technopreneurs in Malaysia.

3.0 RESEARCH METHODS

In this study, the purposive sampling was employed to select 15 participants who are experienced entrepreneurs within several ICT business categories to ensure the relevance and depth in the sampled population. To maintain research reliability and validity, a consistent interview questionnaire was used, complemented by qualitative triangulation methods including document analysis and extensive library research. The data was collected through semi-structured interviews, which were then transcribed and analyzed using ATLAS.ti software, thematic analysis, word clouds, and coding to identify and interpret common themes and patterns. This rigorous approach allowed for an in-depth understanding of the tacit knowledge among the participants, enhancing the comprehensiveness and accuracy of the research findings. The selection criteria of the entrepreneurs are set in the Table 2 as follows:

Table 2. SMEs selection criteria

Criteria	Attributes
No of years of Establishment	Minimum 3 years
Type of company	Sole proprietor and private limited
Size	small and medium enterprises
Yearly Sales Revenue	Minimum RM300k
No of Staffs	5 and above
Industry Focus	ICT

Source: Researcher (2024)

4.0 ANALYSIS AND FINDINGS

The researcher uses thematic method to analyse interview data, transcribing and analysing with ATLAS.ti for better understanding. Word cloud and code networks are also utilized to categorize and study interview content, aiding in discovering correlation patterns between codes.

4.1 The Word Cloud Analysis

Following the outcomes of word map analysis utilizing the frequency function, the researcher proceeded to decipher the codes into various themes concerning ICT entrepreneurship, portraying it as a manifestation of technopreneurs' mission, delineated in the Table 3 as follows:

Table 3. General theme, code and summary of interview

General theme	Codes	Interview Summary
Technopreneur's Sustainable Success	Industry Knowledge	Q3:1 Knowledge of industry practices and technology helped exceed customer expectations by developing innovative solutions, leading to successful long-term partnerships.
	Customer Service	Q3:14 Team used customer knowledge to adjust strategy during company changes, meeting expectations and improving response.
	Resourcefulness	Q3:5 Team faced tech issue in critical project, considered delay, but quickly resolved it using tech expertise and proceeded.
	Crisis Management	Q3:2 Despite early challenges and financial crisis, market knowledge and budgeting skills helped identify issues and strengthen the business.
	Professional Competence	Q3:6 Found critical industry gap during market analysis impacting budget. Utilized experience and skills to refine business strategy and address the gap.
	Strategic Thinking	Q3:3 Used experience to tailor proposal to panelist's preferences during contract pitch, leading to winning the contract.
	Problem Solving	Q3:11 Used reverse engineering and problem-solving skills to integrate non-working technology into project, satisfying clients.
	Innovation	Q3:12 Encountered obstacle in software development, used developer experience to make modifications for successful optimization.

Source: Researcher (2024)

4.1.1 Industry Knowledge

Industry knowledge develops intuitive skills of technopreneurs (Anshari & Hamdan, 2022) which is a form of objective and subjective reasonings that appears to be based on a sensible intuition rather than specific learning. It is a tacit knowledge gained from experience including the application of practical skills from a particular industry. It also depends on an individual's understanding of the processes, developments and methods of the industry. This knowledge tends to be subjective and lies in the individual's memory and contributes to the development of predictive skills that are difficult to transfer directly to others.

Industrial knowledge and problem solving are two closely related components. Industry knowledge refers to an in-depth understanding of a particular industry, including processes, best practices, trends, and requirements and specific regulations to enable businesses to operate within that industry. This knowledge plays an important role in problem solving in an industrial context. Q3:1 "*There was a situation where one of my customers required a specific solution, but it was not stated in the contract. My knowledge of industry practices and technology allows me to develop innovative solutions that exceed their expectations and successfully pursue longer partnerships*"... in the critical role of tacit knowledge.

Industry knowledge helps in the problem-solving process by providing access to relevant professional networks and resources. By understanding industry dynamics and connecting with industry experts, technopreneurs can have better access to the necessary assistance and guidance they need to solve the complex issues and problems.

4.1.2 Adaptability

Adaptability refers to a person's ability to adapt and change according to the changing needs and the dynamic environment (Reeves & Deimler, 2011). As a tacit element, adaptability is a knowledge that cannot be easily condensed or explained or formally expressed in the form of words or procedures or other forms of interpretations. It is formed through experience, exposure and intuition. Adaptability gives ICT technopreneurs the ability to think creatively, find alternative solutions, and boldly take risks in an ever-changing and dynamic environment. They need to have a flexible and open mindfulness to learn new things and apply their knowledge in solving problems or achieving goals.

Adaptability as a tacit skill is part of the tacit resourcefulness element, which is the efficiency to benefit limited resources such as financing and cost, technology, manpower and maximizing individual potential. Q10:6 "*From my observation, most successful technopreneurs are highly adaptable to their environment and agile that allows them to be very creative in finding practical solutions and making the best from their limited resources*"... in the unique set of tacit knowledge.

The ability to adapt to a variety of changing environments allows technopreneurs to efficiently and effectively optimize resources by redesigning strategies, reorganizing existing resources efficiently and creatively.

4.1.3 Resourcefulness

Resourcefulness involves the ability to effectively deploy and leverage limited resources to address challenges or achieve set goals (Zahra, 2021). It involves theoretical and practical wisdom, problem solving, adaptability to an ever-changing environment, and creativity in finding innovative solutions. This knowledge can be gained through experience and learning from a variety of different situations. With a network of cooperation, resourcefulness can be enhanced through various forms of sharing such as information, supply technology, expertise and so on. Q3:5 "*We faced an unexpected technological problem during a critical project, and our team was considering postponing it. But by using my knowledge of the technology and troubleshooting experience, we were able to quickly identify the issues and move forward with the project.*" The resourcefulness can be attributed to entrepreneurial wisdom and senses in using resources, which is an important tacit knowledge in various aspects of management, business and other strategic matters.

4.1.4 Professional Competency

Professional competency is not categorized as a tacit knowledge because it involves relevant knowledge and application of competencies in a particular profession. These competencies are specific skills, knowledge, and abilities that individual acquire through formal education, training, and experience in a professional field. They can be clearly articulated, taught, and assessed. However, professional competency can strongly be linked to a tacit knowledge through its usage in the practical sense.

The tacit knowledge which involves understanding and competence gained from direct, practical, and interacting experience in the work setting environment, is an important element in the development of professional competence. For instance, in the field of ICT, a technopreneur who has competence in programming needs to master tacit knowledge about programming languages, algorithms, or frameworks used in their work environment, then find certain patterns in data, identify creative solutions and the like. This knowledge is not only learned through theory, but also through hands-on practice in developing and solving software problems.

Professional competency explicitly influences innovation activities through creative thinking, application of new ideas, analysis of complex problems and problem solving categorized as tacit knowledge. Q3:6 "*While conducting the market analysis, I found that there is a very critical gap in the industry that could have a significant impact on the budget application put forward. Using our experience and skills (referring to competencies), we successfully fine-tuned our business strategy and focused on filling this gap*"... in the critical role of tacit knowledge.

In the ICT business, innovation is an increasingly important need for organizations to survive and thrive. Tacit knowledge and professional competence are two factors that are interrelated and mutually reinforcing in achieving effective innovation. Therefore, the application and professional development of competency among individuals and organizations is essential to encourage the use of tacit knowledge to produce successful innovations.

4.1.5 Strategic Thinking

Strategic thinking involves the utilization of both tacit and explicit knowledge. While tacit knowledge acquired through experience and intuition might contribute to the ability to think strategically (Brockmann et al, 1998), strategic thinking also relies on explicit knowledge that can be articulated, communicated, and shared (Greiner et al, 2007). Strategic thinking refers to the process of generating and implementing strategies used by organizations to achieve future goals in varying periods for short, medium and long term. It involves in-depth analysis of the internal and external environment of the organization, recognizing opportunities and challenges, as well as planning the necessary measures to achieve competitive excellence and planning strategic resources to face a dynamic future.

Strategic thinking contributes to the successful achievement of the organization's planning and is indispensable for planning during the crisis. Q3:3. *"I recall a scenario where we had to compete for a contract pitch, and I noticed that the panellist had a particular preference for a particular approach. By using my experience and being aware of these cues, we presented our proposal in a way that resonated with them, and we won the contract."*... in the critical role of tacit knowledge.

Strategic thinking is urgently needed when the crisis occurs, strongly associated with innovation and is an attribute to the leadership quality. For technopreneurs to think strategically, they need a deep understanding of the business environment to make the right decisions. Tacit knowledge helps strategic thinkers to understand such things as unspeakable customer needs, ever-changing market trends, and new innovation opportunities.

4.1.6 Customer Service

Customer service mindset, as a concept, can be categorized as a set of practices rather than tacit knowledge. In this case, there may be some intuitive elements of tacit knowledge involved, such as the ability to read non-verbal cues or intuitively understand customer needs. Most parts in the customer service framework and techniques can be explicitly learned, shared, and trained, which is also regarded as a combination of explicit and tacit knowledge and skills (Lin et al, 2011). Tacit knowledge in customer service is acquired by technopreneurs through their continuous experience in customer interaction, constant training, and research on competitors' strategies. This includes the ability to understand a customers' emotions, listen actively to their needs, deal with complaints, and provide effective solutions. Transferring this tacit knowledge to employees is not easy, unless it exposes them to the experience that technopreneurs have gone through practically. It relies on intuition, communication skills, and the ability to adapt to a variety of client situations. Technopreneurs with shared tacit knowledge are able to apply their expertise flexibly and specifically to complex customer issues effectively.

Customer service is part of problem-solving and is influenced by adaptability to a dynamic and ever-changing environment. Q3:14 *"When our company was in the process of implementing new changes, our team found that customers were not responding well. By leveraging my knowledge of customer preferences and engagement techniques, we managed to tweak the strategy slightly to meet customer expectations"*...in the critical role of tacit knowledge.

It is important for organizations to recognize and nurture this tacit knowledge in customer service as an important mindset by providing continuous training, feedback mechanisms, and a supportive work environment. In doing so, organizations can foster a customer-oriented culture and ensure a high-quality and consistent customer experience.

4.1.7 Crisis Management

Crisis management ability can be considered as a combination of explicit and tacit knowledge to form as one of the important skill sets (Moilanen, 2015; Shadrick & Lussier, 2010). While there are certain explicit strategies and guidelines that can be learned and shared, the ability to navigate and effectively handle a crisis situation often relies on the tacit knowledge and experience of the crisis management team. Tacit knowledge in crisis management includes practical understanding, intuition, the ability to make quick decisions under pressure, communicate effectively, coordinate resources, and adapt to changing circumstances.

For technopreneurs in the ICT industry, tacit knowledge in crisis management plays an important role in understanding and overcoming it effectively. Technopreneur's strategic thinking as tacit knowledge is indispensable to navigate crisis, as part of the problem-solving efforts, which is also tacit knowledge. Q3:2 "*While in the early stages I was just starting out, I had a very heavy financial crisis. But I am grateful for my knowledge and understanding of the market and strategic budget-making skills, allowing me to identify the root cause and take necessary measures to bolster my business"*... in the critical role of tacit knowledge.

In this context of crisis management, tacit knowledge can only be gained through practical experience and cognitive understanding. Therefore, ICT technopreneurs should find opportunities to engage in experiences relevant to crisis management, such as through training, reading related books and articles, as well as interacting with crisis management specialists.

4.1.8 Strategic Decision

In this particular study, the researcher found two main roles in the strategic decision-making process, namely data-based and knowledge-based decision making. Data-based decisions involve the process of deliberation and information analysis, assessing alternatives and selecting the best course of action to achieve organizational objectives. It involves data from markets, industry trends and other tangible and more explicit sources.

However, knowledge-based decision making is a tacit knowledge critical to technopreneurs. This is because strategic decisions in entrepreneurship often involve innovation, the development of new products, and the introduction of new technologies in their business through simultaneous assessment of the internal and external environment using intuitive and reasoning knowledge. Q3:10 "*A decision needs to be made whether to venture into the new market segment or to remain in the existing market segment as our core business. Knowledge of business strategies helps me a lot to assess the risks and make the appropriate decisions that benefit this business*"... in the critical role of tacit knowledge.

In the ever-changing environment of the ICT industry, technopreneurs need to combine tacit and explicit knowledge in the process of making strategic decisions. Tacit knowledge enables technopreneurs to understand market communities and create innovative solutions, while explicit knowledge provides them with relevant information for informed decision-making. Through a combination of tacit and explicit knowledge, ICT technopreneurs can increase their chances of success and brave challenges in an ever-changing and evolving industry.

4.1.9 Innovation

Innovation refers to the creation and implementation of new ideas, upgraded processes, new or value-added product developments, or innovative services that lead to advancement, improvement and even increased productivity level (Blok, 2021; Onea, 2021). Innovations are often generated from a combination of tacit knowledge and codified or explicit knowledge such as a deep intuitive understanding of customer needs, creative solutions and creative problem-solving combined with information and data about competitors, consumers and market trends to form good innovative behaviour and mindset.

Innovation directly affects the entrepreneurial success of technopreneurs. In fact, innovations resulting from tacit knowledge will have a very critical and significant role for technopreneurs. Q2:C8 "*Implementing innovative strategies and adaptability to change allows our business to remain relevant in this highly dynamic industry*"... in success factor of technopreneurs.

For technopreneurs, tacit knowledge of innovation is a very valuable elements to drive innovative behaviour of technopreneurs because it helps in creating new ideas, finding solutions to problems, and seeing opportunities that cannot be seen by others, and stay relevant in the industry.

4.1.10 Problem Solving

Problem solving as part reasoning knowledge, is the skill to identify, analyse, and find solutions to problems or challenges faced. Tacit knowledge that may be used in this context is understanding the cause-and-effect relationships such as trial and error and the critical evaluation of an argument.

When faced with a situation of finding a solution to a problem, individuals will use tacit knowledge to assist them in making decisions and finding effective solutions. Q3:11 " *"I once faced a challenge where a particular technology was not working, and we had to figure out a way to integrate it into a project. My expertise in reverse engineering and problem solving allowed us to find a workable solution, which satisfied our clients."*"... in the critical role of tacit knowledge.

In the process of problem solving, tacit knowledge is used to support analytical thinking and assist in making the right decisions to find effective problem solutions. Tacit knowledge becomes the principle that establishes confidence and accuracy in the process of problem solving.

4.2 The Thematic Network Analysis

Employing network thematic analysis, the researcher constructs codes and a network derived from interviews with technopreneurs, illustrated in the Figure 1 as presented below: -

Figure 1. Model of sustainable success of technopreneurs

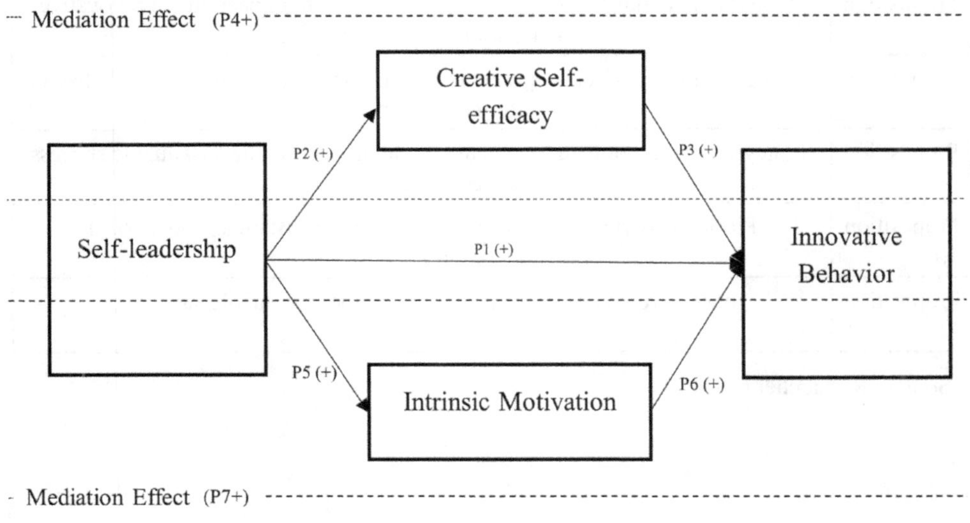

4.2.1 The Research Propositions

Upon analysing the derived code and conducting a thematic network examination, the researcher proceeds to formulate multiple propositions stemming from the re-simulated diagram encompassing variables identified at the primary and secondary tiers within the main code and thematic network, as outlined in Table 4 as follows: -

Table 4. Research proposition

No	Propositions
Proposition 1	Industry knowledge of technopreneurs has an impact on the formation of sustainable success of technopreneurs;
Proposition 2	Industry knowledge of technopreneurs has an impact on the formation of problem-solving skills of technopreneurs;
Proposition 3	Customer service mindset of technopreneurs has an impact on the formation of problem-solving skills of technopreneurs;
Proposition 4	Resourcefulness of technopreneurs has an impact on the formation of problem-solving skills of technopreneurs;
Proposition 5	Crisis management skills has an impact on the formation of problem-solving skills of technopreneurs;
Proposition 6	Professional competence of technopreneurs has an impact on the formation of problem-solving skills of technopreneurs;
Proposition 7	Professional competence of technopreneurs has an impact on the innovative behavior of technopreneurs;
Proposition 8	Strategic thinking of technopreneurs has an impact on the innovative behavior of technopreneurs;
Proposition 9	Strategic thinking of technopreneurs has an impact on the sustainable success of technopreneurs;
Proposition 10	Problem-solving skills has an impact on the sustainable success of technopreneurs;
Proposition 11	Innovative behavior has an impact on the sustainable success of technopreneurs

Source: Researcher (2024)

5.0 THE ROLE OF TACIT KNOWLEDGE IN THE POST-PANDEMIC DIGITAL ECONOMY: WAY FORWARD

5.1 The Role of Tacit Knowledge in the Post-Pandemic Landscape

The COVID-19 pandemic has drastically changed the way organizations operate, especially in the ICT sector. In this period of uncertainty, past experience has taught many technopreneurs to no longer rely solely on explicit or formal knowledge. On the other hand, tacit knowledge in the form of intuition, previous experience, soft skills and the ability to read situations are the main competitive advantages to remain relevant.

For example, in a situation where government policies are changing rapidly and customer needs are also undergoing drastic changes, technopreneurs who can use tacit knowledge to understand customer demand patterns have proven to be able to adapt their products more efficiently. Knowledge such as customer habits, local culture, and certain business patterns cannot be taught through textbooks but only gained through hands-on experience.

This justification is further reinforced when we observe the need for the decision-making process in times of crisis to require an immediate response. In situations like this, technopreneurs rely on their ability to make decisions intuitively based on past patterns they have experienced through previous experience of which, it is a form of tacit knowledge that is difficult to explain formally.

5.2 Tacit Knowledge Sharing Through Digital Platforms

The massive shift from conventional to remote work and online collaboration has posed an important challenge to be studied, for instance, how to maintain and disseminate tacit knowledge in a digital environment? Tacit knowledge is naturally easier to convey in face-to-face interaction through gestures, observation, spontaneous conversation or other appropriate means.

However, there are some digital communication platforms that are now playing an important role as new mediums in imparting tacit knowledge indirectly. For example, informal conversations in social media channels often reveal undocumented internal strategies, best practices, and problem-solving. This knowledge, although not planned, is an important resource for new employees who want to understand the work culture of an ICT firm and it is now trending as people start sharing the atmosphere and work environment at their workplace.

Meanwhile, the use of video recordings, internal forums, and narrative documentation also helps transform some of the tacit knowledge into a tacit-to-explicit form. This is in line with the principles of the SECI model channelled by Nonaka and Takeuchi which emphasizes the importance of externalization in the knowledge management process.

5.3 Gender Perspectives in Tacit Knowledge Acquisition

In the Malaysian context, women's participation in the field of ICT is increasing. However, there is the question of whether there are gender differences in the way tacit knowledge is acquired and applied by different genders. Past studies have shown that women are more likely to develop tacit knowledge through strong interpersonal connections, empathy, and collaborative approaches. On the other hand, men are more likely to learn this knowledge through direct involvement in complex tasks and internal competition.

As a result, organizational strategies to empower tacit knowledge need to take into account these differences in gender-based approaches. For example, creating a workspace that informally supports social interaction and mentoring will help instil tacit knowledge among female employees. Meanwhile, for male employees, challenging technical challenges and cross-departmental exposure opportunities can implicitly accelerate learning.

5.4 Cross-Cultural Influences in Tacit Knowledge Sharing

Malaysia as a multi-racial and multicultural country offers a uniqueness in the context of tacit knowledge sharing. Successful technopreneurs are often those who can align their experiences and intuition with the cultural norms of customers and business partners from different backgrounds.

For example, effective negotiation techniques from different ethnicities with customers from different cultural backgrounds may have significant differences. Knowledge of customs, beliefs or taboos may have significant influences over communication styles and cultural preferences have become an important and inescapable form of knowledge in business, especially from multiracial communities. However, challenges arise when cultural gaps become barriers to effectively delivering tacit knowledge within an organization. Therefore, it is important to develop cross-cultural training strategies as well as mentor-mentee systems that involve the exchange of experiences from various ethnicities within ICT organizations.

6.0 CONCLUSION AND RECOMMENDATION

For an ICT technopreneurs, tacit knowledge is very important because the environment of this industry is changing rapidly and requires the ability to make wise and quick decisions. Tacit knowledge gained through experience and combination with codified knowledge will help technopreneurs to make informed decisions based on their intuition, reasoning and instinctive senses.

Tacit knowledge can also maintain competitive value of the firms. In the ever changing and dynamic ICT business with intense and borderless competition, technopreneurs need to take risks smartly to generate innovation and growth. The tacit knowledge gained through observation, trial and error will help them to make a better decision considering the right risks.

Through understanding of the tacit knowledge, technopreneurs are also able to better assess the various and different business atmosphere. They can read signs of changes in the market and understand customer needs more effectively. Technopreneurs should also value and continue to explore and develop tacit knowledge to achieve sustainable success in an industry that is constantly experiencing rapid growth and changes all around the corner and throughout the periods.

As the role of tacit knowledge is increasingly recognized and acknowledged in the development of technopreneurs' competitiveness, some recommendations are put forward as follows:

a) Enhanced SECI Modelling

The SECI model by Nonaka and Takeuchi (1995) which includes the processes of Socialization, Externalization, Merger, and Internalization has been widely used in knowledge management. However, in today's digital age, there is a need to add another important phase, namely Digitization as a complement to the model. Digitization refers to the effort to structure and store tacit knowledge in digital form through a systematic and easily accessible system. For example, a technopreneur's experience in solving customer issues can be turned into an interactive simulation for the purpose of training new employees. The addition of this phase allows tacit knowledge that is often latent and difficult to transfer to be retained for a long time and made into an organizational asset that can be accessed again at any time.

b) Use of AI Technology and Text Analytics

Artificial intelligence (AI) and text analytics are increasingly being used to capture and analyse informal communications in the workplace which often contain elements of tacit knowledge, especially since there are significant cultural and work differences due to the wave of globalization that has hit the business world today. Through techniques such as natural language processing (NLP), AI is able to identify hidden themes, problem-solving patterns, and informal wisdom from emails, work forums, digital conversations and even informal behaviour patterns. This knowledge can be digitized and fed into an organization's learning system such as training chatbots or experience databases. This technology opens up the space for organizations to automatically capture tacit knowledge and use it to improve operational effectiveness and decision-making processes.

c) Ethics in the Digitization of Tacit Knowledge

While the digitization of tacit knowledge brings many benefits, the ethical aspect should not be taken lightly. Some of the key issues include individual privacy as tacit knowledge is often gained through personal experience. The confidentiality of the organization also needs to be maintained as some information are sensitive. Ownership of knowledge, i.e. the individual's right to knowledge that is contributed informally must also be considered. Digitalization efforts should be implemented with explicit permission from the knowledge owner, as well as with a strong data protection policy. Organizations are advised to develop special ethical guidelines to ensure that tacit knowledge is not misused or exploited by certain parties.

d) Development of the Tacit Efficiency Index

To assess the extent of an organization's ability to manage and leverage tacit knowledge, a Tacit Knowledge Efficiency Index (TKEI) can be developed. The index acts as a diagnostic tool to measure elements such as the effectiveness of informal knowledge sharing, intuition-based decision-making abilities, and an organizational culture that supports informal continuous learning and may also include learning incentives to encourage tacit knowledge transfer. TKEI can help organizations identify skills gaps as well as plan more effective HR investments and training strategies. In this way, the management of tacit knowledge becomes more efficient, planned and in line with the strategic objectives of the organization.

6.1 Practical Implications

The findings of this study have significant practical implications for entrepreneurship related education and studies and technopreneurship training programmes. Tacit knowledge has been found to play an important role in the development of entrepreneurial capabilities such as the identification of opportunities, decision-making and the development of practical skills. Therefore, entrepreneurship education and training programmes should not rely entirely on theoretical and explicit knowledge-based teaching approaches, but should integrate experiential learning such as real case studies, business simulations, project-based learning, mentoring and industry exposure. This approach can help students and technopreneurs develop intuitive abilities, problem-solving skills as well as adaptability in a dynamic ICT environment. Training institutions and policymakers can leverage these findings to design more holistic and practical-oriented entrepreneurial development programs, aligned with the real needs of technopreneurs in achieving business success and sustainability.

6.2 Limitation and Future Research

This study relies on a small sample size of 15 participants from small and medium enterprises (SMEs) in ICT-related industries, which has the potential to limit the level of generalization of the study findings. This study, from the methodological perspectives, used a completely qualitative approach without the support of quantitative analysis, hence the study findings could not be statistically tested for wider empirical validation. These limitations may limit the applicability of the study findings to a larger population of ICT technopreneurs. Therefore, future studies are recommended to conduct more comprehensive research involving a larger and more diverse sample in Malaysia's ICT sector, as well as to use quantitative approaches or mixed methods to empirically test the relationship between tacit knowledge, entrepreneurial ability and technopreneurial sustainable success, thereby increasing the robustness of the study findings. Along with increasingly dynamic technological and social changes, the contribution of tacit knowledge can no longer be taken lightly as it serves as an important catalyst for innovation, business sustainability and operational efficiency in the ICT landscape. Therefore, the recognition and systematic management of tacit knowledge should be made a priority in the development strategy of digital entrepreneurs in Malaysia.

ACKNOWLEDGEMENT

We would like to thank those involved in this study, especially the Ministry of Higher Education Malaysia who has fully funded this study under the Fundamental Research Grant Scheme.

REFERENCES

Abraham, A., & Collins, D. (2017). Defining Coaching Through the Lens of Professional Judgement and Decision Making. In *Proceedings of the 11th ICCE Golobal Coach Conference*.

Anshari, M., & Hamdan, M. (2022). Understanding knowledge management and upskilling in Fourth Industrial Revolution: Transformational shift and SECI model. *VINE Journal of Information and Knowledge Management Systems*, *52*(3), 373–393. DOI: 10.1108/VJIKMS-09-2021-0203

BERNAMA. (2023, July 10). Malaysia muncul hab teknologi, inovasi dinamik. Berita Harian. https://www.bharian.com.my/bisnes/lain-lain/2023/07/1124954/malaysia-muncul-hab-teknologi-inovasi-dinamik

Bidgoli, A. E., Reza, M., Moghadam, S., & Hasangholipour, T. (2022). Designing a strategic financial model for digital start-ups. *Journal of Positive School Psychology*, *2022*(4), 8023–8036. https://journalppw.com/index.php/jpsp/article/view/5159

Blok, V. (2021). What is innovation? Laying the ground for a philosophy of innovation. *Techné: Research in Philosophy and Technology*, *25*(1), 72–96. DOI: 10.5840/techne2020109129

Brockmann, E. N., & Anthony, W. W. P. (1998). The influence of tacit knowledge and collective mind on strategic planning. *Journal of Managerial Issues*, *10*(2), 204–222.

Castaneda, D. I., & Toulson, P. (2021). Is it possible to share tacit knowledge using information and communication technology tools? *Global Knowledge, Memory and Communication*, *70*(8–9), 673–683. DOI: 10.1108/GKMC-07-2020-0102

Chukwujioke Agbim, K., Benapugha Owutuamor, Z., & Orziemgbe Oriarewo, G. (2013). Entrepreneurship Development and Tacit Knowledge : Exploring the Link between Entrepreneurial Learning and Individual Know-How. *Journal of Business Studies Quarterly*, *5*(2), 112–130.

Cuvero, M., Granados, M. L., Pilkington, A., & Evans, R. (2022). Start-ups' use of knowledge spillovers for product innovation: the influence of entrepreneurial ecosystems and virtual platforms. In *R and D Management*. John Wiley and Sons Inc., DOI: 10.1111/radm.12567

DeWaard, H., & Chavhan, R. (2020). Cross-Cultural Mentoring: A Pathway to Building Professional Relationships and Professional Learning Beyond Boundaries. *Journal of Teaching and Learning*, *14*(1), 43–58. DOI: 10.22329/jtl.v14i1.6255

Figurny, G. N. (2021). Phenomenological approaches in the theory of architecture in the context of modern cognitive science. *Voprosy Filosofii*, *2021*(6), 65–73. DOI: 10.21146/0042-8744-2021-6-65-73

Ge, C., Lv, W., & Wang, J. (2023). The Impact of Digital Technology Innovation Network Embedding on Firms' Innovation Performance: The Role of Knowledge Acquisition and Digital Transformation. *Sustainability (Basel)*, *15*(8), 6938. Advance online publication. DOI: 10.3390/su15086938

GlobalData. (2023, June 2). Malaysia ICT Market Size and Forecast (by IT Solution Area, Size Band and Vertical), 2022-2026. Market Research Reports & Consulting | GlobalData UK Ltd. https://www.globaldata.com/store/report/malaysia-ict-market-analysis/

Greiner, M. E., Bohmann, T., & Krcmar, H. (2007). A strategy for knowledge management. *Journal of Knowledge Management*, *11*(6), 3–15. DOI: 10.1108/13673270710832127

Hanif, S., Ahsan, A., & Wise, G. (2020). Icebergs of expertise-based leadership: The role of expert leaders in public administration. *Sustainability (Basel)*, *12*(11), 4544. Advance online publication. DOI: 10.3390/su12114544

Hirano, M., Yamamoto, T., Sakakibara, K., & Kurashige, M. (2017). Social innovation in Sabae city: As a new type of industrial movement in Japan. In PICMET 2016 - Portland International Conference on Management of Engineering and Technology: Technology Management for Social Innovation, Proceedings (pp. 1217–1223). Institute of Electrical and Electronics Engineers Inc. DOI: 10.1109/PICMET.2016.7806512

Kabir, M. N. (2019). *Knowledge-Based Social Entrepreneurship*. Knowledge-Based Social Entrepreneurship., DOI: 10.1057/978-1-137-34809-8

Kippenberger, T. (1997). When is virtual virtuous? *The Antidote*, *2*(6), 28–29. DOI: 10.1108/EUM0000000006443

Kucharska, W., & Erickson, G. S. (2023). Tacit knowledge acquisition & sharing, and its influence on innovations: A Polish/US cross-country study. *International Journal of Information Management*, *71*, 102647. Advance online publication. DOI: 10.1016/j.ijinfomgt.2023.102647

Lin, F. R., Po, R. W., & Orellan, C. V. C. (2011). Mining purchasing decision rules from service encounter data of retail chain stores. *Information Systems and e-Business Management*, *9*(2), 193–221. DOI: 10.1007/s10257-010-0143-3

Lovell, H., & Powells, G. (2020). Smart grid knowledges and the state. *Area*, *52*(3), 583–590. DOI: 10.1111/area.12613

Moilanen, J. H. (2015). The Wisdom of Tacit Knowing-in-Action and Mission Command. *Adult Learning*, *26*(3), 101–108. DOI: 10.1177/1045159515583258

Nonaka, I., & Takeuchi, H. (1995). *The knowledge-creating company: How Japanese companies create the dynamics of innovation*. Oxford University Press. DOI: 10.1093/oso/9780195092691.001.0001

Onea, I. A. (2021). Framework for assessing innovation capacity and business efficiency in Romanian SMEs. *Proceedings of the International Conference on Business Excellence*, 15(1), 1083–1095. DOI: 10.2478/picbe-2021-0102

Polanyi, M. (1966). *The Tacit Dimension*. Doubleday and Company.

Reeves, M., & Deimler, M. (2011). Adaptability: The new competitive advantage. *Harvard Business Review*, *89*(7–8), 7. DOI: 10.1002/9781119204084.ch2

Roundy, P. T. (2020). The wisdom of ecosystems: A transactive memory theory of knowledge management in entrepreneurial ecosystems. *Knowledge and Process Management*, *27*(3), 234–247. DOI: 10.1002/kpm.1635

Shadrick, S. B., & Lussier, J. W. (2010). Training Complex Cognitive Skills: A Theme-Based Approach to the Development of Battlefield Skills. In Development of Professional Expertise (pp. 286–311). Cambridge University Press. DOI: 10.1017/CBO9780511609817.016

Stefanidis, A., Ioannidis, A., & Mourdoukoutas, P. (2007). Entrepreneurial networks in highly globalised industries: The case of the Greek shipping industry. *International Journal of Networking and Virtual Organisations*, *4*(2), 189–200. DOI: 10.1504/IJNVO.2007.013543

Wuytens, N., Schepers, J., Vandekerkhof, P., & Voordeckers, W. (2022). Entrepreneurs Can Know More Than They Can Tell: Conceptualizing and Measuring Tacit Entrepreneurial Knowledge. *Frontiers in Psychology*, *13*, 892223. Advance online publication. DOI: 10.3389/fpsyg.2022.892223 PMID: 35747676

Yao Lartey, P., Shi, J., Jaladi Santosh, R., Owusu Afriyie, S., Akolgo Gumah, I., Husein, M., & Binta Maci Bah, F. (2022). *Importance of Organizational Tacit Knowledge*. Barriers to Knowledge Sharing. In Recent Advances in Knowledge Management. IntechOpen., DOI: 10.5772/intechopen.101997

Yew, J. L. K. (2021). Family Firms, Enterprise Development and Tacit Knowledge Transformation: Small and Medium Enterprises (SMEs) Innovation in Malaysia. *Global Business Review*, 09721509211047648. Advance online publication. DOI: 10.1177/09721509211047648

Zahra, S. A. (2021). The Resource-Based View, Resourcefulness, and Resource Management in Startup Firms: A Proposed Research Agenda. *Journal of Management*, *47*(7), 1841–1860. DOI: 10.1177/01492063211018505

Zhang, M., & Gao, L. (2022). Systems Dynamics-based Study on Contract and Tacit Knowledge Transfer. *Fuza Xitong Yu Fuzaxing Kexue*, *19*(1), 96–103. DOI: 10.13306/j.1672-3813.2022.01.013

Chapter 7
Sustainable Purchase Intentions Toward Organic Food:
Evidence From Generation Z Consumers

Mei Ling Goh
https://orcid.org/0000-0003-3470-4092
Multimedia University, Melaka, Malaysia

Seng Huat Tan
https://orcid.org/0000-0003-0640-4172
Multimedia University, Melaka, Malaysia

ABSTRACT

Organic food industry is an industry that contributes and supports the competitive edge in the framework of the agriculture sector of most of the nations, including Malaysia. The market for organic food is expanding which coupled with the rise of the awareness of consumers for health particularly in the post Covid-19. This can be observed with the earlier research that consumer awareness towards purchasing the eco-friendly and healthy food products is increasing. Research has also shown that the consumers belonging to the Generation Z segment in Malaysia will

DOI: 10.4018/979-8-3693-6195-5.ch007

pay for green products. In order to better understand the sustainable organic food purchase intentions of Generation Z, the present research has two goals. Firstly, it measures the sustainable purchase intentions of Generation Z for organic food, and then it examines the indirect effect of attitude on how health consciousness, environmental concern, and trust for organic labels drive organic food purchase intentions.

1. INTRODUCTION

Increasing consumer consciousness towards consuming healthy food comes in the shape of the size of the worldwide organic food industry. According to Precedence Research (2023), the international market for organic food is valued at USD 183.35 billion in 2023. The key growth driver of organic food market is with increasing awareness towards health and the organic food is viewed as chemical-free products. It has also been stated the health risk involved in eating excessive normal food another consumption driver of organic food products (Precedence Research, 2023). According to Huy et al. (2019), the organic food sector in emerging economies is relatively immature. Nearly 90% of worldwide total organic food market revenue remain anchored in western markets such as North America and Europe (Ayyub et al., 2021).

A 2023 survey by Rakuten Insight revealed that 38% of respondents in Malaysia sometimes bought organic food, which is relatively low (Statista, 2023). Despite this, the sales of organic food are reported to have a steadily growth from 2025 to 2033 (Renub Research, 2025). Organic food, such as fruits, vegetables, packaged foods, beverages, and meat products are among popular items that gain popularity by the consumers. The outbreak of the COVID-19 has heightened the consumers' awareness about the food sources and safety, this sparked the market of organic food (Singh et al., 2024). During the pandemic period, greater interests were shown by consumers on organic food, including consumer behaviour shifts for balanced dietary choices and health concerns (Cramarenco et al., 2023), being more conscious on the advantages of taking organic food through the power of social media, moving the organic food from a niche into broader market (Masih et al., 2025).

The Malaysian organic food industry, with its future potential for expansion, does have a few giant challenges to overcome. Transitioning from traditional to organic methods requires an enormous amount of investment in training, certifications, and eco-friendly farming tools, and most farmers are not familiar with these organic methods of farming and the need for a push to undertake these methods efficiently, resulting in inconsistencies in organic product supply (The Living Centre, 2025). Besides that, the organic food's higher premium price from traditional food could discourage some buyers (Somasundram et al., 2016). The consumers also have low-trust levels in product quality for organics and accreditations system (Aziz et al., 2020). In such a situation that has arisen, greater knowledge for consuming organic foods as a dietary choice is very much important among the Malaysian. This includes Malaysian Generation Z consumers' sustainable purchase intentions which is critical for the market growth of the organic food.

Generation Z, born between 1997 and 2012, are referred to as technology-proficient group, having nurtured with smartphones and social media (Dimock, 2019; Benítez-Márquez et al., 2022). Generation Z appreciates diversity and inclusion, is socially aware, and learned about climate change at an early age (Dimock, 2019; Katz et al., 2022). Millennials or Generation Y comprise those born between 1981 and 1996 (Dimock, 2019). They have been through the growth of digital media and social channels, thus being technology savvy and highly educated. Millennials believe in work-life balance and were heavily impacted by large events in the world and the economic downturn of 2008 during their formative years (Dimock, 2019; Pyöriä et al., 2017).

Purchase intention has long been recognised as one of the fundamental aspects of the industry because it can bring the industry more profitable businesses. If the manufacturers want to increase the consumption of consumers and increase the profits, they need to fulfil the needs of consumers first. The key role of purchase intention is to decide whether the product fulfils the expectations and needs of consumers, as to additionally explore the assessment of goods and services from them. This concept emphasised that if the field of production and services fulfils the expectations of consumers, customer satisfaction will be increased (Xiao et al., 2018).

According to Ernst and Young's Energy transition consumer insights report, consumers from Generation Z in Malaysia are willing to pay for sustainable products (Bernama, 2024, April 30). Su et al. (2019) pointed that Generation Z are also eco-friendlier, and environment concerned. Furthermore, research on young consumer specifically Generation Z in Malaysia is also limited. Notable studies include Poovithira (2024) and Yasin et al. (2025). Poovithira (2024) identified four determinants of purchase intention of Generation Z: environment concern, health consciousness, food safety, and perceived value. Similar study has also been conducted by Yasin et al. (2025) using a cross-sectional study to examine the organic food purchase motivation of young people. Thus, it is crucial to study the organic food buying intention of Generation Z specifically Malaysian. This is also in accordance with the suggestion for future investigations by Ayub et al. (2020) to concentrate on young customers' intentions to buy of the eco-conscious such as organic food.

Bhutto et al. (2023) and Dwivedi et al. (2025) have highlighted the importance of research on Generation Z's buying intention towards organic food since research in this regard is very limited. Although there are vast studies on intention to purchase organic food, most of it has been conducted for Millennials and Generation Y (Hasan & Suciarto, 2020; Patel et al., 2021). Therefore, research specifically focused on Generation Z's buying intentions is severely lacking.

Literature also indicates that limited studies of the health consciousness (Saleki et al., 2020; Nguyen et al., 2021) and trust towards the organic label (Ayub et al., 2020; Saleki et al., 2020; Nguyen et al., 2023) were done on the attitude towards the organic food. Despite all these studies being more on Vietnamese (Nguyen et al, 2023), Chinese (Ahmed et al, 2020), South Korea (Li & Shan, 2025), and Portuguese (Teixeira et al., 2022), studies that have been conducted on the Malaysian side are still poor (Poovithira, 2024; Yasin et al., 2025). It shows that research is needed in the exploration of how the variables impact attitudes of Malaysian Generation Z towards organic food.

As such, this study tries to address the gaps discussed above by scrutinizing the sustainable buying intention of the organic food by Generation Z. This study also tries to scrutinize the effect of attitude that act as a mediator between health consciousness and purchase intention, between environmental concern and purchase intention and between organic-label trust and purchase intention. This research is thought to make an informative input to marketers and producers of organic food, policy makers and researcher to advocate for organic food consumption that will subsequently result in industry growth on the organic food.

2. LITERATURE REVIEW

2.1 Theory of Planned Behaviour (TPB)

Theory of Planned Behaviour model (TPB) (Ajzen, 1985, 1991) is an expansion Theory of Reasoned Action (Ajzen & Fishbein, 1980). TPB model concludes that human beings are rational where a person usually will form a judgment regarding their action based on available information. TPB model concludes that intention of an individual to perform the given behaviour is the core determinant of performing the given behaviour. Intention is the motivational forces that direct behaviour where it is a description of the intention to attempt, or effort to perform the behaviour (Ajzen, 1991). Therefore, in TPB model, intention (behaviour) is an attitude towards the behaviour component, subjective norm and perceived behavioural control. TPB model has been extensively utilized in the context of organic food research such as that of Ahmed et al. (2020), Ferriera and Pereira (2023), Li et al. (2025) and Teixeira et al. (2022).

TPB model has also been augmented by other research by adding other variables to forecast consumer behavioural intention. Ferriera & Pereira (2023) have used health awareness and ecological awareness in their research study on organic food purchasing intention from the Portuguese context. Simultaneously, Ahmed et al. (2020), established environmental concern as mediator of purchase intention and attitude for Chinese consumers aged 18-30 years. Similarly, other researchers like Li and Shan (2025), Nguyen et al. (2023) and Pang et al. (2021), also established that that expanded TPB model can improve interpretative power of purchase intention of consumers in organic food context. Therefore, this study should employ the TPB model since it has been universally acclaimed to be effective in explaining and predicting consumer behaviour, particularly with respect to consuming organic food.

2.2 Purchase Intention

Ajzen (1991) believed that intention is influenced by determinants, i.e., attitude, social influence and perceived behavioural control of someone. Purchase intention is defined as the probability or willingness of a consumer to purchase a product or service (Bhasin, 2025; Nittin, 2015). Also, Spear and Singh (2004) define purchase intention as the probability of a consumer to look or to purchase a product or service. The purchase intention is guided by consumer psychology that indicates the likelihood of a consumer to exhibit a given purchase behavior, as argued by Li et al. (2021) and Zhou et al. (2023). Morinez et al. (2007) highlight that purchase intention is a concern of the consumers' behaviour, perception, and attitude.

On the other hand, Morrison (1979) also highlighted that purchase intentions and purchase behaviour are one and the same. But the strength of the relationship can be changed in various context and time. For example, purchase intentions for involvement products such as cars can be more effective predictors of actual purchasing than involvement products such as household goods (Morrison, 1979). Thus, the knowledge of the determinants of purchase intention is significant in assisting the marketers to have effective and better marketing strategies to gain higher market share and boost the sales of the organisation.

There are vast literature on the purchase intention of consumers in regard to the organic food. Ahmad et al. (2025), Ferreira and Pereira (2023), Jakubowska et al. (2024), Li and Shan (2025), Nguyen and Vo (2023) and Nethra and Tamilmathi (2025) are a few of the recent research works that examine the purchase intention in relation to organic food.

Environmental consciousness, health consciousness, food safety consciousness, perceived value (Poovithira, 2024), and social media (Yasin et al., 2025) were discovered in research to be among the determinants that influence Generation Z's intention to purchase organic food in Malaysia. Generation Z customers will purchase organic food because of perceived benefits and values of organic food, such as quality and long-term health benefits. Similarly, the same goes for Japan's Generation Z, Germany's Generation Z and Canada's Generation Z for organic food purchase in terms of ecological awareness and health perceptions. Social media and social influencers also play their part towards Malaysian Generation Z's attitude and purchasing intention of organic food. The same has been found to occur in Pakistan's Generation Z case (Bhutto et al., 2023). Attitude, subjective norm, and perceived behavioural control are among the main drivers of organic food purchase intention not only in Malaysia but also in other countries like the USA, Australia, and the UK (Džever et al., 2024; Yasin et al., 2025).

2.3 Attitude

Attitude in TPB model is the extent to which one has positive or negative opinions or assumption of commodities or objects (Ajzen, 1991). Maloney et al. (2013) define attitude as the judgment of an event whether they are positive or negative. Regarding to the acceptance of technology, attitude reflects positive or negative emotions of an individual on a particular action (Halim et al., 2021). Bechler et al. (2021) and Haddock et al. (2020) further added that individual's evaluations may change and affect the behaviour differently. A person with a stronger attitude toward the behaviour, will be having a more powerful intention to conduct the behaviour (Abdullah, 2002).

Studies have illustrated that a consumer, who has a positive attitude are more willing to but the organic food (Ahmad et al, 2025; Khan et al., 2023). However, in the analysis of Nguyen et al. (2021), it has been found that consumer who has an unpleasant attitude due facing difficulty to access to the organic food, will not contribute to positive purchase intention. Several previous pieces of research have broadly established that the attitude's impact on consumers' purchase motivation toward organic food (Cheng et al., 2024; Jakubowska et al., 2024; Nethra & Tamilmathi, 2025).

2.4 Subjective Norm

As referred by Ajzen (1991), subjective norm is another factor in TPB model that reflects the level at which individuals believe that significant others anticipate them to engage in the behaviour. According to Park (2000), subjective norms are social in origin which considered the opinions of individuals close to him or her influence a person's decision to commit an act. These opinions are affected by perceptions of societal stress to perform in a certain method (Park, 2000). Asare (2015) has also provided similar definition in which subjective norm is the perceived societal expectations to engage in a behaviour. On the other hand, Fattahi Ardakani et al. (2020) divide subjective norms into two main components, which are the awareness of others' expectations of an individual and their motivation to satisfy these expectations.

Social influence was seen as a predictor of consumer's purchase intention by Canova et al. (2020) in their study on organic food. They further highlighted subjective norm can be referred to the influence caused the expectation by surrounding people such as relatives, friends, and others. This social pressure can thus enhance the tendency to purchase the organic food.

Study by Li and Jaharuddin (2020) have indicated that subjective norms have positive relation to the buying purchase intention towards organic food. They have concluded that social pressure from social circle and household members will increase the likelihood of a consumer to purchase the organic food. There is a series of empirical research revealed that subjective norm has a critical capacity in the establishment of organic food intentions (Ahmed et al., 2020; Cheng et al., 2024; Pang et al., 2021).

2.5 Perceived Behavioural Control

Perceived behavioural control (PBC) refers to how easy or difficult a behaviour that is specified will be perceived to be because of undertaking outcomes (Armitage & Conner 2001). On the other hand, PBC according to Ajzen (1991) termed as the way an individual views the easiness or difficulty of performing a behaviour.

With respect to the organic food, PBC itself involves how consumers feel about their owning the necessary resources, opportunities, and skills to purchase the organic items which subsequently have a significant effect on their purchase behaviour and decisions. When consumers believe that they have the sufficient resources and possibilities for consuming organic food they have the adequate resources and opportunities to obtain organic food, they are more prone to consider buying these products. The factors like availability, affordability, and knowledge of organic products can support this belief, thereby promoting consumers to shop for organic products (Canova et al., 2020). A high level of belief in control can result in more confident consumers when it comes to choosing sustainable and healthy products, thereby creating the boom for the organic food sector.

Various research has revealed evidence of PBC and other TPB precursors having a positive influence on the intentions to purchase organic food. Li and Jaharuddin (2020) established PBC as a robust predictor of purchasing intention for organic food. Through their research, they concluded how consumers will buy those products which possess less barrier as well as more perceived power in controlling the purchase for organic foods. In addition, earlier research has proved that PBC positively influences organic food purchase intention (Amanda & Marsasi, 2024; Zayed et al., 2022).

2.6 Health Consciousness

Due to the increasing enrolment in public education, there has been an increase in the awareness of how people care about their health. Curvelo et al. (2019), and Shahriari et al. (2019) studied consumers and argued that "consumers hold a notion that organic food is always more nutritious in terms of protein, fibre, roughage, and vitamins over the food produced in conventional methods." According to Huang et al (2022), consumers' health consciousness is portrayed as the single most critical psychological trait of one which makes him or her practice healthy behaviour.

Previous studies, for example, Guido (2009) and Guido et al. (2009) claimed that one is ready to take health measures when there is health consciousness. Determined health actions are more likely to be taken by those with high health consciousness according to Kim & Chung (2011). Health consciousness, as pointed out by Asif et al (2018), is regarded to be the integrant characteristic of health-oriented customers which, along with others, greatly determines the purchase of organic foods.

Some previous empirical studies have showed that health consciousness is indirectly linked to purchase intention by having positive effect on attitude (Ferreira & Pereira, 2023; Li & Shan, 2025; Nethra & Tamilmathi, 2025). These studies thereby presented a valid proof that awareness towards health is an attitude determinant of the consumer in relation to organic food.

2.7 Environmental Concern

Individual concern for the environment significantly influences organic food purchasing (Yadav & Pathak, 2016). It would be able to influence purchasing intention on the buying decision of the customer since customers possess an idea that organic food is green-friendly (Kushwah et al., 2019). If consumers are given persuasive information that organic food can reduce environmental risks, they will be persuaded and improve their likelihood of purchasing cthe organic food (Pang et al., 2021). Thus, concern for the environment was the most powerful predictor of attitude of consumer in purchasing organic food (Nguyen et al., 2019).

Research has shown that the environmental awareness as a variable to affect consumers' attitude which further play an important role towards their buying intentions of the organic food (Ahmad et al., 2025). The same results also indicated by some other research (Ferreira & Pereira, 2023; Le-Anh & Nguyen-To, 2020; Teixeira et al., 2022).

2.8 Organic-Label Trust

Consumers are consistently concerned deeply about the trust in organic foods, that can be referred to "an expression of the alternative to have to make an individual decision and just assume that food is safe" (Green et al., 2005). The labelling certificate with a reliable sign shows the organic food's attributes, including healthy, safe, and natural (Almli et al., 2019;

Drexler et al., 2017). Trust is vital in the process the purchase of organic food which successively will rise the likelihood of the purchase of consumers (Nguyen et al., 2021). This trust will build the level of consumer confidence when making an organic food purchase (Ayyub et al., 2018).

Study conducted by Nguyen et al. (2019) have shown that urban Vietnamese was greatly influenced by trust in organic labelling in their decision on the organic food purchase. Huy et al. (2019) have confirmed in their study that lack of trust of consumers in organic labels will result in a low tendency of purchase. Some studies have demonstrated that consumer trust is crucial for green consumption and green product that will impact on attitudes and behaviours (Jeyakumar et al., 2021; Nguyen et al., 2021).

Based on the discussion above, three TPB variables of attitude, subjective norm and perceived behavioural control were assumed to predict organic purchase intention of generation Z. Further, health consciousness, environment concern and trust for organic labels were assumed to predict attitude towards organic food. Accordingly, six hypotheses and research framework (Figure 1) are formulated below.

H1: Consumer attitude towards organic food purchase is positively affected by health consciousness.
H2: Consumer attitude towards organic food purchase is positively affected by environmental concern.
H3: Consumer attitude towards organic food purchase is positively affected by organic-label trust.
H4: Attitude positively affects organic food purchase intention.
H5: Subjective norm positively affects organic food purchase intention.
H6: Perceived behavioural control positively affects organic food purchase intention.
H7: Attitude will act as a mediator between health consciousness and purchase intention.
H8: Attitude will act as a mediator between environmental concern and purchase intention.
H9: Attitude will act as a mediator between organic-label trust and purchase intention.

Figure 1. Research framework

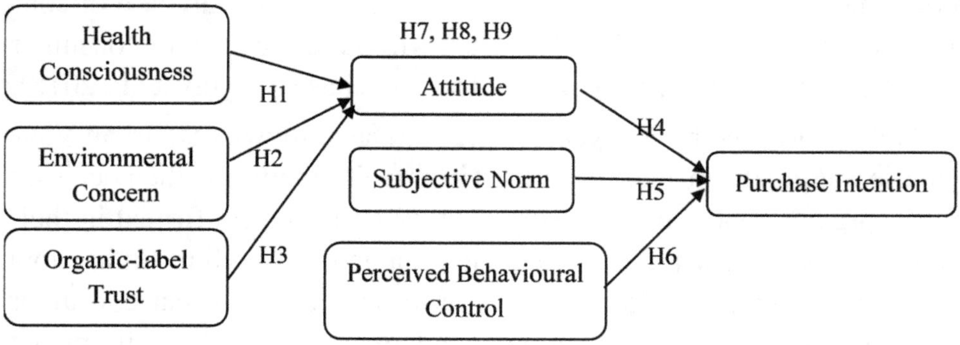

3. RESEARCH METHODS

The population of interest in this study is Malaysia's Generation Z generation born between 1997 and 2012 (Pew Research Centre, 2019). Unit of analysis is consumer Generation Z. This can lead to inadequate information to have complete sampling frame for the use of probability sampling. Hence, convenience sampling, being part of the non-probability sampling, was used in this study as advised by Hulland et al. (2017) and Sarstedt et al. (2017). Furthermore, according to Sekaran & Bougie (2013), convenience sampling facilitates easy gathering of data, rapidly, and in an effective manner. Accordingly, 157 samples were gathered for this research. The participants were selected according to their availability and willingness. The data were gathered through self-report questionnaires, which were sent through Google Forms. Through this, participants were able to complete the questionnaires as they wanted, which was most likely to have a high response rate. The questionnaire seeks to gather data on the in-depth demographic attributes of the respondents. It captures all the measures required to measure the levels of the constructs identified in the research framework, i.e., health consciousness (5 items), concern for the environment (4 items), trust for organic labels (4 items), attitude (3 items), subjective norm (3 items), perceived behavioural control (3 items), and purchase intention (3 items) outlined in Appendix. The constructs are central to understanding determinants influencing purchase intention of organic product purchases. Measurement scales for these dimensions were adapted from the research study of Nguyen et al. (2019) to make the data valid and reliable. Purchase intention used a 7-point Likert scale, whereas independent variables used a 5-point Likert scale. This research design is aimed at minimizing the risk of common method variance, a potential survey research bias, according to Podsakoff et al. (2003) and Tehseen et al. (2017). Partial Least Squares Structural Equation Modeling (PLS-SEM) has been employed in data analysis. This sophisticated statistical procedure was used in order to authenticate both the structural model, whereby the relationships of the constructs are authenticated, and the measurement model, whereby construct validity and reliability are authenticated.

4. RESULTS AND INTERPRETATION

A total of 157 valid answers were gathered in total. The frequency count has shown that 83.40% of all the answers are Chinese while the rest are Malay and Indian. 51.6% holds a university's first degree and 26.8% of them are from the diploma qualification.

4.1 MEASUREMENT MODEL

In Partial Least Square Structural Equation modelling, structural model and measurement model were obtained. In measurement model, standard factor loading (> 0.7), composite reliability (> 0.7) and average variance extracted (> 0.5) are checked (Hari et al., 2021). Since from Table 1, every item has the factor loading that lies between value 0.66 and value 0.91, and composite reliability should be greater than value 0.7 as well as the average variance extracted to be above 0.5. Convergent validity has been confirmed to be up to the standards put forward by Hair et al. (2021).

For discriminant validity, HTMT criterion was used (Henseler et al, 2015). Gold et al, (2001) and Kline (2011) proposed that the HTMT ratio should not exceed 0.9 or 0.85 for all the constructs. All the HTMT values from 0.247 to 0.757 in Table 2 are below the cut-off point of 0.85 of HTMT. This means the discriminant validity is achieved (Gold et al., 2001; Kline, 2011).

Table 1. Convergent validity

Constructs	Items	Factor Loading	CR	AVE
Attitude	ATT1	0.893	0.902	0.756
	ATT2	0.899		
	ATT3	0.813		
	EC1	0.863	0.907	0.71
	EC2	0.85		
Environmental Concern	EC3	0.828		
	EC4	0.83		
Health Consciousness	HC1	0.813	0.915	0.684
	HC2	0.79		
	HC3	0.808		
	HC4	0.842		
	HC5	0.88		
Organic-Label Trust	OLT1	0.895	0.92	0.742
	OLT2	0.846		
	OLT3	0.872		
	OLT4	0.831		
Perceived Behavioural Control	PBC1	0.907	0.857	0.671
	PBC2	0.868		
	PBC3	0.66		
Purchase Intention	PI1	0.899	0.929	0.813
	PI2	0.897		
	PI3	0.91		
Subjective Norm	SN1	0.883	0.898	0.746
	SN2	0.879		
	SN3	0.828		

Note: CR-Composite Reliability, AVE - Average Variance Extracted

Table 2. Discriminant validity using HTMT (2015) criterion

	1	2	3	4	5	6	7
1. Attitude							
2. Environmental Concern	0.473						
3. Health Consciousness	0.247	0.525					
4. Organic-Label Trust	0.543	0.521	0.322				
5. Perceived Behavioural Control	0.526	0.449	0.424	0.42			
6. Purchase Intention	0.596	0.539	0.468	0.315	0.48		
7. Subjective Norm	0.757	0.444	0.283	0.569	0.635	0.655	

4.2 STRUCTURAL MODEL

The structural model analysis was then performed after the measurement model assessment, and the findings are presented in Table 3. The Variance Inflation Factor (VIF) for all constructs varied from 1.288 to 1.95, which is far below the 5 points, indicating that there is no multicollinearity among the independent variables (Hair et al., 2021). Also, the f-square values on the significant path ranging from 0.052 to o.15 are higher than the minimum recommended point of 0.02, as proposed by Cohen (1988).

Table 3. Results of partial least square

Hypothesis	Relationship	Std Beta	Std Error	t-value	Decision	R Square	f Square	VIF
H1	Health Consciousness -> Attitude	-0.003	0.072	0.041	Not Supported	0.277	0.000	1.295
H2	Environmental Concern -> Attitude	0.237	0.098	2.424**	Supported		0.052	1.493
H3	Organic-Label Trust -> Attitude	0.374	0.108	3.469**	Supported		0.15	1.288
H4	Attitude -> Purchase Intention	0.251	0.111	2.26*	Supported	0.38	0.06	1.699
H5	Subjective Norm -> Purchase Intention	0.333	0.11	3.029**	Supported		0.092	1.95
H6	Perceived Behavioural Control -> Purchase Intention	0.142	0.09	1.577	Not Supported		0.023	1.42
Note: * p-value < 0.05, ** p-value <0.01								

Table 4. Results of mediation analysis

Hypothesis	Relationship	Std. Beta	Std. Error	t-value	Confidence Interval Bias Corrected LL	Confidence Interval Bias Corrected UL	Decision
H7	Health Consciousness -> Attitude -> Purchase Intention	-0.001	0.02	0.037	-0.042	0.04	Not Supported
H8	Environmental Concern -> Attitude -> Purchase Intention	0.059	0.044	1.358	0.002	0.164	Not Supported
H9	Organic-label Trust -> Attitude -> Purchase Intention	0.094	0.04	2.362*	0.028	0.186	Supported
*Note: * p-value < 0.05, UL = Upper Level, LL = Lower Level*							

R square is 0.277 for attitude and 0.38 for purchase intention. This indicates that the total variation explained in attitude is 27.7% and purchase intention is 38%. The findings indicate that environmental concern (β = 0.237, t-value = 2.424) and organic label (β = 0.374, t-value = 3.469) has positive influence on the consumers' attitude towards organic food purchase. Health awareness was found to have no significant effect on attitude. This, therefore, affirms hypothesis, H2 and H3 and disconfirms H1.

At the same time, attitude (β = 0.251, t-value = 2.26) and subjective norm (β = 0.333, t-value = 3.029) have positive correlations with the intention to purchase organic food. Perceived behaviour control has no impact on the intention to purchase. Therefore, hypotheses, i.e., H4 and H5 are confirmed by the study except H6.

From Table 4 for mediation analysis testing, t-values are 0.037 (Health Consciousness -> Attitude -> Purchase Intention), 1.358 (Environmental Concern -> Attitude -> Purchase Intention) and 2.362 (Organic-label Trust -> Attitude -> Purchase Intention). There is mediating effect on the path if t-value > 1.96 at 5% significance level. From the t-values derived, attitude plays mediating role in the relationship between organic-label trust and purchase intention. Attitude does not mediate in the other two relationships. This means that the findings support H9 but not for H7 and H8.

5. DISCUSSION AND CONCLUSION

The research validated that health consciousness is unrelated to attitudes towards buying organic food, i.e., Hypothesis 1 (H1) is rejected. This finding differs from previous research (Ferreira & Pereira, 2023; Li & Shan, 2025; Nethra & Tamilmathi, 2025). Health consciousness in this research assesses respondents' self-awareness, vigilance, and general health consciousness. The contradictory results show that respondents do not purchase organic food due to their health consciousness or awareness. Instead, there are some other reasons that could influence their purchasing behavior. That means health consciousness is not considered a significant factor in guiding respondents' attitudes towards purchasing organic food. Past research has shown that Generation Z would care about organic food but the reasons would not be health awareness because of the growing social media impact and brand recognition (Bhutto et al., 2023), lower degree of health empowerment and lesser tendency to look for information related to health though they use digital platform aggressively compared to their previous generations (Jiao et al., 2023), newer technologies bringing about change in health behaviour as a function of generational difference (Balon, 2024).

The findings have indicated that environmental awareness is positively correlated with attitude towards Generation Z consumers' organic food shopping. Therefore, H2 is established. This research is evidenced by the research by Ferreira & Pereira (2023) and Teixeira et al. (2022). This indicates that Generation Z consumer who is environmentally aware and is willing to save the environment from pollution, will improve their attitude towards organic food. Therefore, enhancing their ability to consume organic food as attested by Su et al. (2019) that the consumer who belong to Generation Z are more environmentally conscious compared to other generations. They possess high level of awareness, high commitment and more active in adopting sustainable behaviours (Divinagracia et al., 2024; Lopes, et al., 2024; Juma-Michilena et al., 2024)

Organic-label trust was found to positively influence the attitude towards buying organic food. Therefore, H3 is validated. The findings are aligned with research studies of Jeyakumar et al. (2021) and Nguyen et al. (2021). This has actually established that the Generation Z would possess a good attitude towards buying organic food if they possessed a high trust on the organic food labelling. These empirical results have thus demonstrated that the labelling of organic foods is a credible and reliable indicator of the production of the organic food that will persuade consumer to make a positive assessment on organic food. Organic-label trust is indeed an crucial element to affecting consumption of organic food over non-organic food. This is because the labelling obviously indicates the different types of food among the two to consumers.

The research has indicated that attitude has a positive influence towards the intention in buying organic food among the Generation Z in Malaysia. H4 is thus confirmed. The finding coincides with other literatures (Ahmad et al, 2025; Khan et al., 2023). Attitude towards organic food in this research is seen through the perception of Generation Z towards purchasing the organic food. If they feel that purchasing organic food is a right and a sensible decision and will be profitable to them, then they will be favourably inclined towards purchasing organic food. Hence, this suggested that Generation Z with favourable assessment of the purchase of organic food, would be willing to purchase the organic food. There is a positive attitude toward organic food consumption by Generation Z consumers (Mehdi et al., 2024).

In addition, subjective norm is positively related with organic food purchase intention as well. Thus, H5 is confirmed. The same has been found by Cheng et al. (2024) and Pang et al. (2021) also. Subjective norm is that in this study, belief on the rightness of family members, friends, colleagues and others believe that purchasing organic food is the correct decision to do. Therefore, this explains Generation Z' purchasing intention will be higher if they perceive people around them considering purchasing organic food to be a good action to pursue. The social influence of individuals in their social network then becomes a significant factor on purchasing intention towards organic food. Word of mouth, consumption experience, and recommendation from direct social networks guide their choice and also serve as a cue for them in consuming the organic food.

Finally, perceived behavioural control for buying organic food was shown to exhibit no influence on such buying intention. Thus, H6 is rejected. This finding is in opposition to evidence of existing studies (Amanda & Marsasi, 2024; Zayed et al., 2022). Perceived behavioural control for this study pertains to the extent of control and availability of organic food. It means that consumers will buy organic food when available to them. The low finding in this study suggests that the respondents do not consider perceived behavioural control to be a powerful factor when purchasing organic food. This could be because organic food in Malaysia is easily accessible not just within retail outlets but also in shopping malls, hence it is easy for consumers to buy whenever they want. The diversity in channels of organic food supply will make the consumers perceive that the buying of organic food is an easy and convenience buying behaviour. Therefore, this factor is not significant to them in this research. Maybe future studies can strengthen more on this variable and unearth more data on the impacts on this factor.

For mediating analysis, the outcome that was obtained came up with the fact that attitude is not a mediator between health consciousness and purchase intention. H7 is rejected. The finding contradicts the finding by Li and Shan (2025). Organic food purchase intention was, according to the study conducted by Li and Shan (2025), found to have an indirect effect via attitude on health consciousness. This implies Generation Z who are health-oriented will translate into their organic food purchasing intention but not because of their favourable attitude towards organic food. This can be explained by other variables that future research can explore it.

Apart from that, this study also found that attitude does not mediate between environmental concern and purchasing intention. Thus, H8 is not supported. This is in contrast to Teixeira et al. (2022) where authors find attitude as a mediating factor in the relationship between environment concern and purchasing intention. This means Generation Z with a good attitude not necessarily will increase the tendency of purchasing intention towards organic food. Even though individuals who have an issue with the environment and would wish to preserve it, would be able to buy organic foods.

Mediating analysis otherwise implies that attitude is a mediator of organic-label trust and purchasing intention. H9 is therefore true. This is backed by Patel et al. (2022) whose research discovered that organic certification and trust exert indirect influence via attitude as a mediator. This has hence highlighted the truth that Generation Z consumer with good attitude will buy organic food if they trust the information and certificate on organic food labelling. Finally, the current research has established that organic label trust and environmental concern are the determinants of buying attitude for organic. Attitude and subjective norm turned into the purchase intention determinants of organic food for Generation Z in Malaysia. Organic food attitude is a mediator of organic-label trust and purchase intention but not of the relationship between health consciousness and purchase intention and environmental concern and purchase intention.

As summary, in this study, organic-label trust and concern for the environment have been established as the determinants of attitude for purchasing organic food. Subjective norm and attitude were the determinants of Generation Z's organic food purchasing intention in Malaysia. Organic-food attitude acts as a mediator between organic-label trust and purchase intention but not between that of health consciousness and purchase intention relationship and that of environmental concern and purchase intention relationship. The research has given an insight into the area of sustainable purchase intention of Generation Z consumers of organic food.

6. IMPLICATIONS

6.1 Theoretical Implications

The TPB model has been employed in this study to forecast sustainable purchasing intention towards the organic food from the Generation Z point of view. Environmental concern, organic-label trust, health consciousness was hypothesized to forecast the Generation Z's attitude towards the organic food. The findings revealed have thus augmented the literature understanding of the sustainable purchase intention from the point of view of the consumer of Generation Z. Extended TPB model use is shown to have significantly great explanatory power on Generation Z's organic food buying intention in Malaysia. They may be used as a reference for further studies.

6.2 Managerial Implications

From the managerial perspective, the information from this study would be able useful for several parties like marketing, farming and policy maker in Malaysia.

The marketers design a marketing strategy that emphasize on the environmental benefits of the organic food by underlining the importance of reduction in pesticide usage, conservation of biodiversity and reduction in the carbon footprint to foster environmentally Generation Z. Regarding to this, the company can engage in the community activities like sustainability projects in schools, residential areas and shopping malls. These efforts would be able to help the company to build a trust and loyalty among the environmentally friendly consumers from Generation Z.

To develop the good impression among Generation Z on consuming organic food, business can emphasize the positive points of organic food consumption as for gaining the health benefits and becoming greener. These positives can be put into the advertising activity with the knowledge content of such positives on consuming organic food. It could make the positive impression of Generation Z towards organic and thereby fortify their purchase intention.

Moreover, marketing personnel in the company are capable to impact Generation Z's purchase intention towards organic food by designing advertisement strategies based on social influence. Company can be partnering with celebrities or social media influencers. The collaboration would be powerful enough to impact promoting the purchase intention towards organic food among the social media group, community events and other activities.

Conversely, the company producing organic foods should maintain organic food production at the desired levels of the organic certification. There should be disclosure of the process of food making in an open manner and making it well visible on food packs. Then consumers' trust and confidence will build up. This will set the confidence and loyalty of the customers towards the organic food and ultimately led to the rise in the sales of the organic food.

Then, the social platform of the company can be utilised by the marketers at best to popularize the advantage of organic food and enlighten the consumers regarding the identification and meaning of organic food labels. All these different strategies would have the capacity to consolidate the buying intention of Generation Z.

6.3 Practical Implications

This study would be able to provide some practical implications for the agricultural sector in Malaysia. The increase in the demand for the organic food will encourage more farmers to shift to organic farming. This will then lead a reduction in the chemical use like pesticides and fertiliser that more sustainable and environmentally agriculture section to be promoted. From the economic perspective, the growth in the organic food sector will provide more economic opportunities for the farmers. It will contribute the growth of the economy of the nation.

On the other hand, the government may implement policies and regulations to support the sector of organic food in the country. For example, government needs to ensure the standard for the organic food from farm to table are well maintained. The processes of the certification must also be monitored closely by the related authorities. Furthermore, government can support the organic agriculture in the country by providing more grants, subsidies and training program for the farmers. This is to allow the organic farmers to equip themselves with a better knowledge on the organic farming.

In sum, understanding the purchase intention of Generation Z in Malaysia towards organic food will have the potential to impact organic food businesses and agriculture sector positively. Thus, to uphold a sustainability of the environment, innovation and the growth of the national income.

7. LIMITATIONS AND FUTURE STUDIES

Nevertheless, this research is not without some limitations. To begin with, the convenience sampling of the sample in this research can limit the generalizability of the findings to the overall Malaysian Generation Z population. Probability sampling should be used by future researchers so that the samples are more representative of the total Generation Z population. Secondly, this research was concerned with only Generation Z consumers in Malaysia and hence the generalizability of the findings is lesser. More studies should involve consumers at all society levels to provide inclusive findings and better preparation for marketing. Third, all organic food types are addressed in this research without categorization. Organic food comes from different forms including ready-to-eat food, organic vegetables, and grocery. Subsequent studies need to be focused on a particular type of organic food or classify organic food to enable marketing planners to strategize for effective promotion strategy. Fourth, the research may not have contained sufficient independent variables to effectively gauge Generation Z's buying intention for organic food. To further the knowledge of determinants that affect purchase intention, future research needs to include determinants such as economic status, internet media, cultural issue, ethical issue and others. These determinants were created to affect affecting purchase intention on organic food (Nguyen et al., 2021; Yasin et al., 2025). Lastly, the present study used a cross-sectional design and utilized data gathered at a single point in time. Thus, Generation Z purchase intention change, or consumer behaviour change will not be documented. Thus, henceforth, subsequent studies have to undertake longitudinal research in order to monitor, longitudinally, over time, consumer behaviour change among Generation Z cohort, thus consumer behaviour change on comparative basis is to be corroborated (Caruana et al., 2015).

ACKNOWLEDGEMENT

Special thanks to Pei Xing, Tey for your invaluable contribution to our data collection efforts. Your dedication and meticulous attention to detail have significantly enhanced the quality and accuracy of our project.

REFERENCES

Abdullah, I. (2002). Advertising in Malaysia. *More Advertising Worldwide*, 159–181. DOI: 10.1007/978-3-540-24788-3_9

Ahmad, N., Fahad, M., Zaki, M., Alam, Z., & Khalid, M. (2025). Understanding consumer attitude and purchase intention of organic food products. *Spanish Journal of Marketing - ESIC*, *29*(1), 123–145. DOI: 10.1108/SJME-04-2024-0110

Ahmed, N., Li, C., Khan, A., Qalati, S. A., Naz, S., & Rana, F. (2020). Purchase intention toward organic food among young consumers using theory of planned behaviour: Role of environmental concerns and environmental awareness. *Journal of Environmental Planning and Management*. Advance online publication. DOI: 10.1080/09640568.2020.1785404

Ajzen, I. (1985). From intentions to actions: A theory of planned behaviour. In Kuhl, J., & Beckman, J. (Eds.), *Action-Control: From Cognition to Behaviour* (pp. 11–39). Springer. DOI: 10.1007/978-3-642-69746-3_2

Ajzen, I. (1991). The Theory of Planned Behaviour. *Organizational Behavior and Human Decision Processes*, *50*(2), 179–211. DOI: 10.1016/0749-5978(91)90020-T

Ajzen, I., & Fishbein, M. (1980). *Understanding Attitudes and Predicting Social Behaviour*. Prentice Hall.

Almli, V. L., Asioli, D., & Rocha, C. (2019). Organic Consumer Choices for Nutrient Labels on Dried Strawberries among Different Health Attitude Segments in Norway, Romania, and Turkey. *Nutrients*, *11*(12), 2951–2967. DOI: 10.3390/nu11122951

Amanda, T. A., & Marsasi, E. G. (2024). Exploration of perceived behavioural control and intention to purchase to increase actual behaviour. *Image: Jurnal Riset Manajemen, 12*(1), 14–30. DOI: 10.17509/image.2024.002

Armitage, C. J., & Conner, M. (2001). Efficacy of the Theory of Planned Behaviour: A meta-analytic review. *British Journal of Social Psychology, 40*(4), 471–499. DOI: 10.1348/014466601164939

Asare, M. (2015). Using the Theory of Planned Behaviour to determine the condom use behaviour among college students. *American Journal of Health Studies, 30*(1), 43–50.

Asif, M., Xuhui, W., Nasiri, A., & Ayyub, S. (2018). Determinant factors influencing organic food purchase intention and the moderating role of awareness: A comparative analysis. *Food Quality and Preference, 63*, 144–150. DOI: 10.1016/j.foodqual.2017.08.006

Ayub, A. H., Nik Muhammad Naziman, Y. H., & Samat, M. F. (2020). Factors Influencing Young Consumers' Purchase Intention of Organic Food Product. *Advances in Business Research International Journal, 4*(1), 17–26. DOI: 10.24191/abrij.v4i1.10074

Ayyub, S., Asif, M., & Nawaz, M. A. (2021). Drivers of Organic Food Purchase Intention in a Developing Country: The Mediating Role of Trust. *SAGE Open, 11*(July-September), 1–2. DOI: 10.1177/21582440211045076

Ayyub, S., Wang, X., Asif, M., & Ayyub, R. (2018). Antecedents of Trust in Organic Foods: The Mediating Role of Food Related Personality Traits. *Sustainability (Basel), 10*(10), 3597–3613. DOI: 10.3390/su10103597

Aziz, M. F. B. A., Mispan, M. S. B., & Doni, F. (2020). Organic Food Policy and Regulation in Malaysia: Development and Challenges. In Goh, B., & Price, R. (Eds.), *Regulatory Issues in Organic Food Safety in the Asia Pacific*. Springer., DOI: 10.1007/978-981-15-3580-2_10

Balon, R. (2024). An Explanation of Generations and Generational Changes. *Academic Psychiatry, 48*(3), 280–282. DOI: 10.1007/s40596-023-01921-3

Bechler, C. J., Tormala, Z. L., & Rucker, D. D. (2021). The attitude–behaviour relationship revisited. *Psychological Science*, *32*(8), 1285–1297. DOI: 10.1177/0956797621995206

Benítez-Márquez, M. D., Sánchez-Teba, E. M., Bermúdez-González, G., & Núñez-Rydman, E. S. (2022). Generation Z Within the Workforce and in the Workplace: A Bibliometric Analysis. *Frontiers in Psychology*, *12*, 736820. DOI: 10.3389/fpsyg.2021.736820

Bernama (2024, April 30). *Gen Z, millennials more willing to spend on sustainable products*. https://www.newsarawaktribune.com.my/gen-z-millennials-more-willing-to-spend-on-sustainable-products/

Bhasin, H. (2025). *What is Purchase Intent? Definition, Types & How to Measure*. https://www.marketing91.com/purchase-intention/#:~:text=February%2026%2C%202025%20%7C%20By%20Hitesh,digital%20sources%2C%20and%20other%20analytics

Bhutto, M. Y., Khan, M. A., Sun, C., Hashim, S., & Khan, H. T. (2023). Factors affecting repurchase intention of organic food among generation Z (Evidence from developing economy). *PLoS One*, *18*(3), e0281527. DOI: 10.1371/journal.pone.0281527

Canova, L., Bobbio, A., & Manganelli, A. M. (2020). Buying organic food products: The role of trust in the theory of planned behaviour. *Frontiers in Psychology*, *11*, 575820. DOI: 10.3389/fpsyg.2020.575820

Caruana, E. J., Roman, M., Hernández-Sánchez, J., & Solli, P. (2015). Longitudinal studies. *Journal of Thoracic Disease*, *7*(11), 537–540. DOI: 10.3978/j.issn.2072-1439.2015.10.63

Cheng, S.-J., Jia, H.-X., Wong, P. P. W., & Wang, L. (2024). Factors influencing consumers' purchase intention on organic foods via a Theory of Planned Behaviour approach. *Journal of Tourism, Culinary, and Entrepreneurship*, *3*(1), 98–116. DOI: 10.1234/jtce.2024.001

Cohen, J. (1988). *Statistical Power Analysis for the Behaviours Science* (2nd ed.). Laurence Erlbaum Associates.

Cramarenco, R. E., Burcă-Voicu, M. I., & Dabija, D. C. (2023). Organic food consumption during the COvID-19 pandemic. A bibliometric analysis and systematic review. *Amfiteatru Economic*, *25*(17), 1042–1063. DOI: 10.24818/EA/2023/S17/1042

Curvelo, I. C. G., Watanabe, E. A. D. M., & Alfinito, S. (2019). Purchase intention of organic food under the influence of attributes, consumer trust and perceived value. *Revista de Gestão*, *26*(3), 198–211. DOI: 10.1108/REGE-01-2018-0010

Curvelo, I. C. G., Watanabe, E. A. M., & Alfinito, S. (2019). Purchase intention of organic food under the influence of attributes, consumer trust and perceived value. *Revista de Gestão*, *26*(3), 198–211. DOI: 10.1108/REGE-01-2018-0010

Dimock, M. (2019). *Defining generations: Where Millennials end and Generation Z begins*. Pew Research Centre. https://www.pewresearch.org/short-reads/2019/01/17/where-millennials-end-and-generation-z-begins/

Divinagracia, A., Forones, L. K., P., & E. (2024). Environmental Awareness and Sustainability Perception and Attitude of Generation Z. Psychology and Education: *A Multidisciplinary Journal, 24*(7). DOI: 10.5281/zenodo.13627785

Drexler, D., Fiala, J., Havlíčková, A., Potůčková, A., & Souček, M. (2017). The Effect of Organic Food Labels on Consumer Attention. *Journal of Food Products Marketing*, *24*(4), 441–455. DOI: 10.1080/10454446.2017.1311815

Dwivedi, J., Chandel, S. S., Shrivastava, A., Lepcha, D., & Xess, A. M. (2025). Predicting Generation Z's Purchase Intention towards Organic Food. *Library Progress International*, *45*(1), 80–92.

Džever, S., Marić, D., Leković, K., & Kostić, D. (2024). Generation Z Attitudes towards Organic Food: A Review. *International Scientific Conference Strategic Management and Decision Support Systems in Strategic Management,* 279-286. DOI: 10.46541/978-86-7233-428-9_397

Fattahi Ardakani, M., Salehi-Abargouei, A., Sotoudeh, A., Esmaeildokht, S., & Bahrevar, V. (2020). Do Subjective Norms Predict the Screening of Cancer Patients' First-Degree Relatives? A Systematic Review and Meta-Analysis. *Asian Pacific Journal of Cancer Prevention : APJCP, 21*(6), 1521–1530. DOI: 10.31557/APJCP.2020.21.6.1521

Ferreira, S., & Pereira, O. (2023). Antecedents of Consumers' Intention and Behaviour to Purchase Organic Food in the Portuguese Context. *Sustainability (Basel), 15*(12), 9670. DOI: 10.3390/su15129670

Gold, A. H., Malhotra, A., & Segars, A. H. (2001). Knowledge management: An organizational capabilities perspective. *Journal of Management Information Systems, 18*(1), 185–214. DOI: 10.1080/07421222.2001.11045669

Green, J. M., Draper, A. K., Dowler, E. A., Fele, G., Hagenhoff, V., Rusanen, M., & Rusanen, T. (2005). Public understanding of food risks in four European countries: A qualitative study. *European Journal of Public Health, 15*(5), 523–527. DOI: 10.1093/eurpub/cki016

Guido, G. (2009). *Behind Ethical Consumption.* Peter Lang Verlag., https://www.peterlang.com/document/1051940 DOI: 10.3726/978-3-0351-0499-8

Guido, G., Prete, M. I., Peluso, A. M., Maloumby-Baka, R. C., & Buffa, C. (2009). The role of ethics and product personality in the intention to purchase organic food products: A structural equation modeling approach. *International Review of Economics, 57*(1), 79–102. DOI: 10.1007/s12232-009-0086-5

Haddock, G., Thorne, S., & Wolf, L. (2020). Attitudes and behavior. In *Oxford Research Encyclopedia of Psychology*. Oxford University Press., DOI: 10.1093/acrefore/9780190236557.013.449

Hair Jr, J. F., Hult, G. T. M., Ringle, C. M., & Sarstedt, M. (2021). *A Primer on Partial Least Squares Structural Equation Modeling* (PLS-SEM). Sage Publication.

Halim, E., Chandra, A. N., Salim, J., Margarita, V., Destiano, R., & Hebrard, M. (2021). Predicting the Determinants of Continuance Intention to Use E-Wallet in Indonesia Post-COVID-19 Pandemic. *International Conference on Information Management and Technology* (ICIMTech), 2021. DOI: 10.1109/ICIMTech53080.2021.9534968

Hasan, H. N., & Suciarto, S. (2020). The Influence of Attitude, Subjective Norm and Perceived Behavioral Control towards Organic Food Purchase Intention. *Journal of Management and Business Environment*, *1*(2), 132–153. DOI: 10.24167/jmbe.v1i2.2260

Henseler, J., Ringle, C. M., & Sarstedt, M. (2015). A New Criterion for Assessing Discriminant Validity in Variance-Based Structural Equation Modeling. *Journal of the Academy of Marketing Science*, *43*(1), 115–135. DOI: 10.1007/s11747-014-0403-8

Huang, Z., Zhu, Y. D., Deng, J., & Wang, C. L. (2022). Marketing Healthy Diets: The Impact of Health Consciousness on Chinese Consumers' Food Choices. *Sustainability (Basel)*, *14*(4), 2059. DOI: 10.3390/su14042059

Hulland, J., Baumgartner, H., & Smith, K. M. (2017). Marketing survey research best practices evidence and recommendations from a review of JAMS articles. *Journal of the Academy of Marketing Science*, *46*(1), 92–108. DOI: 10.1007/s11747-017-0532-y

Huy, L., Chi, M., Lobo, A., Nguyen, N., & Long, P. (2019). Effective Segmentation of Organic Food Consumers in Vietnam Using Food-Related Lifestyles. *Sustainability (Basel)*, *11*(5), 1237–1251. DOI: 10.3390/su11051237

Jakubowska, D., Dąbrowska, A. Z., Pachołek, B., & Sady, S. (2024). Behavioural intention to purchase sustainable food: Generation Z's perspective. *Sustainability (Basel)*, *16*(17), 7284. DOI: 10.3390/su16177284

Jeyakumar, N. R., Liang, J., & Meemken, E. M. (2021). Mediating Role of Organic Labeling Awareness and Food Safety Attitudes in the Correlation Between Green Product Awareness and Purchase Intentions. *SAGE Open*, *11*(4), 1–12. DOI: 10.1177/21582440211061565

Jiao, W., Chang, A., Ho, M., Lu, Q., Liu, M. T., & Schulz, P. J. (2023). Predicting and empowering health for generation Z by comparing health information seeking and digital health literacy: Cross-sectional questionnaire study. *Journal of Medical Internet Research, 25*, e47595. DOI: 10.2196/47595

Juma-Michilena, I. J., Ruiz-Molina, M. E., Gil-Saura, I., & Belda-Miquel, S. (2024). Pro-environmental behaviours of generation Z: A cross-cultural approach. *International Review on Public and Nonprofit Marketing*, *21*(3), 1–29. DOI: 10.1007/s12208-024-00395-9

Katz, R., Ogilvie, S., Shaw, J., & Woodhead, L. (2022). *What to know about Gen Z. Stanford Report.* https://news.stanford.edu/stories/2022/01/know-gen-z

Khan, M., Ahmad, N., & Zaki, M. (2023). Values, attitude, and desire in organic food purchase intention in Mexico. *Frontiers in Sustainable Food Systems*, *7*, 1516788. DOI: 10.3389/fsufs.2024.1516788

Kim, H. Y., & Chung, J. E. (2011). Consumer purchase intention for organic personal care products. *Journal of Consumer Marketing*, *28*(1), 40–47. DOI: 10.1108/07363761111101930

Kline, R. (2011). Principles and Practice of Structural Equation Modeling, 3nd edition.pdf (Third). The Guilford Press.

Kushwah, S., Dhir, A., & Sagar, M. (2019). Ethical consumption intentions and choice behaviour towards organic food. Moderation role of buying and environmental concerns. *Journal of Cleaner Production*, *236*, 117519. DOI: 10.1016/j.jclepro.2019.06.350

Le-Anh, T., & Nguyen-To, T. (2020). Consumer purchasing behaviour of organic food in an emerging market. *International Journal of Consumer Studies*, *44*(6), 563–573. DOI: 10.1111/ijcs.12588

Li, J., & Jaharuddin, N. S. (2020). Customer purchase intentions and actual purchase for organic food: A moderated mediation model of perceived value and trust. *Journal of Cleaner Production*, *242*, 118320. DOI: 10.1016/j.jclepro.2019.118320

Li, X., Zhang, X., & Wang, Y. (2021). Cognitive legitimacy and perceived benefits in the adoption of innovative products. *Journal of Business Research, 139*, 123–134. DOI: 10.1016/j.jbusres.2021.09.012

Li, Y., Guo, F., Xu, J., & Yu, Z. (2025). Buying organic food products: The role of trust in the theory of planned behaviour. *Frontiers in Psychology, 11*, 575820. Advance online publication. DOI: 10.3389/fpsyg.2020.575820

Li, Y., & Shan, B. (2025). Exploring the role of health consciousness and environmental awareness in purchase intentions for green-packaged organic foods: An extended TPB model. *Frontiers in Nutrition, 12*, 1528016. Advance online publication. DOI: 10.3389/fnut.2025.1528016

Lopes, J. M., Gomes, S., Suchek, N., & Nogueira, S. (2024). The hidden reasons behind generation Z's green choices. *Discover Sustainability, 5*(1), 1–17. DOI: 10.1007/s43621-024-00764-8

Maloney, E. K., Lapinski, M. K., & Neuberger, L. (2013). Predicting Land Use Voting Behaviour: Expanding our Understanding of the Influence of Attitudes and Social Norms. *Journal of Applied Social Psychology, 43*(12), 2377–2390. DOI: 10.1111/jasp.12186

Masih, J., Singh, H., & Masih, C. (2025). Post-pandemic organic food trends: Sustainable eating explored through social media analysis. *Academy of Marketing Studies Journal, 29*(1), 1–14.

Mehdi, S. M., Rūtelionė, A., & Bhutto, M. Y. (2024). The Role of Environmental Values, Environmental Self-Identity, and Attitude in Generation Z's Purchase Intentions for Organic Food. *Environmental Research, Engineering and Management, 80*(2), 75–87. DOI: 10.5755/j01.erem.80.2.36649

Morinez, J., Smith, A., & Lee, K. (2007). Purchase intention and consumer behaviour. *JMR, Journal of Marketing Research, 44*(3), 567–579.

Morrison, D. G. (1979). Purchase intentions and purchase behaviour. *Journal of Marketing, 43*(2), 65–74. DOI: 10.1177/002224297904300207

Nethra, H. M., & Tamilmathi, D. (2025). A study on consumers' attitude towards purchase decision of organic food products with reference to Bengaluru City. *South Eastern European Journal of Public Health, XXVII*, 215–224. DOI: 10.70135/seejph.vi.5163

Nguyen, H., Nguyen, N., Nguyen, B., Lobo, A., & Vu, P. (2019). Organic Food Purchases in an Emerging Market: The Influence of Consumers' Personal Factors and Green Marketing Practices of Food Stores. *International Journal of Environmental Research and Public Health, 16*(6), 1037–1053. DOI: 10.3390/ijerph16061037

Nguyen, P. M., & Vo, N. D. (2023). Exploring organic food purchase behaviours of gen z: An application of TPB and MOA model in a transition country. *Foundations of Management, 15*(1), 35–50. DOI: 10.2478/fman-2023-0003

Nguyen, T. M., Park, J. H., & Choi, W. L. (2021). Factors Influencing Consumer Purchase Intention toward Organic Food Products: An Empirical Study in Vietnam Market. *Journal of Channel and Retailing, 26*(1), 127–147. DOI: 10.17657/jcr.2021.01.31.6

Nittin, R. (2015). The impact of marketing strategies on purchase intention. *International Journal of Marketing Studies, 7*(4), 45–58.

Pang, S. M., Tan, B. C., & Lau, T. C. (2021). Antecedents of Consumers' Purchase Intention towards Organic Food: Integration of Theory of Planned Behaviour and Protection Motivation Theory. *Sustainability (Basel), 13*(9), 5218–5233. DOI: 10.3390/su13095218

Park, H. S. (2000). Relationships among attitudes and subjective norms: Testing the theory of reasoned action across cultures. *Communication Studies, 51*(2), 162–175. DOI: 10.1080/10510970009388516

Patel, H. R., Sharma, M., & Purohit, R. (2021). Factors Influencing Millennials' Purchase Intention of Organic Food. *International Journal of Future Generation Communication and Networking, 14*(1), 2032–2046.

Patel, H. R., Sharma, M., & Purohit, R. (2022). Role of Organic Certification and Trust in Organic Food Buying Intention: Attitude as a Mediator. *Ramanujan International Journal of Business and Research, 7*(2), 46–55. DOI: 10.51245/rijbr.v7i2.2022.324

Pew Research Centre. (2019). *Defining generations: Where Millennials end, and Generation Z begins.* https://www.pewresearch.org/short-reads/2019/01/17/where-millennials-end-and-generation-z-begins/

Podsakoff, P. M., MacKenzie, S. B., Lee, J. Y., & Podsakoff, N. P. (2003). Common method biases in behavioral research: A critical review of the literature and recommended remedies. *The Journal of Applied Psychology*, *88*(5), 879–903. DOI: 10.1037/0021-9010.88.5.879

Poovithira, P. (2024). Factors influencing intention of buying organic food products among generation Z in Malaysia. Master's thesis, University Utara Malaysia.

Precedence Research. (2023). *Organic Food Market* (By Product: Fruits and vegetables, Dairy products, Meat, fish and poultry, Frozen foods, Others; By Distribution Channel: Online, Offline) - Global Industry Analysis, Size, Share, Growth, Trends, Regional Outlook, and Forecast 2023-2032. https://www.precedenceresearch.com/organic-food-market

Pyöriä, P., Ojala, S., Saari, T., & Järvinen, K. (2017). The Millennial Generation: A New Breed of Labour? *SAGE Open*, *7*(1), 1–14. DOI: 10.1177/2158244017697158

Renub Research. (2025). *Malaysia Organic Food Market Outlook*. https://www.renub.com/malaysia-organic-food-market-p.php

Saleki, R., Quoquab, F., & Mohammad, J. (2020). Factor affecting consumer's intention to purchase organic food: Empirical study from Malaysian context. *International Journal of Business Innovation and Research*, *23*(2), 183–204. DOI: 10.1504/IJBIR.2020.110096

Sarstedt, M., Bengart, P., Shaltoni, A. M., & Lehmann, S. (2017). The use of sampling methods in advertising research: A gap between theory and practice. *International Journal of Advertising*, *37*(4), 1–14.

Sekaran, U., & Bougie, R. (2013). *Research Methods for Business: A Skill-Building Approach* (6th ed.). Wiley.

Shahriari, E., Torres, I. M., Zúñiga, M. A., & Yarlou, P. M. (2019). Values Driving Organic Food Purchase Intention: A Comparative Analysis between a Developing Eastern Country (Iran) and a Developed Western Country (US). *Journal of International Consumer Marketing*, *31*(4), 317–329. DOI: 10.1080/08961530.2018.1561345

Singh, P., Verma, M., & Singh, R. (2024). Studies on Impact and Opinion of Organic Food Products of Human Life during [European Journal of Nutrition & Food Safety]. *COVID*, •••, 19.

Somasundram, C., Razali, Z., & Santhirasegaram, V. (2016). A Review on Organic Food Production in Malaysia. *Horticulturae*, *2*(12), 1–5. DOI: 10.3390/horticulturae2030012

Statista (2023). *Frequency of purchasing organic food among consumers in Malaysia as of September 2023*. https://www.statista.com/statistics/1010541/frequency-buying-organic-food-malaysia/

Su, C.-H., Tsai, C.-H., Chen, M.-H., & Lv, W. Q. (2019). U.S. Sustainable Food Market Generation Z Consumer Segments. *Sustainability (Basel)*, *11*(13), 3607–3620. DOI: 10.3390/su11133607

Tehseen, S., Ramayah, T., & Sajilan, S. (2017). Testing and Controlling for Common Method Variance: A Review of Available Methods. *Journal of Management Sciences*, *4*(2), 142–168. DOI: 10.20547/jms.2014.1704202

Teixeira, S. F., Barbosa, B., Cunha, H., & Oliveira, Z. (2022). Exploring the antecedents of organic food purchase intention: An extension of the theory of planned behaviour. *Sustainability (Basel)*, *14*(1), 242–254. DOI: 10.3390/su14010242

The Living Centre. (2025). *Organic Farming in Malaysia: A Growing Trend for Sustainable Living*. https://thelivingcentre.my/organic-farming-in-malaysia-a-growing-trend-for-sustainable-living/

Xiao, A., Yang, S., & Iqbal, Q. (2018). Factors Affecting Purchase Intentions in Generation Y: An Empirical Evidence from Fast Food Industry in Malaysia. *Administrative Sciences*, *9*(4), 1–16. DOI: 10.3390/admsci9010004

Yadav, R., & Pathak, G. S. (2016). Intention to purchase organic food among young consumers: Evidence from a developing nation. *Appetite*, *96*, 122–128. DOI: 10.1016/j.appet.2015.09.017

Yasin, N. H. M., Che Shalifullizam, N. I. F., & Tuan, S. A. (2025). T. N. Z., Yusoff, M. N. D., Zulkefli, N. S., Raja Omar, R. N., Rasdi. M. A., L. (2025). Consumer Purchase Intention of Organic Food: A Cross-Sectional Study Among Young Adults. *AIP Conference Proceedings*, *3271*, 050014. DOI: 10.1063/5.0260060

Zayed, M. F., Gaber, H. R., & el Essawi, N. (2022). Examining the Factors that Affect Consumers' Purchase Intention of Organic Food Products in a Developing Country. *Sustainability (Basel)*, *14*(10), 5868–5883. DOI: 10.3390/su14105868

Zhou, L., Huang, M., & Li, J. (2023). Psychological factors influencing purchase intention. *Journal of Business Research*, *56*(1), 78–89.

APPENDIX

Items in Questionnaire

Health Consciousness

1. I am very self-conscious about my health.
2. I am alert to changes in my health.
3. I am usually aware of my health.
4. I take responsibility for the state of my health.
5. I am aware of the state of my health as I go through the day.

Environmental Concern

1. I am very concerned about the environment in Malaysia.
2. My main concern is about the environmental degradation in Malaysia.
3. I am very concerned about how to protect the environment in Malaysia.
4. I often think about helping protect the environment in Malaysia.

Organic-Label Trust

1. The characteristics of the organic food labelling are trustworthy.
2. The characteristics of the organic food labelling are rigorous in production and inspection.
3. The characteristics of the organic food labelling are honest.
4. The characteristics of the organic food labelling are in compliance with the law.

Attitude

1. Buying organic food is a right choice.
2. Buying organic food can bring many benefits.
3. I think that purchasing organic food is wise.

Subjective Norms

1. My family buy organic food.
2. My friends and colleagues think that I should buy organic food.
3. People who are important to me think that using organic food is good for health.

Perceived Behavioural Control

1. I believe that I have complete control of buying organic food.

2. For me to buy organic food is easy.
3. It's mostly up to me whether or not to buy organic food.

Purchase Intention

1. The next time I shop for vegetables and/or fruits, I am very likely to choose organic vegetables and/ or fruits.
2. The next time when I shop for meat, I am very likely to choose organic meat.
3. Whenever I can, I will have the intention of buying organic food.

Chapter 8
The Influence of Women on Boards on the Nexus Between Environmental Performance and Firm Value in Malaysia

Yenyen Yip
Multimedia University, Malaysia

ABSTRACT

This study examines the association between environmental performance and firm value in the presence of female directors based on Malaysian context. The present study utilises 74 listed firms on Bursa Malaysia covering 2012-2020. Results obtained from Pool-OLS panel regression analysis reveal that the presence of female directors positively influences the nexus between environmental performance and firm value in Malaysia. This paper contributes not only to academic discourse but also offers practical implications for businesses aiming to enhance their environmental performance, particularly in developing countries like Malaysia. The utilization of Malaysian data provides novel empirical evidence within an emerging market, enhancing our understanding of the intricate relationships between gender diversity, environmental performance, and firm value.

DOI: 10.4018/979-8-3693-6195-5.ch008

INTRODUCTION

Companies have been pushed to expand the number of females on corporate boards due to the global need for more diverse boards. Some countries have enacted laws requiring female participation on boards, including Belgium, Germany, Iceland, Norway, Italy, Australia, Spain, and France (Verhoeven et al., 2022). The Malaysian government began an initiative in 2004 to advance gender equality, and at the time, Prime Minister Abdullah Badawi expressed support for a 30% female quota for senior management roles in the public sector (Zahid et al., 2020). In the latest step, the Malaysia Code of Corporate Governance (MCCG)-2021 explicitly states that there must be thirty percent women on all boards.

In MCCG 2021, it is clearly written that all boards must have 30% females on board. Notably, boards falling short of this requirement are obligated to disclose the reasons behind the deficiency, outline potential corrective actions, and provide an estimated timeframe for achieving the specified gender representation. This institutionalized commitment underscores Malaysia's dedication to fostering gender diversity at the highest levels of corporate leadership. In 2021, Malaysia's female board members reached 27.4%, surpassing Singapore and Indonesia's share, according to Statista Research department.

Ibrahim and Angelidis (1994) claim that female directors have a greater inclination towards philanthropy than their male counterparts. Williams (2003) posits that the existence of females on boards has a favourable correlation with the corporate charitable activities . Using feminist ethics literature and social role theory, Boulouta (2013) investigates the connection between gender diversity on boards and corporate social responsibility (CSR) performance. She discovers that the presence of female directors in corporate boards exhibit less harmful social practices. According to Biswas et al. (2018), companies that have a larger gender representation on their boards typically do better environmentally.

Recently, the topic of how a firm's value may be impacted by its environmentally responsible practices has drawn the attention of regulators, scholars, and researchers. Prior research, such as that of Friedman (1970), states that since the purpose of a business is to increase profits for its shareholders, extra money spent on environmental preservation or socially conscious initiatives is detrimental to firm's net worth. There has been a shift in this philosophy, nevertheless, in recent times. Businesses are directing resources towards addressing environmental concerns and avoiding actions or activities that endanger customers or workers out of a concern for the sustainability of their business.

In general, businesses should improve social well-being to get societal acceptance (Zuraida et al., 2018). Companies can attain product uniqueness by participating in environmental conservation initiatives, which will ultimately result in increased firm value (Wahba & Elsayed, 2015). However, putting environmental conservation programmes into action necessitates a large resource consumption. For this reason, some businesses may use CSR to improve their reputation or engage in "greenwashing" (Wang & Sarkis, 2017). As a result of the low resource allocation for strategic CSR efforts, the connection between environmental performance and business performance may be insignificant.

The objective of this research is to investigate whether the presence of women on corporate boards improves the link between environmental performance and firm value in Malaysian companies. Considering that female investors are more socially conscious than male investors (Sparkes, 2002), it makes sense that having a higher proportion of female members on corporate boards would improve environmental performance, which in turn improves business outcomes. The study's findings, which are based on 74 Malaysian listed companies from 2012 to 2022, indicate that companies with more female directors typically perform better environmentally, which ultimately enhances the value of the entire company.

The contribution of this study as follows: Firstly, this is one of a few studies which investigates the impact of female directors in influencing the association between environmental performance and firm value based on Malaysian context. It brings new insight regarding the impact of gender diversity in emerging market like Malaysia. Secondly, this research reports that the presence of women on boards imposes a favourable impact on environmental performance which eventually enhances firm value. This finding offers additional understanding on the impact of gender diversity on firm value, thus enlarging the pool of literature concerning gender diversity. Third, this study endeavours to provide statistical and economic credibility to the Code's recommendations. This is likely to motivate businesses to take meaningful initiatives to increase female representation on boards in order to capitalise on the opportunity for improved performance and corporate governance. Fourth, the outcome of this research is expected to provide supporting basis to the Malaysian capital market regulators on the reasonableness in revising the Malaysian Code of Corporate Governance in 2021 to require 30% of women participation on corporate boards. The organisation of this study is as follows: The subsequent section covers the literature review and hypothesis development. The third section presents the data and technique employed. The fourth section discusses the results of the study and lastly, the fifth section offers a conclusion to this study.

LITERATURE REVIEW AND HYPOTHESIS DEVELOPMENT

Adams and Ferreira (2009) suggest that women directors who have distinct values and experiences may assist in enhancing the corporate sustainability decision-making. According to Carter et al. (2003), female directors are more adaptive to stakeholder-oriented approach, accommodating wider interests of various stakeholders and environmental issues. Study by Wang et al's (2021) reports that the presence of female directors positively associated with CSR reporting in China, highlighting importance of gender on corporate financial reporting associated to CSR initiatives. Research by Gupta et al.'s (2020) demonstrate that firms with female directors participation are more likely to engage in proactive CSR practices, i.e. environmental-related performance. Study by Elmagrhi et al. (2019) indicates that the number of female directors has a favourable impact on the overall corporate environmental performance. All these pieces of evidence suggest that gender, i.e. female directors have substantial impact on the development and implementation of CSR strategies.

Study by Waddock and Graves's (1998) shows that companies with strong environmental performance are perceived more positively by socially responsible investors. This finding supports stakeholder theory, which contends that resolving environmental issues improves stakeholders' views of the company's performance. Eccles et al. (2014) posit that investors and consumers often perceive companies that have a strong track record of environmental performance more positively, which in turn leads to high firm value. Derwall et al. (2005) find that significant environmental performance can minimise systemic risk while increasing long-term market value. Gupta et al.'s (2020) study in India found that environmental sustainability is linked to financial performance. Liu et al. (2020) propose that female directors may influence CSR, in which affecting company performance. The authors find that female directors' influence is more pronounced when they are vested with greater authority promoting CSR. Findings from Xie et al. (2020) demonstrate that women on boards promotes proactive environmental strategies, which assist corporations to create competitive advantage which subsequently linked to financial performance. Based on a sample of Asian firms, Rehman et. al (2020) find that the presence of female directors increase the probability of a firm to adopt environmental management system (EMS). Besides, the authors also claim that women on boards enhancing the nexus between EMS and corporate financial performance. Focus on hospitality and tourism industry, study by Uyar et al. (2020) show that the presence of female directors is positively associated with superior CSR performance in all dimensions including environmental performance. However, they fail to find any significant connection between CSR and financial performance. Take together, this study proposes that environmental stewardship, as facilitated by the influence of women directors, contributes to better corporate value.

Based on the above discussions, the hypothesis of this study is developed as follows:

H1: The presence of female directors affects the relationship between environmental performance and firm value.

METHODOLOGY

The sample of this study consists of 74 Malaysian listed firms from 2012 to 2020. The environmental performance of firms is measured by the environmental score extracted from the Bloomberg database, which ranges from 0 (lowest) to 100 (highest). It indicates how successfully a business avoids environmental hazards by implementing optimal management practices. The information concerning percentage of female directors are compiled from firms' annual report and Bloomberg. All financial data are obtained from Bloomberg database. ROA (return on assets), the dependent variable, is taken as an indicator for firm value whereas the environmental performance is employed as the independent variable. Further, the percentage of female directors on board is taken as the moderating variable while control variables such as institutional ownership, board size and firm age, which are known to have influence on firm value have been included in the baseline model. Table 1 presents the measurement of variables of this study.

Table 1. Measurement of variables

Variable Name	Label	Descriptions
Dependent variable		
Return on assets (ROA)	ROA	Net income divided by total assets
Independent variable		
Environmental performance	ENV	Environmental score compiled by Bloomberg
		ranges from 0 (lowest) to 100 (highest)
Moderating variable		
Female directors	GENDER	Percentage of female directors
Control variables		
Institutional ownership	INS	% of outstanding shares held by the institutions
Firm age	AGE	The number of years since the firm was established.
Board size	BSIZE	Number of directors on board

The regression model of this study is structured as follows:

$$ROA_{i,t} = \alpha + \beta_1 ENV_{i,t} + \beta_2 GENDER_{i,t} + \beta_3 (ENV*GENDER)_{i,t} + \beta_4 INS_{i,t} + \beta_5 AGE_{i,t} + \beta_6 BSIZE_{i,t} + \varepsilon_{i,t}$$

(1) where ENV*GENDER denotes the interaction term. Other variables are as defined earlier.

REGRESSION RESULTS

The descriptive statistics for each variable are displayed in Table 2. Table 2 shows that the sample companies were able to generate a profit of RM7.33 on average for each RM (Ringgit Malaysia) invested in assets (ROA). The environmental score (ENV) has a standard deviation of 15.93 and a mean, minimum, and maximum of 21.99, 1.55, and 80.84, respectively. While the average number of female directors (GENDER) is 18.27 percent, the average board size (BSIZE) is nine directors, with a range of five to twenty. On average, the institutional owners (INS) hold 60.1% of shares in the sample firms. Also, the average firm age (AGE) since its establishment is 47 years, ranging from a minimum of 9 to a maximum of 115 years.

Table 2. Descriptive statistics

Variable	Mean	Std. Dev.	Min	Max
ROA	7.33	9.57	0	75.4
ENV	21.99	15.93	1.55	80.84
GENDER	18.27	12.32	0	57.14
INS	60.10	25.61	0	95.02
AGE	47.22	24.49	9	115
BSIZE	8.99	1.92	5	20

Table 3 reports the correlations coefficients between return on assets (ROA), environmental score (ENV), percentage of female directorship (GENDER) and other control variables. The results indicate no correlation problem between the independent variables, as most variables have correlation values of less than 0.8, indicating no sign of serious multicollinearity (Gujarati, 2003).

Table 3. Correlation

	ROA	ENV	GENDER	INS	AGE	BSIZE
ROA	1					
ENV	0.4301	1				
GENDER	0.1181	0.3422	1			
INS	0.0634	0.0212	-0.0744	1		
AGE	0.2353	0.028	-0.0491	-0.005	1	
BSIZE	-0.1925	-0.0579	0.0325	0.0163	-0.0079	1

Table 4 presents the results of this study based on the pooled-OLS model. The positive coefficient of the ENV*GENDER interaction is statistically significant at the 5% level, indicating that the presence of female directors enhances the impact of environmental performance on firm financial performance, thereby supporting H1. Besides, the results indicate that ENV is positively associated with firm value at 1% significantly level suggesting that environmental performance improves market acceptance and hence improves business outcomes. Among the control variables, AGE is positively associated with firm value, whereas BSIZE shows a negative association. No significant relationship was found between INS and firm value. This suggests that firms with a longer establishment history and smaller board sizes tend to perform better financially.

These results are in line with past studies, which indicate that women directors consider the concerns of environmentally conscious stakeholders (Carter, 2003), engage in proactive CSR practices (Gupta et al., 2020; Liu et al., 2020), promote proactive environmental strategies (Xie et al., 2020; Uyar et al., 2020), and increase the adoption rate of EMS. These findings suggest that any efforts to consider, engage, promote and adopt CSR practices may improvise financial performance (Gupta et al., 2020; Xie et al., 2020; Rehman et al., 2020), enhance competitive advantage (Xie et al., 2020), and reduce business risk (Derwall et al., 2005).

In brief, the outcome supports the premise that the female directors influences environmental stewardship, leading to improved company value.

Table 4. The effect of gender diversity on the relationship between environmental performance and firm performance

Variables	Pooled-OLS
ENV	0.180***
	(0.0464)
GENDER	-0.0828
	(0.0630)
ENV*GENDER	0.00418**
	(0.00204)
INS	0.0243
	(0.0193)
AGE	0.0798***
	(0.0163)
BSIZE	-0.770***
	(0.237)
Constant	4.375
	(2.858)
Observations	346
R-squared	0.278

Note: Figures in the parentheses are standard errors. Asterisk ** and *** indicate the respective 10%, 5% and 1% significance level.

CONCLUSION

This study examines how the presence of female directors affects environmental performance and firm value in Malaysia. This study has examined 74 Malaysian companies and suggest that having female directors strengthen the connection between environmental performance and firm value. The results indicate that female directors address company performance concerned with environmental sustainability to align with stakeholders' interest. Female directors tend to focus on addressing proactive environmental measures, reducing business risks and increasing company value. This study highlights the importance of female directors in strategizing corporate environmental efforts, ultimately improving firm value. By enhancing CSR initiatives, and diverting environmental risks, female directors are prominent in promoting good sustainability practices and a higher company value. As companies continue to explore and adapt to a changing global landscape, the study suggests recognising the contributions of female directors for more resilient and valuable organizations.

In conclusion, the results lend support and validate MCCG 2021 that requires 30% of female participation in the Malaysian boards. This may also serve as a basis for market regulators to improvise board diversity in Malaysia.

This research suffers several limitations that should be taken into account as possible directions for future research. Firstly, the study considers Malaysian firms only. It would be meaningful to extend this study into other countries worldwide. Secondly, this research utilises ROA as the only measurement of firm value. Future research may focus on other comprehensive dimensions of firm value such as Tobin Q ratio, return on equities (ROE) etc.

ACKNOWLEDGMENT

This research was supported by Multimedia University, Malaysia under the IRFUND, project SAP ID MMUI/230094.

REFERENCES

Adams, R. B., & Ferreira, D. (2009). Women in the boardroom and their impact on governance and performance. *Journal of Financial Economics*, *94*(2), 291–309. DOI: 10.1016/j.jfineco.2008.10.007

Biswas, P. K., Mansi, M., & Pandey, R. (2018). Board composition, sustainability committee and corporate social and environmental performance in Australia. *Pacific Accounting Review*, *30*(4), 517–540. DOI: 10.1108/PAR-12-2017-0107

Boulouta, I. (2013). Hidden connections: The link between board gender diversity and corporate social performance. *Journal of Business Ethics*, *113*(2), 185–197. DOI: 10.1007/s10551-012-1293-7

Carter, D. A., Simkins, B. J., & Simpson, W. G. (2003). Corporate governance, board diversity, and firm value. *Financial Review*, *38*(1), 33–53. DOI: 10.1111/1540-6288.00034

Derwall, J., Guenster, N., Bauer, R., & Koedijk, K. (2005). The eco-efficiency premium puzzle. *Financial Analysts Journal*, *61*(2), 51–63. DOI: 10.2469/faj.v61.n2.2716

Eccles, R. G., Ioannou, I., & Serafeim, G. (2014). The impact of corporate sustainability on organizational processes and performance. *Management Science*, *60*(11), 2835–2857. DOI: 10.1287/mnsc.2014.1984

Elmagrhi, M. H., Ntim, C. G., Elamer, A. A., & Zhang, Q. (2019). A study of environmental policies and regulations, governance structures, and environmental performance: The role of female directors. *Business Strategy and the Environment*, *28*(1), 206–220. DOI: 10.1002/bse.2250

Friedman, M. (1970). The social responsibility of business is to increase its profits. *New York Times*, 13 September, pp. 122–126.

Gujarati, D. (2003). *Essentials of Econometrics.* Irwin McGraw-Hill.

Gupta, A. K., & Gupta, N. (2020). Effect of corporate environmental sustainability on dimensions of firm performance–Towards sustainable development: Evidence from India. *Journal of Cleaner Production, 253*, 119948. DOI: 10.1016/j.jclepro.2019.119948

Ibrahim, N. A., & Angelidis, J. P. (1994). Effect of board members' gender on corporate social responsiveness orientation. *Journal of Applied Business Research, 10*(1), 35–40. DOI: 10.19030/jabr.v10i1.5961

Liu, Y., Lei, L., & Buttner, E. H. (2020). Establishing the boundary conditions for female board directors' influence on firm performance through CSR. *Journal of Business Research, 121*, 112–120. DOI: 10.1016/j.jbusres.2020.08.026

Rehman, S., Orij, R., & Khan, H. (2020). The search for alignment of board gender diversity, the adoption of environmental management systems, and the association with firm performance in Asian firms. *Corporate Social Responsibility and Environmental Management, 27*(5), 2161–2175. DOI: 10.1002/csr.1955

Sparkes, R. (2002). *Socially Responsible Investment: A Global Revolution.* John Wiley.

Uyar, A., Kilic, M., Koseoglu, M. A., Kuzey, C., & Karaman, A. S. (2020). The link among board characteristics, corporate social responsibility performance, and financial performance: Evidence from the hospitality and tourism industry. *Tourism Management Perspectives, 35*, 100714. DOI: 10.1016/j.tmp.2020.100714

Verhoeven, D., Musial, K., Hambusch, G., Ghannam, S., & Shashnov, M. (2022). Net effects: Examining strategies for women's inclusion and influence in ASX200 company boards. *Applied Network Science, 7*(1), 48. DOI: 10.1007/s41109-022-00490-y

Waddock, S., & Graves, S. B. (1998). The corporate social performance–financial performance link. *Strategic Management Journal, 18*(4), 303–319. DOI: 10.1002/(SICI)1097-0266(199704)18:4<303::AID-SMJ869>3.0.CO;2-G

Wahba, H., & Elsayed, K. (2015). The mediating effect of financial performance on the relationship between social responsibility and ownership structure. *Future Business Journal, 1*(1-2), 1–12. DOI: 10.1016/j.fbj.2015.02.001

Wang, C., Deng, X., Álvarez-Otero, S., Sial, M. S., Comite, U., Cherian, J., & Oláh, J. (2021). Impact of women and independent directors on corporate social responsibility and financial performance: Empirical evidence from an emerging economy. *Sustainability (Basel), 13*(11), 6053. DOI: 10.3390/su13116053

Wang, Z., & Sarkis, J. (2017). Corporate social responsibility governance, outcomes, and financial performance. *Journal of Cleaner Production, 162*, 1607–1616. DOI: 10.1016/j.jclepro.2017.06.142

Williams, R. J. (2003). Women on corporate boards of directors and their influence on corporate philanthropy. *Journal of Business Ethics, 42*(1), 1–10. DOI: 10.1023/A:1021626024014

Xie, J., Nozawa, W., & Managi, S. (2020). The role of women on boards in corporate environmental strategy and financial performance: A global outlook. *Corporate Social Responsibility and Environmental Management, 27*(5), 2044–2059. DOI: 10.1002/csr.1945

Zahid, M., Rahman, H. U., Ali, W., Khan, M., Alharthi, M., Qureshi, M. I., & Jan, A. (2020). Boardroom gender diversity: Implications for corporate sustainability disclosures in Malaysia. *Journal of Cleaner Production, 244*, 118683. DOI: 10.1016/j.jclepro.2019.118683

Zuraida, Z., Houqe, M. N., & Van Zijl, T. (2018). Value relevance of environmental, social and governance disclosure. In *Research Handbook of Finance and Sustainability* (pp. 458–483). Edward Elgar Publishing. DOI: 10.4337/9781786432636.00033

ADDITIONAL READING

Amorelli, M. F., & García-Sánchez, I. M. (2021). Trends in the dynamic evolution of board gender diversity and corporate social responsibility. *Corporate Social Responsibility and Environmental Management*, *28*(2), 537–554. DOI: 10.1002/csr.2079

Ardito, L., Dangelico, R. M., & Messeni Petruzzelli, A. (2021). The link between female representation in the boards of directors and corporate social responsibility: Evidence from B corps. *Corporate Social Responsibility and Environmental Management*, *28*(2), 704–720. DOI: 10.1002/csr.2082

Awwad, B. S., Binsaddig, R., Kanan, M., & Al Shirawi, T. (2023). Women on boards: An empirical study on the effects on financial performance and corporate social responsibility. *Competitiveness Review*, *33*(1), 147–160. DOI: 10.1108/CR-06-2022-0084

De Masi, S., Słomka-Gołębiowska, A., Becagli, C., & Paci, A. (2021). Toward sustainable corporate behavior: The effect of the critical mass of female directors on environmental, social, and governance disclosure. *Business Strategy and the Environment*, *30*(4), 1865–1878. DOI: 10.1002/bse.2721

Elmagrhi, M. H., Ntim, C. G., Elamer, A. A., & Zhang, Q. (2019). A study of environmental policies and regulations, governance structures, and environmental performance: The role of female directors. *Business Strategy and the Environment*, *28*(1), 206–220. DOI: 10.1002/bse.2250

Farza, K., Ftiti, Z., Hlioui, Z., Louhichi, W., & Omri, A. (2022). The effect of corporate board characteristics on environmental innovation. *Environmental Modeling and Assessment*, *27*(6), 1021–1042. DOI: 10.1007/s10666-022-09836-3

Khidmat, W. B., Habib, M. D., Awan, S., & Raza, K. (2022). Female directors on corporate boards and their impact on corporate social responsibility (CSR): Evidence from China. *Management Research Review*, *45*(4), 563–595. DOI: 10.1108/MRR-09-2020-0560

Moreno-Ureba, E., Bravo-Urquiza, F., & Reguera-Alvarado, N. (2022). An analysis of the influence of female directors on environmental innovation: When are women greener? *Journal of Cleaner Production*, *374*, 133871. DOI: 10.1016/j.jclepro.2022.133871

Wang, Y., Wilson, C., & Li, Y. (2021). Gender attitudes and the effect of board gender diversity on corporate environmental responsibility. *Emerging Markets Review*, *47*, 100744. DOI: 10.1016/j.ememar.2020.100744

Xie, J., Nozawa, W., & Managi, S. (2020). The role of women on boards in corporate environmental strategy and financial performance: A global outlook. *Corporate Social Responsibility and Environmental Management*, *27*(5), 2044–2059. DOI: 10.1002/csr.1945

Yadav, P., & Prashar, A. (2023). Board gender diversity: Implications for environment, social, and governance (ESG) performance of Indian firms. *International Journal of Productivity and Performance Management*, *72*(9), 2654–2673. DOI: 10.1108/IJPPM-12-2021-0689

KEY TERMS AND DEFINITIONS

Corporate Sustainability: The idea of a company using resources so that current needs are met without diminishing the ability for future generations to meet their own. This is all about creating a combination of economic success with social responsibility and environmental stewardship so that businesses can thrive and still look after the planet, its people.

CSR Reporting: Corporate Social Responsibility (CSR) reporting is referred to companies sharing and divulging their social, environmental impacts on society. Ultimately, this transparency does a number of things – keeps businesses honest and on track to ensure they are following ethical guidelines, gives stakeholders the tools required to assess for themselves how well different companies align with their understanding of ethics in practice which enables consumers or investors alike, provide an informed choice.

Environmental Management System (EMS): EMS is a systematic, structured framework utilized by organizations to accomplish and improve their environmental performance. Regulated companies use EMS as a systematic approach to strive for compliance while maximizing their resources and minimizing pollution. It is seen as an approach that is aligned with the global and even national aspirations towards sustainable development for Malaysia companies. Overall, research have shown that firms are more likely to enjoy good environmental performance when well-developed EMS frameworks function properly.

Environmental Performance: Environmental performance indicates how well a company does in affecting the environment. It means things such as reducing waste, using less energy, and conserving resources. Good environmental performance could also be a sign to the market of how firmly a company is committed to sustainability, which should go down well with stakeholders.

Feminist Ethics Literature: A body of literature that values feminine traits, such as empathy, care, and interconnectedness, as essential aspects of ethical decision-making.

Firm Value: Firm value is what the market believes a company to be worth. It includes financial indicators such as share prices, market capitalisation and more qualitative considerations like brand reputation or stakeholder trust, all of which can be positively affected by good governance practices.

Gender Diversity: Gender diversity in corporate governance often means gender parity on company boards, between women and men. Diversity provide access to different points of view and styles that may impact how a company responds to environmental or social issues etc.

Greenwashing: Greenwashing occurs when a company lies or exaggerates its eco-friendly behaviour.

Malaysian Corporate Code of Corporate Governance (MCCG): The MCCG is a framework that sets out best practices in corporate governance for Malaysian companies, which will, in turn lead to public trust towards the operation of the companies.

Social Role Theory: The theory suggests that men and women engage in behaviours consistent with their role. By nature, men are dominant agents whereas women nurture social desires. In the context of board dynamics, social role theory could mean that female directors emphasize on sustainability and corporate responsibility.

Chapter 9
Perceived Readiness for Technological Change in Rural Micro and Small Enterprises (MSEs) in Peninsular Malaysia's Traditional Food Sector: A Thematic Survey

Shahrul Nizam Yunos
https://orcid.org/0009-0009-1590-6597
MILA University, Malaysia

Ridzuan Masri
https://orcid.org/0000-0002-3584-9771
MILA University, Malaysia

Nur Zulaikha Mohamed Sa'dom
https://orcid.org/0000-0002-4100-517X
MILA University, Malaysia

DOI: 10.4018/979-8-3693-6195-5.ch009

ABSTRACT

This study investigates the perceived readiness for technological change among rural entrepreneurs operating in the traditional food sector. A total of 14 entrepreneurs were selected as respondents for interviews to gather critical data. The sample selection considered various demographic factors such as business type, business experience, and the unique traditional food products offered by each entrepreneur. The study results reveal a range of opinions and readiness levels among respondents. Some entrepreneurs demonstrate a positive and open attitude towards technology use, seeing it as a tool to enhance operational efficiency and reach a wider market. Conversely, some respondent's express doubts about technology's ability to integrate the values and uniqueness of their traditional food products. The findings of this study offer valuable insights for stakeholders in the traditional food industry to design interventions or programs suitable for enhancing the readiness and capabilities of rural entrepreneurs in technology adoption.

1.0 INTRODUCTION

The traditional food industry in Malaysia is part of the nation's culinary heritage. With a diverse influence from the Malay, Chinese, Indian, and indigenous cultures, Malaysian traditional food reflects the cultural diversity and traditions of the country. From delightful snacks such as *'keropok'*, *'kerepek'*, *'kuih raya'*, and *'dodol'*, to hearty dishes like *'nasi lemak'*, *'laksa'*, *'satay'*, and *'roti canai'*, authentic Malaysian cuisine offers a variety of flavours, textures, and tastes. These traditional dishes are often passed down through generations, with each family adding their unique touch. The traditional food industry in Malaysia not only provides delicious meals but also preserves the cultural heritage and national identity, gaining recognition worldwide. In fact, Malaysia is known as a food paradise (Remie et al, 2021). The rapid emergence of traditional food in domestic and foreign markets has accelerated, especially as the country's tourism and hospitality sectors develop, creating rapid industrial opportunities in various urban and rural sectors (Elfrida et al, 2020).

The food sector has long been recognized as a vital industry in Malaysia, significantly contributing to the country's cultural and economic heritage and boosting local and international tourism industries. The national food sector, particularly in the context of traditional food, thrives in rural areas where traditional recipes and techniques are passed down from generation to generation. However, many traditional foods have also made their way to major cities in Malaysia, and some have even been exported to countries like Japan, Europe, and Western nations (Zainudin, 2018). In recent years, especially post-Covid-19, there has been a growing interest in the development and promotion of Malaysian traditional food products, both domestically and internationally (Abdullah & Nor Azam, 2021).

Social media platforms like TikTok and YouTube have seen numerous short videos focusing on food segments that have captured the attention of foreigners from countries like Korea, Russia, the United States, Japan, Europe, and others, who provide comments and reviews on Malaysian traditional foods. This interest stems from a desire to explore and promote the country's cultural heritage while attracting their own followers. Additionally, local residents are seen as passionate and actively involved in preserving cultural heritage, promoting sustainable food production, and seizing opportunities from the increasing global trend towards traditional and creatively unique flavours (MIDA, 2020).

1.1 Research Problem

While there have been studies on the traditional food industry in Malaysia, with most focusing on the effectiveness of marketing strategies, advertising, and supply chains (Yahaya et al, 2019), the specific context of readiness to adapt to technological changes among rural entrepreneurs has not been fully explored (EPU, 2019), especially in this traditional food sector. Furthermore, the readiness to adapt to technological changes and how this affects their preparedness to face future development momentum remains understudied. Understanding these challenges will provide valuable insights into the growth potential and development in the traditional food industry in rural areas, thereby assisting the country in reducing poverty and unemployment issues.

The traditional food sector in rural Malaysia, predominantly consisting of micro and small Bumiputera enterprises, holds significant economic value ranging from hundreds of millions to billions of ringgit annually. This industry plays a crucial role in preserving the country's cultural heritage and supporting its economic growth. Information obtained from the Ministry of International Trade and Industry (MITI) in 2023 emphasizes the substantial growth of Malaysia's halal exports in 2022, reaching a value of RM59.46 billion. Forecasts indicate that the market value of the Halal food industry in Malaysia is expected to reach RM500 billion by 2030 (Shahira, 2023).

Despite the lack of precise data on the value of traditional food industries, the readiness of rural entrepreneurs to embrace technological advancements in their businesses remains uncertain (Thomas, 2023). This uncertainty is primarily due to various significant constraints posed by the fast-paced technological landscape and evolving market demands in rural areas (Ferrari et al, 2022). Therefore, the research problem lies in the need to explore and analyse the perceptions and readiness of rural entrepreneurs in the traditional food industry towards adopting and integrating technological innovations in their production, packaging, marketing, distribution processes, and all related process chains. There is a significant research gap in understanding the awareness level, attitudes, knowledge, skills, and resources available for them to integrate technological advancements in rural areas, and information on this study is also very limited in the Malaysian context.

Hence, this study aims to bridge this knowledge gap by examining the perceptions and readiness of rural entrepreneurs towards technological changes in the traditional food industry within Micro and Small Enterprises (MSEs). The study will explore factors that can contribute to their future success, as well as the obstacles they face in enhancing their businesses. By identifying these factors, the study will provide recommendations to support the growth and sustainability of traditional food enterprises in rural areas.

From the presented problem statement, the Table 1 shows the research questions, research objectives, and interview questions that will guide this study further.

Table 1. Research questions, objectives and interview questions

Research Questions	Research Objectives	Interview Questions
What is the level of readiness of rural entrepreneurs in the traditional food sector to adopt and implement technological change?	To understand the level of readiness among rural entrepreneurs in the traditional food sectors;	How confident are you in your technological skills and ability to innovate in adopting and implementing technological changes in your traditional food business?

2.0 LITERATURE REVIEW

2.1 Perceived Readiness

The perceived readiness of rural entrepreneurs towards technological change and its potential benefits is an important aspect to consider in understanding the adoption and implementation of new technologies in rural areas. Several studies have attempted to assess the readiness of rural entrepreneurs towards technological change and have identified various factors contributing to their perceived readiness. For example, a study by Noor et al (2020) exploring rural social entrepreneurship programs in Malaysia, particularly focusing on the Social Entrepreneur Club (SEC) component, found that rural entrepreneurs with access to Information and Communication Technology (ICT) were more inclined to embrace technological change. This research essentially supports the Social Entrepreneurship Club (SEC) aimed at transforming rural entrepreneurs into social entrepreneurs by enhancing their economic activities and fostering social capital using ICT through the establishment of telecentres that provide space for rural communities to enhance their ICT knowledge and skills. SEC, operating under the Rural Internet Centre (RIC), engages rural communities in entrepreneurial activities and promotes socialization. However, some rural entrepreneurs show limited interest in becoming social entrepreneurs and prefer to remain as entrepreneurs despite ICT support. The success of SEC depends on the participation of entrepreneurs, geographical location, and support from telecentre managers. The research findings essentially indicate that SEC functions as an economic development strategy, creating jobs, increasing income and business opportunities, and facilitating social networks to build social capital within and outside rural communities. Additionally, SEC acts as a community connector and can serve as an indicator of rural community well-being.

Similarly, a study by Cunningham et al (2023) revealed that rural entrepreneurs with prior experience with technology and who view it as a tool to enhance business efficiency and productivity are more willing to adopt new technologies. However, there is still a literature gap regarding the perceived readiness among rural entrepreneurs towards technological change. One potential gap is the focus on the technological literacy of rural entrepreneurs.

While studies have examined the impact of education and experience on their readiness, more research is needed to explore specific technological literacy levels among rural entrepreneurs. Understanding their current knowledge and skills in using technology can help shape appropriate training programs and support to enhance their readiness for technological change.

Although some studies have briefly mentioned perceived benefits, a more in-depth analysis is needed to understand how rural entrepreneurs specifically view the potential benefits and how these perceptions influence their readiness. Identifying specific benefits, such as increased market access, cost savings, or better product quality, can provide insights into the motivation level towards technological change among rural entrepreneurs.

2.2 Challenges Faced by Rural Entrepreneurs

Rural areas are known to face unique challenges when it comes to technological change and its utilization by entrepreneurs in this field. This literature review will explore the challenges faced by rural entrepreneurs towards technological change and highlight some potential gaps in existing research.

One of the main challenges faced by rural entrepreneurs is financial constraints. Limited access to capital and resources makes it difficult for them to invest in new technology and keep up with the rapid advancements in technology. As highlighted by Romero-Castro (2023), a lack of financial resources is a major reason why rural entrepreneurs often lag in adopting new technologies. These constraints limit their ability to invest in the tools and equipment needed for technological change.

Another significant challenge faced by rural entrepreneurs is the lack of technological infrastructure in rural areas. Poor connectivity, limited access to logistical capabilities, and inadequate technological infrastructure make it challenging for entrepreneurs to access and use new technology. As stated by Fanelli (2021), insufficient technological infrastructure acts as a barrier to technological change in rural areas. These technological infrastructure gaps need to be addressed in specific ways, rather than broadly, to encourage the adoption of new technology by rural entrepreneurs.

Limited knowledge and skills are also major challenges faced by rural entrepreneurs in adopting technological change. Many rural entrepreneurs lack the necessary knowledge and skills to effectively adopt and use new technology in their businesses. According to a report by the Economic Research Institute for ASEAN and East Asia - ERIA (2018), limited knowledge and skills act as barriers to technological change in rural areas. These knowledge and skills gaps need to be addressed through targeted training programs and capacity-building initiatives aimed at rural entrepreneurs.

The information in the Table 2 shows the literature summary that highlights the gaps regarding rural entrepreneurs that need further exploration:

Table 2. Summary of the literature review and gaps

Author	Year	Country	Types of industry	Identified Knowledge gaps
Lekhanya	2018;	Afrika Selatan	General SMEs	Limited focus on rural areas and specific challenges in adopting new technologies;
Prasetyo *et al,*	2022	Indonesia	General SMEs	General challenges in adopting new technologies;
Morris *et al*	2022	Wales, UK	General SMEs	Digital divide between urban and rural area using demographic characteristics (descriptive)
Elkafrawi	2020	Mesir	Micro business	Reciprocal relationship between women entrepreneurs and their rural context
de Guzman *et al*	2020	USA	Micro and small business	Perception towards youth entrepreneurship in rural area
Kusumastuti et al,	2022	Indonesia	Social business	Construction of knowledge related to social innovation
Xu *et al*	2023	China	Agriculture farmers	Agricultural technology extension and social networks on farmers' adoption of technology

2.3 Technological Readiness of Rural Entrepreneurs in the Context of Southeast Asia and International Comparisons

Studies related to technology readiness and technology application among rural entrepreneurs have received increasing attention, particularly in developing countries and countries in Southeast Asia. While socioeconomic contexts and business structures vary by country, rural entrepreneurs generally face similar challenges in adapting to technological change, including the digital divide, skills limitations, as well as the need to maintain traditional practices and values in business operations.

In Indonesia, studies such as Fahmi & Savira (2023) found that micro and small enterprises in rural areas show a moderate level of technology readiness despite realizing the benefits of digitalization on business productivity and sustainability. Key constraints identified include low levels of digital literacy, limited financial capital, as well as concerns about the risks of technological change. The study asserts that the willingness felt by entrepreneurs plays an important role in determining whether a technology will be accepted or rejected.

The study also found that rural entrepreneurs' attitudes towards digitalisation are influenced by the capability approach, which is a combination of skills, social support and learning opportunities. Entrepreneurs who possess confidence in their digital abilities tend to show a higher level of willingness to explore new technologies, while those with less exposure show a cautious and skeptical attitude.

In the context of Vietnam, Le et al. (2023) reported that the level of digital readiness among small and medium-sized enterprises is influenced by the perception of the ease of use of technology, the availability of training, as well as the suitability of technology with existing operating structures. Although the study did not focus entirely on rural areas, the findings suggest that internal organizational factors and individual perceptions are key elements in shaping technology readiness. This study also indicates that the adoption of Industry 4.0 technology in small and medium-sized firms in Vietnam is more influenced by internal factors such as technological knowledge, management readiness and organizational confidence than purely external factors. This shows that technological readiness is not only related to infrastructure, but also closely related to the perception and capabilities of the entrepreneurs themselves.

These entrepreneurial studies related to the use of technology at the ASEAN and international levels as shown in table 2 above, show that rural entrepreneurs in the Asian continent and beyond share similar challenges to rural entrepreneurs as found in Malaysia, particularly in terms of the digital divide, lack of technical skills, and concerns about the impact of technology on the authenticity of traditional products. However, most previous studies have focused more on the factors of technology adoption and digitalisation outcomes, while studies that examine perceived readiness in-depth, particularly in the context of micro and small enterprises of traditional food in rural Malaysia, are still limited that require further and updated exploration.

In addition to individual readiness factors, the literature also shows that the adoption of technology among rural entrepreneurs is influenced by various structural barriers such as financial constraints, lack of training, and weakness of technological infrastructure. Several studies have also highlighted the importance of institutional and government policy support in improving technology readiness, particularly through financial assistance, skills training, and rural infrastructure development. However, the role of these factors is often discussed separately from the perspective of the readiness felt by the entrepreneurs themselves, particularly in the context of micro and small enterprises of traditional food in Malaysia.

3.0 METHODOLOGY

3.1 Method

A qualitative approach has been chosen as the research strategy, as it allows for in-depth exploration (Tomaszewski et al, 2020) of the perceptions and readiness of rural entrepreneurs in MSEs traditional food towards technological change. This strategy aligns with the interpretivist paradigm, as it emphasizes understanding and meaning. In this cross-sectional study, the researcher collects data from multiple individuals at the same time aiming to gain a broad overview of participants' views, experiences, and perceptions at a specific period. Through the cross-sectional approach, the researcher can understand the differences or similarities between different individual respondents and explore variations in their views or experiences separately and collectively. In this study, face-to-face interviews will be conducted with rural entrepreneurs. The interviews will be conducted using a semi-structured format, allowing for a structured and focused flow of conversation. Data will be transcribed, coded, and analysed thematically to reveal patterns and themes that emerge.

3.2 Sampling

The study population consists of rural entrepreneurs in the traditional food sector in rural areas in the central region of Malaysia. Purposive sampling involves selecting participants with specific characteristics or experiences relevant to the research objectives. Due to this sector is predominantly operated by Bumiputera ethnic groups in most rural areas, Therefore, the researcher selects participants who are Bumiputera entrepreneurs specifically involved in the traditional food sector. The table 3 highlights the criteria used for purposive sampling.

Table 3. Purposive sampling criteria

Variables	Criterion
Geographical location	Rural Areas of the Central Region of Peninsular Malaysia (Selangor, Melaka and Negeri Sembilan)
Business Type	Traditional food production/distribution/packaging/ reseller
Business Categories	Micro and small businesses
Establishment	Sole proprietorship and private limited
Year of incorporation	Minimum 3 years
Income per year	< RM 300,000 (SME Corp)
Premises	Shop lot / house factory / mini warehouse

3.3 Sample Size

To ensure a thorough and comprehensive qualitative research process, the researcher will use a method where interviews will be concluded once feedback from participants reaches saturation, indicating the point at which no new themes are generated from the information obtained. A study conducted by Guest et al (2006) in health sciences found that saturation was reached after interviewing the first 12 out of 60 selected participants. Additionally, a study by Francis et al (2010) using the Theory of Planned Behaviour (TPB) empirically determined that saturation was reached after the 17th participant regarding all the theory constructs established at the initial stage. Therefore, the researcher expects saturation to be reached between 12-17 participants. Hence, a total of 14 participants have been selected for this study on rural entrepreneurs to achieve a balance in interview saturation outcomes.

3.4 Validity and Reliability

Member checking involves sharing research findings with participants to validate their accuracy and interpretations (Stahl & King, 2020). By involving participants in the analysis and interpretation of data, the researcher can confirm the accuracy of findings and ensure they align with participants' perspectives. This process enhances the validity of the research by increasing the credibility and reliability of the findings. Peer review involves obtaining feedback and input from other researchers or experts in the field to validate interpretations and findings. This external review process helps identify any potential biases or errors in the analysis and enhances the reliability of the study (Kuo, 2022).

4.0 ANALYSIS AND FINDINGS

4.1 MSEs Demographic Information

The demographic profile of rural entrepreneurs as depicted in Table 4-1 below provides a clear picture of the economic landscape in which these rural entrepreneurs operate. Mostly engaged in conventional business models, the rural entrepreneurs included in the interviews are seen to meet local needs through traditional trading methods, such as market stalls and small-scale manufacturing facilities. The details about selected participants can be observed in the Table 4.

Table 4. Demographic information

No	Age	Type of Business	Gross Income / Year	Registration	Period of Business
P 1	54	Keropok Lekor Maker	RM80K – RM120K	Sole Proprietorship	30 years
P2	46	Homemade Rendang Paste Artisan	RM 50K-RM90K	Partnership	15 years
P3	38	Satay Vendor	RM50K-RM 75K	Sole Proprietorship	8 years
P4	50	Nasi Lemak Stall	RM90K-RM100K	Sole Proprietorship	20 years
P5	63	Serunding Manufacturer	RM110K-RM130K	Sole Proprietorship	21 years
P6	35	Asam Pedas Fish Cuisine	RM 180K-RM200K	Private Limited Company	10 years
P7	45	Frozen Handmade Kuih-Muih	RM 80K-RM90K	Sole Proprietorship	22 years
P8	39	Gulai Kawah Specialists	RM 100K-RM150K	Partnership	12 years

continued on following page

Table 4. Continued

No	Age	Type of Business	Gross Income / Year	Registration	Period of Business
P9	33	Lemang Vendor	RM40K-RM60K	Sole Proprietorship	5 years
P10	52	Roasted Local Coffee Beans	RM200K-RM250K	Private Limited Company	25 years
P11	29	Traditional Malay Kuih Online Store	RM50K-RM70K	Sole Proprietorship	3 years
P12	48	Laksa	RM75-RM 85K	Sole Proprietorship	18 years
P13	41	Traditional Biscuits and Snacks	RM95K-RM120K	Sole Proprietorship	16 years
P14	37	Cendol and Ice Kacang Maker	RM65K-RM75K	Sole Proprietorship	11 years

In terms of finances, rural entrepreneurs in the traditional food sector experience a wide range of income constraints. With fluctuations from RM40,000 to RM200,000 per year, the economic advancement of these businesses varies significantly. The diversity in income levels may reflect various factors such as operational scale, local demand for products, efficiency in their business processes, uniqueness of offerings, and the entrepreneurs' ability to tap into broader markets, possibly through avenues like local tourism or regional food exhibitions.

4.2 General Theme

The general theme of the perceived technology readiness is indicated in the Figure 1.

Figure 1. General theme of perceived technology readiness

Thematic analysis of traditional food entrepreneurs reveals a common thread of openness towards adopting technology to enhance business practices while maintaining a strong respect for tradition. At one end of the spectrum, the study found individuals who are beginning their journey towards the relevance of technology, recognizing the value it brings to their traditional businesses such as keropok lekor and nasi lemak. They are willing to learn and utilize technology with some guidance to remain competitive and reach a broader customer base.

In the middle, there are those with experience in using technology, especially for marketing channels like social media and digital payments. They are willing to embrace further technological advancements to improve efficiency and enhance their operations, such as those involved in rendang and Asam Pedas businesses. However, they aim to strike a balance to ensure the authenticity of their products is not compromised.

Further along the spectrum, researchers encountered entrepreneurs who have leveraged technology to a significant extent. They use online platforms and digital marketing for products like traditional Malay *kuih* and local coffee beans, realizing the positive impact on their reach and customer engagement. These individuals demonstrate not only willingness but also dedication to invest more time and develop their technological skills.

Ultimately, some entrepreneurs exhibit high confidence in their technological skills and have successfully integrated technology to enhance and modernize their businesses. This group includes entrepreneurs selling traditional cookies and snacks, They not only use online ordering and payment systems but also consistently seek innovative ways to expand their businesses.

4.3 Codes and Categories

Traditional food entrepreneurs in rural areas are gradually facing the tide of technological change in various ways, with their attitudes often falling somewhere between two mentalities: optimistic and hesitant mindsets (Rosen, 2000) as illustrated in the Figure 2.

Figure 2. Code and category of technology readiness

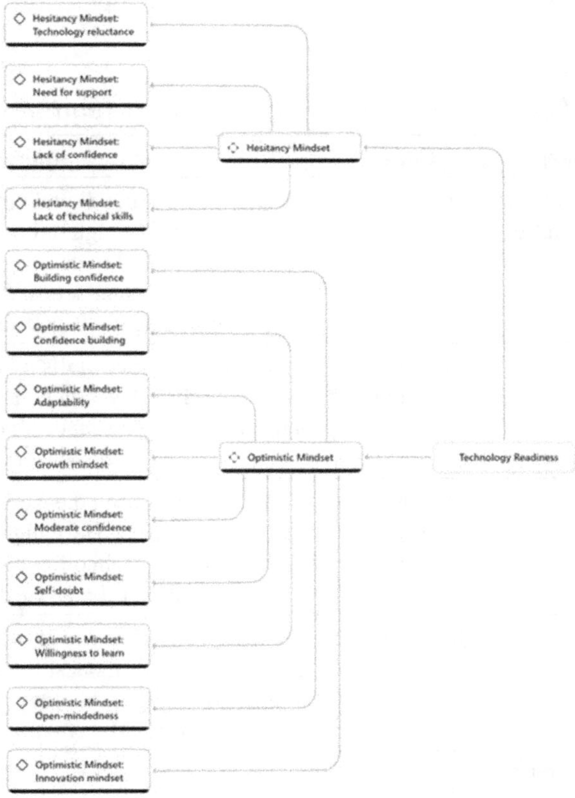

Rural entrepreneurs with an optimistic mindset tend to embrace technology as a crucial business enhancer (Al Issa, 2022). This group views technology as a gateway to new opportunities, often enthusiastic about leveraging digital tools for market expansion, process optimization, and product innovation. On the other hand, a mindset of doubt entails a cautious and sometimes resistant attitude towards technological advancements (Molloy & Ronnie, 2021). This may stem from a combination of factors: lack of familiarity with new tools, limited access to training, or scepticism about the tangible benefits of digital usage. Entrepreneurs of this nature may perceive technology as a threat to their traditional way of operating, potentially disrupting established practices and personal customer relationships that are key features of rural food businesses (Fernandes & Burcharth, 2024). Table 6 below provides a summary of interview findings as follows.

Table 7. Main themes, categories and technology readiness coding

Main Theme	Category	Code	Interview Summary
Perceived Technology Readiness	Optimistic Mindset	Adaptability	P6:Q3 - Since using digital payments, sales of spicy acid fish through online have increased and are interested in developing knowledge of culinary manufacturing technology (Restaurateur - *Ikan asam pedas*).
		Confidence building	P3:Q3 - Have limited skills in the application to receive purely 'satay' orders. Ready to embrace innovation but need support to boost confidence (*Satay* Maker).
		Business growth	P10:Q3 – Has used the website for digital marketing of coffee. Have high confidence and ready to invest in technology (Manufacturer and Trader, Local Coffee)
		Innovation	P12:Q3 – Has used social media and online delivery but has a modest level of confidence in manufacturing technology, yet is willing to innovate (Maker – *Mee Laksa*)

continued on following page

Table 7. Continued

Main Theme	Category	Code	Interview Summary
		Open-mindedness	P4:Q3: Has used the app for the delivery of nasi lemak, but still lacks the confidence to use technological innovations in the nasi lemak business. Requires support and guidance to innovate (Operators - *Nasi Lemak*)
		Willingness to learn	P9:Q2: Technology confidence is low but ready to learn about technology as sales methods are still conventional (Entrepreneur - *Lemang*)
	Hesitancy Mindset	Lack of confidence	P11:Q3 – Has made full use of the online store and is confident of machine handling, yet feels the business approach is still lagging behind. Requires new knowledge to increase sales (Entrepreneur - traditional *kuih-muih*)
		Lack of technical skills	P13:Q3 – Has used internet platforms to sell, but is still hesitant to use technology to maintain traditional tastes (Entrepreneur - traditional cookies and snacks)
		Need for support	P5:Q3 – Less confidence in technology because it wants to preserve original tastes, yet is willing to explore computerized manufacturing technology (*Serunding* Maker)
		Technology reluctance	P1:Q2 – Maintain the traditionality and originality. Not interested with extensive technology, and lack confident (Entreprenuer – *Keropok Lekor*)

5.0 DISCUSSION

5.1 Optimistic Mindset

The approach of rural entrepreneurs towards adopting technology and innovation can be characterized in the following contexts based on the generated codes:

5.1.1 Adaptability

Rural entrepreneurs can quickly adapt their operations to incorporate new technology. They understand that adaptability is not a one-time event but a continuous process, crucial to staying relevant and competitive. In the realm of rural entrepreneurship, assimilating new technology is a vital strategy to remain sustainable and competitive. Rural entrepreneurs must demonstrate wise steps that adapting to technological innovations is not a sporadic effort but a continuous dynamic process. Knowledge of this plays a crucial role in ensuring their traditional food businesses remain relevant and competitive in the evolving market landscape.

5.1.2 Building Self-Confidence

Empowering rural entrepreneurs, especially in the traditional food business sector, relies on the development of their self-confidence through smart technology integration. Rural entrepreneurs often face barriers to technology adoption due to infrastructure limitations and digital literacy gaps (Shukla et al, 2023). However, when these entrepreneurs experience success on a small scale by leveraging technology, whether through streamlined supply chain management, enhanced marketing via social media platforms, or improved financial transactions through mobile banking, they often witness gradual improvements in operational capacity and market reach. Building self-confidence, as emphasized by Bandura (2000), becomes a driver for transitioning from technology interest to technology mastery. Mastery in this aspect encourages rural entrepreneurs to continuously improve their business models, harnessing the potential of technology to preserve their culinary heritage while enhancing their efforts.

5.1.3 Business Growth

Technology integration can enhance productivity (Begazo et al., 2023) in these traditional food businesses. This can be achieved through task automation, digital inventory management, or the adoption of modern cooking techniques to increase output and efficiency. Furthermore, such innovations can significantly enhance the quality of their traditional offerings, ensuring consistency and compliance with food safety regulations, thereby strengthening consumer trust and repeat purchases (Ali et al, 2024). Rural entrepreneurs who incorporate technology and innovation into their business strategies often witness growth in their operations. This is evidenced not only by quantitative revenue spikes but also by qualitative improvements in their product offerings, leading to healthy business growth (Tuitjer et al, 2022). Strategies that integrate traditional food businesses with modern technology can support a sustainable growth trajectory for traditional food businesses in rural areas.

5.1.4 Innovation

Innovation is a crucial element that underpins the acceptance and success of technology integration (Eze et al, 2021) in the rural entrepreneurship sector. Entrepreneurs in this sector are not mere passive recipients of technological changes; instead, they actively engage in experimental efforts to enhance the culinary experience. This innovative spirit is demonstrated through exploring new methods, integrating unique flavours, or pioneering innovative business models driven by technological advancements. Such innovative tendencies encourage these traditional food entrepreneurs to look beyond conventional boundaries, using technology such as precision cooking tools to achieve unparalleled flavour profiles or utilizing social media analytics to identify emerging culinary trends. Additionally, they may experiment with non-traditional ingredients to enhance traditional recipes, striking a balance between tradition and innovation.

5.1.5 Open-Mindedness

Rural entrepreneurs need to have an open-minded attitude to accept various solutions and new technological platforms different from conventional practices. This responsiveness enables them to explore and assimilate technological innovations optimally in line with their unique business pressures and the complex culinary preferences of their traditional food customers. With such a mindset, these entrepreneurs are not constrained by traditional paradigms but are instead open to examining and integrating modern tools ranging from mobile business aspects to enhance market reach, to food preservation techniques that can extend the shelf life of their culinary products without compromising taste or authenticity. With an open-minded approach, they can distinguish the essential from the non-essential, ensuring that technology serves as a bridge to their goals rather than a barrier.

5.1.6 Willingness to Learn

The tendency to embrace more creative business methodologies with suitable technology is crucial for rural entrepreneurs, who engage in business not only for profit but also as a driver of sustainable economic growth (Morris et al, 2022). In an era where global trade and culinary innovation go hand in hand, these rural entrepreneurs must demonstrate a willingness to learn continuously and systematically to expand their knowledge and navigate market transitions in a competitive and dynamic environment. This learning effort goes beyond acquiring food and traditional cuisine materials and providing unique dishes. It needs to encompass a comprehensive understanding of technological advancements such as digital marketing, e-commerce platforms, and supply chain optimization. Rural entrepreneurs who show a willingness to learn something new demonstrate forward-thinking. They need to actively explore expertise through continuous professional development, leveraging workshops, online courses, and peer collaborations. By doing so, they can not only maintain the authenticity of their culinary heritage but also adapt their business strategies to align with contemporary consumer expectations and the competitive business landscape.

5.2 Hesitant Mindset

On the other hand, in the rural entrepreneurship environment, there are entrepreneurs who approach technology cautiously, characterized by the following:

5.2.1 Lack of Confidence

The lack of confidence seen among rural entrepreneurs in using technology to produce traditional food often traces back to negative experiences with technology. This includes deeper doubts about their ability to learn and effectively use new systems, mostly due to infrastructure limitations and exposure. These entrepreneurs may have had prior engagements such as using digital platforms or machining technology, leading to reluctance to integrate them into their daily operations. Not to mention, the investment costs they must bear. Given the traditional nature of their small businesses, these entrepreneurs may view technological advancements as a challenge to their traditional ways. Transitioning from conventional methods to technology-based practices and unfamiliar innovations demand not only acquiring new skills but also fundamental changes in thinking. This can be worrisome, especially without sufficient support and learning to bridge this gap.

5.2.2 Lack of Technical Skills

Rural entrepreneurs in the traditional food sector often face challenges due to insufficient technical skills, a situation exacerbated by the complexity of handling modern technology. Gaps in digital literacy may widen, with the need to navigate new and highly complex devices and platforms (Wolfert et al, 2021). These complexities often hinder these entrepreneurs from implementing technology-related measures to coordinate between their operations and market development. A prime example of this challenge can be seen when trying to market their products online or manage inventory through digital systems. The skills required for these tasks, which should not be overly complicated, can become extremely challenging if not followed by proper induction and training processes. This scenario leads to a continuous cycle of technological phobia, where skill deficiencies lead to rejection, further reinforcing the required skills deficit.

5.2.3 Need for Support

Rural entrepreneurs in the traditional food sector recognize the potential benefits of integrating technology into their businesses, but hesitant thoughts, largely driven by perceived support context deficits at the personal and community levels. Reluctance to embrace technological advancements does not stem from resistance to change but from a sense of isolation in the digital journey (Tang & Zhu, 2020). The challenge is not only to learn to use new tools but also about not having a strong support system to rely on during the transition. Entrepreneurs of this kind often operate in supportive communities that may not fully practice digital norms, thus lacking peer examples to emulate. Additionally, they may not have immediate access to personal networks with the knowledge or experience to guide them through and experience the dynamic technology landscape themselves.

5.2.4 Technology Reluctance

Rural entrepreneurs often exhibit reluctance to incorporate technology into their businesses (Ferrari et al, 2022b). Change may bring surprises and fears of the unknown perception that technological adaptation may disrupt deeply rooted practices passed down through generations that hold historical and cultural significance. This reluctance is further exacerbated by concerns about the costs associated with acquiring new technology, staff training, and maintaining digital infrastructure. For most entrepreneurs, especially in rural areas, these financial implications pose significant risks to the typical thin profit margins of small-scale operations (Amouri et al, 2021). There is a deep preference for traditional methods, seen not only as cooking techniques but as a cultural heritage passed down through generations. These methods are part of their identity and community cohesion. Entrepreneurs are concerned that technology use may dilute the authenticity of their products, often a unique selling point that attracts consumers seeking genuine indigenous flavours.

5.2.5 Barriers to Technology Adoption and the Role of Government Support

In addition to individual readiness factors, the literature also shows that the adoption of technology among rural entrepreneurs is influenced by various structural barriers such as financial constraints, lack of training, and weakness of technological infrastructure. Several studies have also highlighted the importance of institutional and government policy support in improving technology readiness, particularly through financial assistance, skills training, and rural infrastructure development. However, the role of these factors is often discussed separately from the perspective of the readiness felt by the entrepreneurs themselves, particularly in the context of micro and small enterprises of traditional food in Malaysia.

5.3 Research Proposition and Recommendations

Based on the qualitative analysis findings, the following recommendations are developed based on the evolved framework as indicated in the Table 7.

Table 8. Study propositions based on objectives

Objectives of the Study	Qualitative Study Proposition
Understand the perceived readiness of rural entrepreneurs in the traditional food sectors to embrace technological change;	Technology readiness is perceived through a combination of an optimistic mindset towards the benefits of new technology and hesitant thinking related to uncertainty and potential risks.

In the context of rural entrepreneurship, especially in the traditional food business sectors, technology readiness plays a crucial role in determining business success. The development and use of new technology can be key to increasing productivity and effectiveness, but at the same time, it also brings challenges and risks. Some entrepreneurs have an optimistic view of the benefits of new technology, seeing it as an opportunity to enhance their business operations and expand their markets. They view technology as a tool to achieve success in this fast-paced and competitive market.

On the other hand, there is also strong resistance and doubt among some entrepreneurs, especially in rural areas. Lack of access to resources such as training and financing, along with infrastructure limitations like weak internet connectivity, heighten uncertainty about investing in new technology. The risk of adopting technology without fully understanding its implications is also a factor driving this hesitant attitude. Resistance to change and reliance on old ways of doing business can hinder the acceptance of technological innovation.

Adapting technology readiness in the context of rural entrepreneurship in traditional food businesses requires a balanced approach. It necessitates raising awareness of the potential benefits of technology in enhancing the quality and production of traditional foods, as well as providing support mechanisms to reduce risks and uncertainties. Technology education and skills training focusing on the specific needs of the traditional food industry can help alleviate fears of technology failure. Developing infrastructure and adequate investment in technology tailored to the specific needs of traditional food businesses are also crucial steps.

To achieve this balance, collaboration among entrepreneurs, communities, government, and educational institutions is essential. The government's role in providing fiscal incentives, technology investment subsidies, and initiatives to improve rural internet infrastructure can help reduce the financial burden on entrepreneurs and stimulate interest in technology adoption. Therefore, a combination of belief in the benefits of technology and reducing doubts and risks through appropriate support and education can shape a bright future for traditional food entrepreneurship in rural areas.

6.0 CONCLUSION

The effectiveness of technology readiness among rural entrepreneurs is associated with their positive perspectives and caution towards the benefits and risks of new technology. This technology readiness is assessed based on the balance between the challenges faced - such as infrastructure deficiencies, access to resources, or skills gaps - and the utility of technology. The perceived technological influences drive rural entrepreneurs to embrace technological changes. Innovation, efficiency, maintenance, and optimization of traditional food businesses are some positive effects of technological changes for these entrepreneurs.

In this context, various stakeholders need to play specific strategic roles. For example, the government plays a crucial role in ensuring appropriate infrastructure is built and improved, as well as providing incentives or financial assistance to rural entrepreneurs to adopt new technologies. Additionally, the government can encourage policies that promote innovation and the preservation of traditional efforts through technology. Entrepreneurship development programs for rural entrepreneurs in Malaysia are designed to benefit local communities by providing the necessary resources, training, and support to start and grow businesses.

It is essential for rural entrepreneurs to have access to up-to-date information on these programs through local government agency offices, official websites, or engage with local entrepreneurship and business organizations to fully leverage the programs offered by the Malaysian government in supporting the development of small and medium entrepreneurs in rural areas.

The technological readiness of rural entrepreneurs is not only influenced by individual attitudes and capabilities but is also shaped by structural factors such as financial constraints, training, infrastructure, as well as government policy support. Therefore, an integrated approach involving institutional support and capacity building is essential to increase technological readiness in the rural traditional food sector.

REFERENCES

Abdullah, K. M., & Nor Azam, N. R. A. (2021). Innovated Malay Traditional Food Products: Do Consumers Accept the Authentic Quality? *International Journal of Academic Research in Business & Social Sciences, 11*(16). Advance online publication. DOI: 10.6007/IJARBSS/v11-i16/11228

Al Issa, H. E. (2022). Psychological capital for success: The mediating role of entrepreneurial persistence and risk-taking. *Journal of Entrepreneurship in Emerging Economies, 14*(4), 525–548.

Ali, R., Irfan, S., & Hamid, S. (2024). Emerging themes in food tourism: A systematic literature review and research agenda. *British Food Journal, 126*(1), 372–408. DOI: 10.1108/BFJ-11-2022-0939

Amouri, A., Festa, G., Shams, S. R., Sakka, G., & Rossi, M. (2021). Technological propensity, financial constraints, and entrepreneurial limits in young entrepreneurs' social business enterprises: The tunisian experience. *Technological Forecasting and Social Change, 173*, 121126. DOI: 10.1016/j.techfore.2021.121126

Bandura, A. (2000). Self-efficacy: The foundation of agency. Control of human behavior, mental processes, and consciousness: Essays in honor of the 60th birthday of August Flammer, 16.

Begazo, T., Blimpo, M., & Dutz, M. (2023). *Digital Africa: Technological Transformation for Jobs*. World Bank Publications. DOI: 10.1596/978-1-4648-1737-3

Cunningham, J. A., Damij, N., Modic, D., & Olan, F. (2023). MSME technology adoption, entrepreneurial mindset and value creation: A configurational approach. *The Journal of Technology Transfer, 48*(5), 1–25. DOI: 10.1007/s10961-023-10022-0

De Guzman, M. R. T., Kim, S., Taylor, S., & Padasas, I. (2020). Rural communities as a context for entrepreneurship: Exploring perceptions of youth and business owners. *Journal of Rural Studies, 80*, 45–52. DOI: 10.1016/j.jrurstud.2020.06.036

Economic Research Institute for ASEAN and East Asia-ERIA. (2018). *Study on MSMEs Participation in the Digital Economy in ASEAN*. Economic Research Institute for ASEAN and East Asia.

Elfrida, T., Sazali, S. A., & Abu Bakar, M. N. (2020). The Representation of Baba-Nyonya Cuisine in the Context of Halal Tourism Industry in Malacca, Malaysia. *Humanus, 19*(1), 61. DOI: 10.24036/humanus.v19i1.107681

Elkafrawi, N. M. (2020) Women Entrepreneurship Development in Egyptian Rural Context: A Structuration Perspective. Doctoral thesis, University of Huddersfield.

EPU. (2019). National Fourth Industrial Revolution (4IR) Policy. *Economic Planning Unit, Prime Minister's Department, 1*, 1–72.

Eze, S. C., Chinedu-Eze, V. C., Awa, H. O., & Alharthi, R. H. E. (2021). Factors stimulating value micro-businesses attribute to digital marketing technology (DMT) adoption. *PLoS One, 16*(12), e0260145. DOI: 10.1371/journal.pone.0260145 PMID: 34855805

Fahmi, F. Z., & Savira, M. (2023). Digitalization and rural entrepreneurial attitude in Indonesia: A capability approach. *Journal of Enterprising Communities: People and Places in the Global Economy, 17*(2), 454–478. DOI: 10.1108/JEC-06-2021-0082

Fanelli, R. M. (2021). Barriers to adopting new technologies within rural small and medium enterprises (SMEs). *Social Sciences (Basel, Switzerland), 10*(11), 430. DOI: 10.3390/socsci10110430

Fernandes, E., & Burcharth, A. (2024). Why traditional firms from the same industry reject digital transformation: Structural constraints of perception and attention. *Long Range Planning, 57*(2), 102426. DOI: 10.1016/j.lrp.2024.102426

Ferrari, A., Bacco, M., Gaber, K., Jedlitschka, A., Hess, S., Kaipainen, J., Koltsida, P., Toli, E., & Brunori, G. (2022). Drivers, barriers and impacts of digitalisation in rural areas from the viewpoint of experts. *Information and Software Technology, 145*, 106816. Advance online publication. DOI: 10.1016/j.infsof.2021.106816

Francis, J. J., Johnston, M., Robertson, C., Glidewell, L., Entwistle, V., Eccles, M. P., & Grimshaw, J. M. (2010). What is an adequate sample size? Operationalising data saturation for theory-based interview studies. *Psychology & Health*, *25*(10), 1229–1245. DOI: 10.1080/08870440903194015 PMID: 20204937

Guest, G., Bunce, A., & Johnson, L. (2006). How Many Interviews Are Enough?: An Experiment with Data Saturation and Variability. *Field Methods*, *18*(1), 59–82. DOI: 10.1177/1525822X05279903

Kuo, C.-L. (2022). Peer Review for Academic Research. *Archives of Otorhinolaryngology-Head & Neck Surgery*, *6*(1). Advance online publication. DOI: 10.24983/scitemed.aohns.2022.00155

Kusumastuti, R., Silalahi, M., Sambodo, M. T., & Juwono, V. (2022). *Understanding rural context in the social innovation knowledge structure and its sector implementations*. Management Review Quarterly., DOI: 10.1007/s11301-022-00288-3

Le, V. L. T., Nguyen, T. H., & Pham, K. D. (2023). What drives Industry 4.0 technologies Adoption? Evidence from a SEM-neural network approach in the context of Vietnamese firms. *Sustainability (Basel)*, *15*(7), 5969. DOI: 10.3390/su15075969

Lekhanya, L. M. (2018). The Digitalisation of Rural Entrepreneurship. In *Entrepreneurship - Trends and Challenges*. InTech., DOI: 10.5772/intechopen.75925

Malaysian Investment Development Authority (MIDA). (2020). Food Industry in Malaysia. *Food Industries*, *13*, •••. http://www.mida.gov.my/home/administrator/system_files/modules/photo/uploads/20180903103354_Food Industry 2018_V4.pdf

Molloy, L., & Ronnie, L. (2021). Mindset shifts for the Fourth Industrial Revolution: Insights from the life insurance sector. *SA Journal of Human Resource Management*, *19*, 13. DOI: 10.4102/sajhrm.v19i0.1543

Morris, J., Morris, W., & Bowen, R. (2022). Implications of the digital divide on rural SME resilience. *Journal of Rural Studies*, *89*, 369–377. DOI: 10.1016/j.jrurstud.2022.01.005

Noor, M. M., Hashim, N., & Jamin, R. M. (2020). Implications of ICT for development on enhancing rural entrepreneur program (rep) at telecentres in Malaysia. *International Journal of Business and Society*, *21*(2), 629–642. DOI: 10.33736/ijbs.3275.2020

Prasetyo, P. E., & Setyadharma, A. (2022). Digitalization Technology for Sustainable Rural Entrepreneurship and Inequality. *Journal of Human Resource and Sustainability Studies*, *10*(03), 464–484. DOI: 10.4236/jhrss.2022.103028

Remie Mohd Johan, M., Azalanshah Md Syed, M., & Mohd Adnan, H. (2021). Mobile eateries SMEss: Occidentals & Malaysia chronicles. Journal of Tourism. *Hospitality & Culinary Arts*, *13*, 85–102.

Romero-Castro, N., López-Cabarcos, M. A., & Piñeiro-Chousa, J. (2023). Finance, technology, and values: A configurational approach to the analysis of rural entrepreneurship. *Technological Forecasting and Social Change*, *190*, 122444. Advance online publication. DOI: 10.1016/j.techfore.2023.122444

Rosen, R. H. (2000). *Global literacies: Lessons on business leadership and national cultures*. Simon and Schuster.

Shahira, N. (2023, May 8). Eksport produk halal Malaysia dijangka meningkat tahun ini – HDC. Buletin TV3. https://www.buletintv3.my/detik-niaga/eksport-produk-halal-malaysia-dijangka-meningkat-tahun-ini-hdc/

Shukla, S., Bisht, K., Tiwari, K., & Bashir, S. (2023). Comparative Study of the Global Data Economy. In *Data Economy in the Digital Age* (pp. 63–86). Springer Nature Singapore. DOI: 10.1007/978-981-99-7677-5_4

Stahl, N. A., & King, J. R. (2020). Understanding and Using Trustworthiness in Qualitative Research. *Journal of Developmental Education*, *44*(1), 26–28. DOI: 10.4135/9781483329574

Tang, W., & Zhu, J. (2020). Informality and rural industry: Rethinking the impacts of E-Commerce on rural development in China. *Journal of Rural Studies*, *75*, 20–29. DOI: 10.1016/j.jrurstud.2020.02.010

Thomas, B. (2023). Exploring the facilitators of e-commerce adoption among rural entrepreneurs in Sabah. *Journal of BIMP-EAGA Regional Development*, *9*(1), 1–11. DOI: 10.51200/jbimpeagard.v9i1.4365

Tomaszewski, L. E., Zarestky, J., & Gonzalez, E. (2020). Planning Qualitative Research: Design and Decision Making for New Researchers. *International Journal of Qualitative Methods*, *19*, 1609406920967174. Advance online publication. DOI: 10.1177/1609406920967174

Tuitjer, G., & Küpper, P. (2022). Local and vertical networking as drivers of innovativeness and growth in rural businesses. *Journal of Rural Studies*, *95*, 412–422. DOI: 10.1016/j.jrurstud.2022.09.014

Wolfert, S., van Wassenaer, L., van der Burg, S., Ryan, M., Klerkx, L., Rijswijk, K., ... & Beers, G. (2021). Navigating the Twilight Zone: Pathways towards digital transformation of food systems. Wageningen University & Research.

Xu, J., Cui, Z., Wang, T., Wang, J., Yu, Z., & Li, C. (2023). Influence of Agricultural Technology Extension and Social Networks on Chinese Farmers' Adoption of Conservation Tillage Technology. *Land (Basel)*, *12*(6), 1215. DOI: 10.3390/land12061215

Yahaya, T. A. H., Kamarudin, D., & Hassan, N. S. M. (2019). *Marketing Strategy, Technological Innovation and Inventory Management Towards Malaysia's Food Industry Performance*. Cognitive-Crcs., DOI: 10.15405/epsbs.2019.08.53

Zainudin, F. (2018, April 18). Hidangan Malaysia tambat selera Jepun. Retrieved from https://www.bharian.com.my/authors/oleh-faiza-zainudin

Compilation of References

Abdullah, I. (2002). Advertising in Malaysia. *More Advertising Worldwide*, 159–181. DOI: 10.1007/978-3-540-24788-3_9

Abdullah, K. M., & Nor Azam, N. R. A. (2021). Innovated Malay Traditional Food Products: Do Consumers Accept the Authentic Quality? *International Journal of Academic Research in Business & Social Sciences*, *11*(16). Advance online publication. DOI: 10.6007/IJARBSS/v11-i16/11228

Abraham, A., & Collins, D. (2017). Defining Coaching Through the Lens of Professional Judgement and Decision Making. In *Proceedings of the 11th ICCE Golobal Coach Conference*.

Adam, H. (2021). Fintech and Entrepreneurship Boosting in Developing Countries: A Comparative Study of India and Egypt. *Studies in Computational Intelligence*, *974*, 141–156. DOI: 10.1007/978-3-030-73057-4_12

Adams, R. B., & Ferreira, D. (2009). Women in the boardroom and their impact on governance and performance. *Journal of Financial Economics*, *94*(2), 291–309. DOI: 10.1016/j.jfineco.2008.10.007

Ahluwalia, S., Mahto, R. V., & Guerrero, M. (2020). BcT and startup financing: A TCE perspective. *Technological Forecasting and Social Change*, *151*(February 2019), 119854. DOI: 10.1016/j.techfore.2019.119854

Ahmad, N., Fahad, M., Zaki, M., Alam, Z., & Khalid, M. (2025). Understanding consumer attitude and purchase intention of organic food products. *Spanish Journal of Marketing - ESIC*, *29*(1), 123–145. DOI: 10.1108/SJME-04-2024-0110

Ahmed, N., Li, C., Khan, A., Qalati, S. A., Naz, S., & Rana, F. (2020). Purchase intention toward organic food among young consumers using theory of planned behaviour: Role of environmental concerns and environmental awareness. *Journal of Environmental Planning and Management*. Advance online publication. DOI: 10.1080/09640568.2020.1785404

Ajzen, I. (1985). From intentions to actions: A theory of planned behaviour. In Kuhl, J., & Beckman, J. (Eds.), *Action-Control: From Cognition to Behaviour* (pp. 11–39). Springer. DOI: 10.1007/978-3-642-69746-3_2

Ajzen, I. (1991). The Theory of Planned Behaviour. *Organizational Behavior and Human Decision Processes, 50*(2), 179–211. DOI: 10.1016/0749-5978(91)90020-T

Ajzen, I., & Fishbein, M. (1980). *Understanding Attitudes and Predicting Social Behaviour*. Prentice Hall.

Al Issa, H. E. (2022). Psychological capital for success: The mediating role of entrepreneurial persistence and risk-taking. *Journal of Entrepreneurship in Emerging Economies, 14*(4), 525–548.

Al Muhairi, M., & Nobanee, H. (2019). Sustainable Financial Management. SSRN Electronic Journal. DOI: 10.2139/ssrn.3472417

Alameri, M., Alshamsi, F., Alsaedi, S., Alkaabi, A., Alamri, R., Alshamsi, M., & Nobanee, H. (2021). Financial Analysis of Hilton Holdings. doi:-DOI: 10.2139/ssrn.3930493

Albeshr, S., & Nobanee, H. (2020). Blockchain Applications in Banking Industry: A Mini-Review. SSRN *Electronic Journal*. DOI: 10.2139/ssrn.3539152

Ali, R., Irfan, S., & Hamid, S. (2024). Emerging themes in food tourism: A systematic literature review and research agenda. *British Food Journal, 126*(1), 372–408. DOI: 10.1108/BFJ-11-2022-0939

Allam, Z., & Jones, D. S. (2019). The Potential of Blockchain within Air Rights Development as a Prevention Measure against Urban Sprawl. *Urban Science (Basel, Switzerland)*, *3*(1), 38. Advance online publication. DOI: 10.3390/urbansci3010038

Almli, V. L., Asioli, D., & Rocha, C. (2019). Organic Consumer Choices for Nutrient Labels on Dried Strawberries among Different Health Attitude Segments in Norway, Romania, and Turkey. *Nutrients*, *11*(12), 2951–2967. DOI: 10.3390/nu11122951

Amanda, T. A., & Marsasi, E. G. (2024). Exploration of perceived behavioural control and intention to purchase to increase actual behaviour. *Image: Jurnal Riset Manajemen*, *12*(1), 14–30. DOI: 10.17509/image.2024.002

Amouri, A., Festa, G., Shams, S. R., Sakka, G., & Rossi, M. (2021). Technological propensity, financial constraints, and entrepreneurial limits in young entrepreneurs' social business enterprises: The tunisian experience. *Technological Forecasting and Social Change*, *173*, 121126. DOI: 10.1016/j.techfore.2021.121126

Anshari, M., & Hamdan, M. (2022). Understanding knowledge management and upskilling in Fourth Industrial Revolution: Transformational shift and SECI model. *VINE Journal of Information and Knowledge Management Systems*, *52*(3), 373–393. DOI: 10.1108/VJIKMS-09-2021-0203

Anthony, I. A. N., Yuan, J., & Xia, S. U. N. (2021). Promoting China – European Union Cooperation on Green. SIPRI Policy Brief, 2021, 0–8. https://www.jstor.org/stable/resrep29591

Arif, U., & Sohail, M. T. (2020). Asset pricing with higher co-moments and CVaR: Evidence from pakistan stock exchange. *International Journal of Economics and Financial Issues*, *10*(5), 243–255. DOI: 10.32479/ijefi.10351

Armitage, C. J., & Conner, M. (2001). Efficacy of the Theory of Planned Behaviour: A meta-analytic review. *British Journal of Social Psychology*, *40*(4), 471–499. DOI: 10.1348/014466601164939

Arrow, K. J. (1988). The Organization of Economic Activity. *Small Business Economics*, ●●●, v.

Asare, M. (2015). Using the Theory of Planned Behaviour to determine the condom use behaviour among college students. *American Journal of Health Studies*, *30*(1), 43–50.

Asif, M., Xuhui, W., Nasiri, A., & Ayyub, S. (2018). Determinant factors influencing organic food purchase intention and the moderating role of awareness: A comparative analysis. *Food Quality and Preference*, *63*, 144–150. DOI: 10.1016/j.foodqual.2017.08.006

Ayub, A. H., Nik Muhammad Naziman, Y. H., & Samat, M. F. (2020). Factors Influencing Young Consumers' Purchase Intention of Organic Food Product. *Advances in Business Research International Journal*, *4*(1), 17–26. DOI: 10.24191/abrij.v4i1.10074

Ayyub, S., Asif, M., & Nawaz, M. A. (2021). Drivers of Organic Food Purchase Intention in a Developing Country: The Mediating Role of Trust. *SAGE Open*, *11*(July-September), 1–2. DOI: 10.1177/21582440211045076

Ayyub, S., Wang, X., Asif, M., & Ayyub, R. (2018). Antecedents of Trust in Organic Foods: The Mediating Role of Food Related Personality Traits. *Sustainability (Basel)*, *10*(10), 3597–3613. DOI: 10.3390/su10103597

Aziz, M. F. B. A., Mispan, M. S. B., & Doni, F. (2020). Organic Food Policy and Regulation in Malaysia: Development and Challenges. In Goh, B., & Price, R. (Eds.), *Regulatory Issues in Organic Food Safety in the Asia Pacific*. Springer., DOI: 10.1007/978-981-15-3580-2_10

Balon, R. (2024). An Explanation of Generations and Generational Changes. *Academic Psychiatry*, *48*(3), 280–282. DOI: 10.1007/s40596-023-01921-3

Bandura, A. (2000). Self-efficacy: The foundation of agency. Control of human behavior, mental processes, and consciousness: Essays in honor of the 60th birthday of August Flammer, 16.

Bank for International Settlements. (2023). *Sound practices: implications of fintech developments for banks and bank supervisors*. BIS.

Bartoletti, M., & Pompianu, L. (2017). An analysis of bitcoin OP_RETURN metadata. *Lecture Notes in Computer Science (Including Subseries Lecture Notes in Artificial Intelligence and Lecture Notes in Bioinformatics), 10323 LNCS*, 218–230. DOI: 10.1007/978-3-319-70278-0_14

Baumol, W. J. (2016). *Review : Williamson ' s The Economic Institutions of Capitalism Author (s): William J . Baumol Published by : Wiley on behalf of RAND Corporation Stable URL :* https://www.jstor.org/stable/2555390 *Williamson ' s The Economic Institutions of Capitalism. 17*(2), 279–286.

Bechler, C. J., Tormala, Z. L., & Rucker, D. D. (2021). The attitude–behaviour relationship revisited. *Psychological Science, 32*(8), 1285–1297. DOI: 10.1177/0956797621995206

Begazo, T., Blimpo, M., & Dutz, M. (2023). *Digital Africa: Technological Transformation for Jobs.* World Bank Publications. DOI: 10.1596/978-1-4648-1737-3

Belleflamme, P., Lambert, T., & Schwienbacher, A. (2014). Crowdfunding: Tapping the right crowd. *Journal of Business Venturing, 29*(5), 585–609. DOI: 10.1016/j.jbusvent.2013.07.003

Benabou, R., & Tirole, J. (2010). Individual and corporate social responsibility. *Economica, 77*(305), 1–19. DOI: 10.1111/j.1468-0335.2009.00843.x

Benítez-Márquez, M. D., Sánchez-Teba, E. M., Bermúdez-González, G., & Núñez-Rydman, E. S. (2022). Generation Z Within the Workforce and in the Workplace: A Bibliometric Analysis. *Frontiers in Psychology, 12*, 736820. DOI: 10.3389/fpsyg.2021.736820

Benston, G. J., & Smith, C. W. (1976). A Transactions Cost Approach to the Theory of Financial Intermediation the Thirty-Fourth Annual Meeting of the American Finance Association Dallas, Texas Published by : Wiley for the American Finance Association Stable URL : https://www.jstor.org/stable/. *The Journal of Finance, 31*(2), 215–231.

Bernama (2024, April 30). *Gen Z, millennials more willing to spend on sustainable products.* https://www.newsarawaktribune.com.my/gen-z-millennials-more-willing-to-spend-on-sustainable-products/

BERNAMA. (2023, July 10). Malaysia muncul hab teknologi, inovasi dinamik. Berita Harian. https://www.bharian.com.my/bisnes/lain-lain/2023/07/1124954/malaysia-muncul-hab-teknologi-inovasi-dinamik

Bhasin, H. (2025). *What is Purchase Intent? Definition, Types & How to Measure.* https://www.marketing91.com/purchase-intention/#:~:text=February%2026%2C%202025%20%7C%20By%20Hitesh,digital%20sources%2C%20and%20other%20analytics

Bhutto, M. Y., Khan, M. A., Sun, C., Hashim, S., & Khan, H. T. (2023). Factors affecting repurchase intention of organic food among generation Z (Evidence from developing economy). *PLoS One*, *18*(3), e0281527. DOI: 10.1371/journal.pone.0281527

Bidgoli, A. E., Reza, M., Moghadam, S., & Hasangholipour, T. (2022). Designing a strategic financial model for digital start-ups. *Journal of Positive School Psychology*, *2022*(4), 8023–8036. https://journalppw.com/index.php/jpsp/article/view/5159

Biswas, P. K., Mansi, M., & Pandey, R. (2018). Board composition, sustainability committee and corporate social and environmental performance in Australia. *Pacific Accounting Review*, *30*(4), 517–540. DOI: 10.1108/PAR-12-2017-0107

Blok, V. (2021). What is innovation? Laying the ground for a philosophy of innovation. *Techné: Research in Philosophy and Technology*, *25*(1), 72–96. DOI: 10.5840/techne2020109129

Boulouta, I. (2013). Hidden connections: The link between board gender diversity and corporate social performance. *Journal of Business Ethics*, *113*(2), 185–197. DOI: 10.1007/s10551-012-1293-7

Brockmann, E. N., & Anthony, W. W. P. (1998). The influence of tacit knowledge and collective mind on strategic planning. *Journal of Managerial Issues*, *10*(2), 204–222.

Buchner, B., Stadelmann, M., Wilkinson, J., Mazza, F., Rosenberg, A., & Abramskiehn, D. (2014). The Global Landscape of Climate Finance 2014. Climate Policy Initiative Report

Buitenhek, M. (2016). Understanding and applying BcT in banking: Evolution or revolution? *Journal of Digital Banking*, *1*(2), 111–119. https://www.henrystewartpublications.com/sites/default/files/02_Buitenhek_JDB_V1.2.pdf. DOI: 10.69554/TXYN8464

Burhan, A. H. N., & Rahmanti, W. (2012). The impact of sustainability reporting on company performance. Journal of Economics, Business, &. *Accountancy Ventura*, *15*(2), 257–272. DOI: 10.14414/jebav.v15i2.79

Busch, T., Bauer, R., & Orlitzky, M. (2016). Sustainable Development and Financial Markets: Old Paths and New Avenues. *Business & Society*, *55*(3), 303–329. DOI: 10.1177/0007650315570701

Busch, T., & Lewandowski, S. (2018). Corporate carbon and financial performance a meta-analysis. *Journal of Industrial Ecology*, *22*(4), 745–759. DOI: 10.1111/jiec.12591

Canova, L., Bobbio, A., & Manganelli, A. M. (2020). Buying organic food products: The role of trust in the theory of planned behaviour. *Frontiers in Psychology*, *11*, 575820. DOI: 10.3389/fpsyg.2020.575820

Carriere-Swallow, Y., Haksar, V., & Patnam, M. (2021). India's Approach to Open Banking: Some Implications for Financial Inclusion. SSRN *Electronic Journal*. DOI: 10.5089/9781513570686.001

Carter, D. A., Simkins, B. J., & Simpson, W. G. (2003). Corporate governance, board diversity, and firm value. *Financial Review*, *38*(1), 33–53. DOI: 10.1111/1540-6288.00034

Caruana, E. J., Roman, M., Hernández-Sánchez, J., & Solli, P. (2015). Longitudinal studies. *Journal of Thoracic Disease*, *7*(11), 537–540. DOI: 10.3978/j.issn.2072-1439.2015.10.63

Castaneda, D. I., & Toulson, P. (2021). Is it possible to share tacit knowledge using information and communication technology tools? *Global Knowledge, Memory and Communication*, *70*(8–9), 673–683. DOI: 10.1108/GKMC-07-2020-0102

Catalini, C., & Gans, J. S. (2020). Some simple economics of the blockchain. *Communications of the ACM*, *63*(7), 80–90. DOI: 10.1145/3359552

Chane, A. (2018). La finance verte en Chine, une composante essentielle de la transition vers une économie bas-carbone. Idées Économiques et Sociales, N° 192(2), 42–45.).DOI: 10.3917/idee.192.0042

Cheng, S.-J., Jia, H.-X., Wong, P. P. W., & Wang, L. (2024). Factors influencing consumers' purchase intention on organic foods via a Theory of Planned Behaviour approach. *Journal of Tourism, Culinary, and Entrepreneurship*, *3*(1), 98–116. DOI: 10.1234/jtce.2024.001

Chen, Y. (2018). Blockchain tokens and the potential democratization of entrepreneurship and innovation. *Business Horizons*, *61*(4), 567–575. DOI: 10.1016/j.bushor.2018.03.006

Chiles, T. H., & Mcmackin, J. F. (2016). Integrating Variable Risk Preferences, Trust, and TCE Author (s): Todd H. Chiles and John F. McMackin Source : The Academy of Management Review, Vol. 21, No. 1 (Jan., 1996), pp. 73-99 Published by. *Academy of Manageme.*, *21*(1), 73–99.

Christensen, H. B., Hail, L., & Leuz, C. (2021). Mandatory CSR and sustainability reporting: Economic analysis and literature review. *Review of Accounting Studies*, *26*(3), 1176–1248. DOI: 10.1007/s11142-021-09609-5

Chukwujioke Agbim, K., Benapugha Owutuamor, Z., & Orziemgbe Oriarewo, G. (2013). Entrepreneurship Development and Tacit Knowledge : Exploring the Link between Entrepreneurial Learning and Individual Know-How. *Journal of Business Studies Quarterly*, *5*(2), 112–130.

Clark, G. L., Feiner, A., & Viehs, M. (2015). *From the Stockholder to the Stakeholder: How Sustainability Can Drive Financial Outperformance*. University of Oxford and Arabesque Partners.

Coase, R. H. (1937). The Nature of the Firm. *Economica*, *4*(16), 386–405. DOI: 10.1111/j.1468-0335.1937.tb00002.x

Cohen, J. (1988). *Statistical Power Analysis for the Behaviours Science* (2nd ed.). Laurence Erlbaum Associates.

Cole, R. A. (1998). The importance of relationships to the availability of credit. *Journal of Banking & Finance*, *22*(6–8), 959–977. DOI: 10.1016/S0378-4266(98)00007-7

Conner, K. R. (1991). A Historical Comparison of Resource-Based Theory and Five Schools of Thought Within Industrial Organization Economics: Do We Have a New Theory of the Firm? *Journal of Management*, *17*(1), 121–154. DOI: 10.1177/014920639101700109

Cramarenco, R. E., Burcă-Voicu, M. I., & Dabija, D. C. (2023). Organic food consumption during the COvID-19 pandemic. A bibliometric analysis and systematic review. *Amfiteatru Economic*, *25*(17), 1042–1063. DOI: 10.24818/EA/2023/S17/1042

Cunningham, J. A., Damij, N., Modic, D., & Olan, F. (2023). MSME technology adoption, entrepreneurial mindset and value creation: A configurational approach. *The Journal of Technology Transfer*, *48*(5), 1–25. DOI: 10.1007/s10961-023-10022-0

Curvelo, I. C. G., Watanabe, E. A. D. M., & Alfinito, S. (2019). Purchase intention of organic food under the influence of attributes, consumer trust and perceived value. *Revista de Gestão*, *26*(3), 198–211. DOI: 10.1108/REGE-01-2018-0010

Cuvero, M., Granados, M. L., Pilkington, A., & Evans, R. (2022). Start-ups' use of knowledge spillovers for product innovation: the influence of entrepreneurial ecosystems and virtual platforms. In *R and D Management*. John Wiley and Sons Inc., DOI: 10.1111/radm.12567

Dahlberg, T., Mallat, N., Ondrus, J., & Zmijewska, A. (2006). Mobile Payment Market and Research - Past, Present, and Future. *Presentation at Helsinki Mobility Roundtable, Helsinki, Finland, June 1-2, 2002*(January 2006), 1–16.

David, R. J., & Han, S. K. (2004). A systematic assessment of the empirical support for TCE. *Strategic Management Journal*, *25*(1), 39–58. DOI: 10.1002/smj.359

Davidson, S., De Filippi, P., & Potts, J. (2018). Disrupting Governance: The New Institutional Economics of Distributed Ledger Technology. SSRN *Electronic Journal*, 1–27. DOI: 10.2139/ssrn.2811995

De Guzman, M. R. T., Kim, S., Taylor, S., & Padasas, I. (2020). Rural communities as a context for entrepreneurship: Exploring perceptions of youth and business owners. *Journal of Rural Studies*, *80*, 45–52. DOI: 10.1016/j.jrurstud.2020.06.036

Derwall, J., Guenster, N., Bauer, R., & Koedijk, K. (2005). The eco-efficiency premium puzzle. *Financial Analysts Journal*, *61*(2), 51–63. DOI: 10.2469/faj.v61.n2.2716

Deschryver, P. (2020). Accélérer la transition énergétique: le rôle de la finance verte et ses enjeux pour l'Europe. In Ifri. https://www.ifri.org/fr/publications/etudes-de-lifri/accelerer-transition-energetique-role-de-finance-verte-enjeux-leurope

Déséglise, C., & Freijido, D. L. (2019). Financing sustainable infrastructure at scale. *Journal of International Affairs*, *73*(1), 33–48.

Devi, N. (2022). Green Business Developments in India- A Study on the Eco-Friendly Initiatives Towards Sustainable Developments. *International Journal of Innovative Research in Technology*, *9*(3), 385–388.

DeWaard, H., & Chavhan, R. (2020). Cross-Cultural Mentoring: A Pathway to Building Professional Relationships and Professional Learning Beyond Boundaries. *Journal of Teaching and Learning*, *14*(1), 43–58. DOI: 10.22329/jtl.v14i1.6255

Dikau, S., & Volz, U. (2021). "Central Banking, Climate Change, and Green Finance." Asian Development Bank Institute.https://www.adb.org/sites/default/files/publication/908751/climate-change-climate-finance-experience-directions.pdf

Dimock, M. (2019). *Defining generations: Where Millennials end and Generation Z begins*. Pew Research Centre. https://www.pewresearch.org/short-reads/2019/01/17/where-millennials-end-and-generation-z-begins/

Divinagracia, A., Forones, L. K., P., & E. (2024). Environmental Awareness and Sustainability Perception and Attitude of Generation Z. Psychology and Education: *A Multidisciplinary Journal, 24*(7). DOI: 10.5281/zenodo.13627785

Donovan, K. (2012). Mobile money for financial inclusion. *Information and Communications for development, 61*(1), 61-73.

Drexler, D., Fiala, J., Havlíčková, A., Potůčková, A., & Souček, M. (2017). The Effect of Organic Food Labels on Consumer Attention. *Journal of Food Products Marketing*, *24*(4), 441–455. DOI: 10.1080/10454446.2017.1311815

Duranti, L., & Rogers, C. (2016). Trust in Records and Data Online. *Integrity in Government through Records Management: Essays in Honour of Anne Thurston*, 203–214. DOI: 10.4324/9781315589077-21

Dutta, A., Bouri, E., Rothovius, T., & Uddin, G. S. (2023). Climate risk and green investments: New evidence. Energy, 265(February 2022), 126376. DOI: 10.1016/j.energy.2022.126376

Dwivedi, J., Chandel, S. S., Shrivastava, A., Lepcha, D., & Xess, A. M. (2025). Predicting Generation Z's Purchase Intention towards Organic Food. *Library Progress International*, *45*(1), 80–92.

Džever, S., Marić, D., Leković, K., & Kostić, D. (2024). Generation Z Attitudes towards Organic Food: A Review. *International Scientific Conference Strategic Management and Decision Support Systems in Strategic Management,* 279-286. DOI: 10.46541/978-86-7233-428-9_397

Eccles, R. G., Ioannou, I., & Serafeim, G. (2014). The Impact of Corporate Sustainability on Organizational Processes and Performance. *Management Science*, *60*(11), 2835–2857. DOI: 10.1287/mnsc.2014.1984

Economic Research Institute for ASEAN and East Asia-ERIA. (2018). *Study on MSMEs Participation in the Digital Economy in ASEAN*. Economic Research Institute for ASEAN and East Asia.

Elfrida, T., Sazali, S. A., & Abu Bakar, M. N. (2020). The Representation of Baba-Nyonya Cuisine in the Context of Halal Tourism Industry in Malacca, Malaysia. *Humanus, 19*(1), 61. DOI: 10.24036/humanus.v19i1.107681

Elkafrawi, N. M. (2020) Women Entrepreneurship Development in Egyptian Rural Context: A Structuration Perspective. Doctoral thesis, University of Huddersfield.

Elmagrhi, M. H., Ntim, C. G., Elamer, A. A., & Zhang, Q. (2019). A study of environmental policies and regulations, governance structures, and environmental performance: The role of female directors. *Business Strategy and the Environment, 28*(1), 206–220. DOI: 10.1002/bse.2250

EMF. (2015). Towards a circular economy: Business rationale for an accelerated transition. Ellen MacArthur Foundation (EMF), 20. https://www.ellenmacarthurfoundation.org/circular-economy-articles

EPU. (2019). National Fourth Industrial Revolution (4IR) Policy. *Economic Planning Unit, Prime Minister's Department, 1*, 1–72.

Eyraud, L., Clements, B., & Wane, A. (2013). Green investment: Trends and determinants. *Energy Policy, 60*, 852–865. DOI: 10.1016/j.enpol.2013.04.039

Eze, S. C., Chinedu-Eze, V. C., Awa, H. O., & Alharthi, R. H. E. (2021). Factors stimulating value micro-businesses attribute to digital marketing technology (DMT) adoption. *PLoS One, 16*(12), e0260145. DOI: 10.1371/journal.pone.0260145 PMID: 34855805

Fahmi, F. Z., & Savira, M. (2023). Digitalization and rural entrepreneurial attitude in Indonesia: A capability approach. *Journal of Enterprising Communities: People and Places in the Global Economy, 17*(2), 454–478. DOI: 10.1108/JEC-06-2021-0082

Falcone, P. M., & Sica, E. (2019). Assessing the opportunities and challenges of green finance in Italy: An analysis of the biomass production sector. *Sustainability (Basel), 11*(2), 517. Advance online publication. DOI: 10.3390/su11020517

Fanelli, R. M. (2021). Barriers to adopting new technologies within rural small and medium enterprises (SMEs). *Social Sciences (Basel, Switzerland), 10*(11), 430. DOI: 10.3390/socsci10110430

Fanning, K., & Centers, D. P. (2016). Blockchain and its coming impact on financial services. *Journal of Corporate Accounting & Finance, 27*(5), 53–57. DOI: 10.1002/jcaf.22179

Fareed, Z., Salem, S., Adebayo, T. S., Pata, U. K., & Shahzad, F. (2021). Role of Export Diversification and Renewable Energy on the Load Capacity Factor in Indonesia: A Fourier Quantile Causality Approach. *Frontiers in Environmental Science, 9*, 1–9. DOI: 10.3389/fenvs.2021.770152

Fattahi Ardakani, M., Salehi-Abargouei, A., Sotoudeh, A., Esmaeildokht, S., & Bahrevar, V. (2020). Do Subjective Norms Predict the Screening of Cancer Patients' First-Degree Relatives? A Systematic Review and Meta-Analysis. *Asian Pacific Journal of Cancer Prevention : APJCP, 21*(6), 1521–1530. DOI: 10.31557/APJCP.2020.21.6.1521

Fernandes, E., & Burcharth, A. (2024). Why traditional firms from the same industry reject digital transformation: Structural constraints of perception and attention. *Long Range Planning, 57*(2), 102426. DOI: 10.1016/j.lrp.2024.102426

Ferrari, A., Bacco, M., Gaber, K., Jedlitschka, A., Hess, S., Kaipainen, J., Koltsida, P., Toli, E., & Brunori, G. (2022). Drivers, barriers and impacts of digitalisation in rural areas from the viewpoint of experts. *Information and Software Technology, 145*, 106816. Advance online publication. DOI: 10.1016/j.infsof.2021.106816

Ferreira, S., & Pereira, O. (2023). Antecedents of Consumers' Intention and Behaviour to Purchase Organic Food in the Portuguese Context. *Sustainability (Basel), 15*(12), 9670. DOI: 10.3390/su15129670

Figurny, G. N. (2021). Phenomenological approaches in the theory of architecture in the context of modern cognitive science. *Voprosy Filosofii, 2021*(6), 65–73. DOI: 10.21146/0042-8744-2021-6-65-73

Financial Stability Board. (2017). Final Report: Recommendations of the Task Force on Climate-Related Financial Disclosure. https://www.fsb-tcfd.org/wp content/uploads/2017/06/FINAL-2017-TCFD-Report-11052018.pdf

Flammer, C. (2020). Green Bonds: Effectiveness and Implications for Public Policy. In Environmental and Energy Policy and the Economy (Vol. 1). DOI: 10.1086/706794

Flammer, C. (2013). Corporate Social Responsibility and Shareholder Reaction: The Environmental Awareness of Investors. *Academy of Management Journal*, *56*(3), 758–781. DOI: 10.5465/amj.2011.0744

Francis, J. J., Johnston, M., Robertson, C., Glidewell, L., Entwistle, V., Eccles, M. P., & Grimshaw, J. M. (2010). What is an adequate sample size? Operationalising data saturation for theory-based interview studies. *Psychology & Health*, *25*(10), 1229–1245. DOI: 10.1080/08870440903194015 PMID: 20204937

Friede, G., Busch, T., & Bassen, A. (2015). ESG and Financial Performance: Aggregated Evidence from More than 2000 Empirical Studies. *Journal of Sustainable Finance & Investment*, *5*(4), 210–233. DOI: 10.1080/20430795.2015.1118917

Friedman, M. (1970). The social responsibility of business is to increase its profits. *New York Times*, 13 September, pp. 122–126.

Frimousse, S., & Peretti, J. M. (2021). La contribution de la finance verte et durable à la performance extra-financière. *Question (s) de management*, *36*(6), 141-166.

Galaz, V., Crona, B., Dauriach, A., Scholtens, B., & Steffen, W. (2018). Finance and the Earth system – Exploring the links between financial actors and non-linear changes in the climate system. *Global Environmental Change*, *53*(January), 296–302. DOI: 10.1016/j.gloenvcha.2018.09.008

Ge, C., Lv, W., & Wang, J. (2023). The Impact of Digital Technology Innovation Network Embedding on Firms' Innovation Performance: The Role of Knowledge Acquisition and Digital Transformation. *Sustainability (Basel), 15*(8), 6938. Advance online publication. DOI: 10.3390/su15086938

Ghoshal, S., & Moran, P. (1996). Bad for Practice : A Critique of the Transaction Cost Theory Author (s): Sumantra Ghoshal and Peter Moran Source : The Academy of Management Review, Vol. 21, No. 1 (Jan., 1996), pp. 13-47 Published by : Academy of Management Stable URL : http. *Academy of Management Review, 21*(1), 13–47. https://www.jstor.org/stable/258627. DOI: 10.2307/258627

Giancaspro, M. (2017). Is a 'smart contract' really a smart idea? Insights from a legal perspective. *Computer Law & Security Review, 33*(6), 825–835. DOI: 10.1016/j.clsr.2017.05.007

GlobalData. (2023, June 2). Malaysia ICT Market Size and Forecast (by IT Solution Area, Size Band and Vertical), 2022-2026. Market Research Reports & Consulting | GlobalData UK Ltd. https://www.globaldata.com/store/report/malaysia-ict-market-analysis/

Gochhwal, R. (2017). Unified Payment Interface—An Advancement in Payment Systems. *American Journal of Industrial and Business Management, 07*(10), 1174–1191. DOI: 10.4236/ajibm.2017.710084

Gold, A. H., Malhotra, A., & Segars, A. H. (2001). Knowledge management: An organizational capabilities perspective. *Journal of Management Information Systems, 18*(1), 185–214. DOI: 10.1080/07421222.2001.11045669

Gray, R. (1994). Transactions Costs and New Institutions: Will CBLTs Have a Role in the Saskatchewan Land Market? *Canadian Journal of Agricultural Economics/Revue Canadienne d'agroeconomie, 42*(4), 501–509. DOI: 10.1111/j.1744-7976.1994.tb00044.x

Green, J. M., Draper, A. K., Dowler, E. A., Fele, G., Hagenhoff, V., Rusanen, M., & Rusanen, T. (2005). Public understanding of food risks in four European countries: A qualitative study. *European Journal of Public Health, 15*(5), 523–527. DOI: 10.1093/eurpub/cki016

Greenstone, M., List, J. A., & Syverson, C. (2012). *The effects of environmental regulation on the competitiveness of US manufacturing (No. w18392)*. National Bureau of Economic Research. DOI: 10.3386/w18392

Greiner, M. E., Bohmann, T., & Krcmar, H. (2007). A strategy for knowledge management. *Journal of Knowledge Management*, *11*(6), 3–15. DOI: 10.1108/13673270710832127

GSMA. (2023). State of mobile internet connectivity 2023.

Guest, G., Bunce, A., & Johnson, L. (2006). How Many Interviews Are Enough?: An Experiment with Data Saturation and Variability. *Field Methods*, *18*(1), 59–82. DOI: 10.1177/1525822X05279903

Guido, G. (2009). *Behind Ethical Consumption*. Peter Lang Verlag., https://www.peterlang.com/document/1051940 DOI: 10.3726/978-3-0351-0499-8

Guido, G., Prete, M. I., Peluso, A. M., Maloumby-Baka, R. C., & Buffa, C. (2009). The role of ethics and product personality in the intention to purchase organic food products: A structural equation modeling approach. *International Review of Economics*, *57*(1), 79–102. DOI: 10.1007/s12232-009-0086-5

Gujar (2020). A Study of Sustainable Business Practices in the Indian Pharmaceutical Industry. (Doctoral Thesis). Pacific University, Udaipur, India.

Gujarati, D. (2003). *Essentials of Econometrics*. Irwin McGraw-Hill.

Guo, Y., & Liang, C. (2016). Blockchain application and outlook in the banking industry. *Financial Innovation*, *2*(1), 24. Advance online publication. DOI: 10.1186/s40854-016-0034-9

Gupta, A. K., & Gupta, N. (2020). Effect of corporate environmental sustainability on dimensions of firm performance–Towards sustainable development: Evidence from India. *Journal of Cleaner Production*, *253*, 119948. DOI: 10.1016/j.jclepro.2019.119948

Gupta, S., & Kumar, D. (2020). Upi - An Innovative Step for Making Digital Payment Effective and Consumer Perception on Unified Payment Interface. *The International Journal of Analytical and Experimental Modal Analysis, 12*(1), 2482–2491.

Haddock, G., Thorne, S., & Wolf, L. (2020). Attitudes and behavior. In *Oxford Research Encyclopedia of Psychology*. Oxford University Press., DOI: 10.1093/acrefore/9780190236557.013.449

Hair Jr, J. F., Hult, G. T. M., Ringle, C. M., & Sarstedt, M. (2021). *A Primer on Partial Least Squares Structural Equation Modeling* (PLS-SEM). Sage Publication.

Halim, E., Chandra, A. N., Salim, J., Margarita, V., Destiano, R., & Hebrard, M. (2021). Predicting the Determinants of Continuance Intention to Use E-Wallet in Indonesia Post-COVID-19 Pandemic. *International Conference on Information Management and Technology* (ICIMTech), 2021. DOI: 10.1109/ICIMTech53080.2021.9534968

Hanif, S., Ahsan, A., & Wise, G. (2020). Icebergs of expertise-based leadership: The role of expert leaders in public administration. *Sustainability (Basel), 12*(11), 4544. Advance online publication. DOI: 10.3390/su12114544

Han, J., & Gao, H. Y. (2024). Green finance, social inclusion, and sustainable economic growth in OECD member countries. *Humanities & Social Sciences Communications, 11*(1), 1–8. DOI: 10.1057/s41599-024-02662-w

Hasan, H. N., & Suciarto, S. (2020). The Influence of Attitude, Subjective Norm and Perceived Behavioral Control towards Organic Food Purchase Intention. *Journal of Management and Business Environment, 1*(2), 132–153. DOI: 10.24167/jmbe.v1i2.2260

Henseler, J., Ringle, C. M., & Sarstedt, M. (2015). A New Criterion for Assessing Discriminant Validity in Variance-Based Structural Equation Modeling. *Journal of the Academy of Marketing Science, 43*(1), 115–135. DOI: 10.1007/s11747-014-0403-8

Hirano, M., Yamamoto, T., Sakakibara, K., & Kurashige, M. (2017). Social innovation in Sabae city: As a new type of industrial movement in Japan. In PICMET 2016 - Portland International Conference on Management of Engineering and Technology: Technology Management for Social Innovation, Proceedings (pp. 1217–1223). Institute of Electrical and Electronics Engineers Inc. DOI: 10.1109/PICMET.2016.7806512

Horbach, J., Rammer, C., & Rennings, K. (2012). Determinants of Eco-innovations by Type of Environmental Impact—The Role of Regulatory Push/Pull, Technology Push and Market Pull. *Ecological Economics*, *78*, 112–122. DOI: 10.1016/j.ecolecon.2012.04.005

Huang, Z., Zhu, Y. D., Deng, J., & Wang, C. L. (2022). Marketing Healthy Diets: The Impact of Health Consciousness on Chinese Consumers' Food Choices. *Sustainability (Basel)*, *14*(4), 2059. DOI: 10.3390/su14042059

Hulland, J., Baumgartner, H., & Smith, K. M. (2017). Marketing survey research best practices evidence and recommendations from a review of JAMS articles. *Journal of the Academy of Marketing Science*, *46*(1), 92–108. DOI: 10.1007/s11747-017-0532-y

Huy, L., Chi, M., Lobo, A., Nguyen, N., & Long, P. (2019). Effective Segmentation of Organic Food Consumers in Vietnam Using Food-Related Lifestyles. *Sustainability (Basel)*, *11*(5), 1237–1251. DOI: 10.3390/su11051237

Iansiti, M., & Lakhani, K. R. (2017, January). The truth about blockchain: It will take years to transform business, but the journey begins now. *Harvard Business Review*, 117–128.

Ibrahim, N. A., & Angelidis, J. P. (1994). Effect of board members' gender on corporate social responsiveness orientation. *Journal of Applied Business Research*, *10*(1), 35–40. DOI: 10.19030/jabr.v10i1.5961

Inderst, G., Kaminker, Ch., & Stewart, F. (2012). Defining and Measuring Green Investments: Implications for Institutional Investors Asset Allocations. OECD Working Papers on Finance, Insurance and Private Pensions, No.24, OECD Publishing.

Innoventures, S., & Wyman, O. (2015). *The Fintech 2.0 Paper: rebooting financial services.* Santander InnoVentures.

International Monetary Fund. (2024). Digital money and financial inclusion in emerging economies.

International Renewable Energy Agency (IRENA). (2019). Global Energy Transformation: A Roadmap to 2050.

International Renewable Energy Agency. (2019). "Renewable Energy and Jobs – Annual Review 2019

IPCC. (2014). Climate change 2014, synthesis report. IPCC, Geneva, Switzerland. Retrieved 17 June,2019,fromhttp://www.ipcc.ch/pdf/assessmentreport/ar5/syr/SYR_AR5_FINAL_full_ wcover.pdf

Jain, M. (2019). Fintech in India- Powering Mobile Payments. *Kpmg*, (August), 1–36.

Jakubowska, D., Dąbrowska, A. Z., Pachołek, B., & Sady, S. (2024). Behavioural intention to purchase sustainable food: Generation Z's perspective. *Sustainability (Basel)*, *16*(17), 7284. DOI: 10.3390/su16177284

Jeffers, E. (2015). Pourquoi faut-il une finance durable et soutenable ? Revue d'économie Financière, N° 117(1), 225–236. .DOI: 10.3917/ecofi.117.0225

Jeyakumar, N. R., Liang, J., & Meemken, E. M. (2021). Mediating Role of Organic Labeling Awareness and Food Safety Attitudes in the Correlation Between Green Product Awareness and Purchase Intentions. *SAGE Open*, *11*(4), 1–12. DOI: 10.1177/21582440211061565

Jiao, W., Chang, A., Ho, M., Lu, Q., Liu, M. T., & Schulz, P. J. (2023). Predicting and empowering health for generation Z by comparing health information seeking and digital health literacy: Cross-sectional questionnaire study. *Journal of Medical Internet Research*, *25*, e47595. DOI: 10.2196/47595

Juma-Michilena, I. J., Ruiz-Molina, M. E., Gil-Saura, I., & Belda-Miquel, S. (2024). Pro-environmental behaviours of generation Z: A cross-cultural approach. *International Review on Public and Nonprofit Marketing*, *21*(3), 1–29. DOI: 10.1007/s12208-024-00395-9

Kabir, M. N. (2019). *Knowledge-Based Social Entrepreneurship*. Knowledge-Based Social Entrepreneurship., DOI: 10.1057/978-1-137-34809-8

Kaminker, C., & Stewart, F. (2012). The Role of Institutional Investors in Financing Clean Energy. *OECD Working Papers on Finance, Insurance and Private Pensions*, No. 23.

Kaminker, C., et al. (2013), « L'investissement institutionnel dans les infrastructures vertes: Études de cas », OECD Working Papers on Finance, Insurance and Private Pensions, n° 35, Éditions OCDE, Paris, DOI: 10.1787/20797117

Kandpal, V., & Mehrotra, R. (2019). Financial inclusion: The role of fintech and digital financial services in India. *Indian Journal of Economics & Business*, *19*(1), 85–93.

Kang, J. (2018). Mobile payment in Fintech environment: Trends, security challenges, and services. *Human-Centric Computing and Information Sciences*, *8*(1), 32. Advance online publication. DOI: 10.1186/s13673-018-0155-4

Karamitsos, I., Papadaki, M., & Al Barghuthi, N. B. (2018). Design of the Blockchain Smart Contract: A Use Case for Real Estate. *Journal of Information Security*, *09*(03), 177–190. DOI: 10.4236/jis.2018.93013

Katz, R., Ogilvie, S., Shaw, J., & Woodhead, L. (2022). *What to know about Gen Z. Stanford Report*. https://news.stanford.edu/stories/2022/01/know-gen-z

Kempf, H. (2020). Verdir la politique monétaire. *Revue d'Économie Politique*, *130*(3), 311–343. DOI: 10.3917/redp.303.0311

Khadka, R. (2020). *The impact of BcT in banking: How can blockchain revolutionize the banking industry? October*, 37.

Khan, H. H., Malik, M. N., Konecna, Z., Chofreh, A. G., Goni, F. A., & Klemes, J. J. (2022). Blockchain technology for agricultural supply chains during the COVID-19 pandemic: Benefits and cleaner solutions. *Journal of Cleaner Production*, *347*, 131268. DOI: 10.1016/j.jclepro.2022.131268

Khan, M., Ahmad, N., & Zaki, M. (2023). Values, attitude, and desire in organic food purchase intention in Mexico. *Frontiers in Sustainable Food Systems*, *7*, 1516788. DOI: 10.3389/fsufs.2024.1516788

Kim, H. Y., & Chung, J. E. (2011). Consumer purchase intention for organic personal care products. *Journal of Consumer Marketing*, *28*(1), 40–47. DOI: 10.1108/07363761111101930

Kippenberger, T. (1997). When is virtual virtuous? *The Antidote*, *2*(6), 28–29. DOI: 10.1108/EUM0000000006443

Kitzmueller, M., & Shimshack, J. (2012). Economic perspectives on corporate social responsibility. *Journal of Economic Literature*, *50*(1), 51–84. DOI: 10.1257/jel.50.1.51

Klein, M. (2011). *Mobile Banking and Financial Inclusion The Regulatory Lessons. May*.

Kline, R. (2011). Principles and Practice of Structural Equation Modeling, 3nd edition.pdf (Third). The Guilford Press.

Kołodziej, M. (2021). Development Factors of BcT Within Banking Sector. *Springer Proceedings in Business and Economics*, 125–138. DOI: 10.1007/978-3-030-73667-5_8/COVER

Krishna, S. (2021). Digital identity, datafication and social justice: Understanding Aadhaar use among informal workers in south India. *Information Technology for Development*, *27*(1), 67–90. DOI: 10.1080/02681102.2020.1818544

Kucharska, W., & Erickson, G. S. (2023). Tacit knowledge acquisition & sharing, and its influence on innovations: A Polish/US cross-country study. *International Journal of Information Management, 71*, 102647. Advance online publication. DOI: 10.1016/j.ijinfomgt.2023.102647

Kuo, C.-L. (2022). Peer Review for Academic Research. *Archives of Oto-rhinolaryngology-Head & Neck Surgery, 6*(1). Advance online publication. DOI: 10.24983/scitemed.aohns.2022.00155

Kushwah, S., Dhir, A., & Sagar, M. (2019). Ethical consumption intentions and choice behaviour towards organic food. Moderation role of buying and environmental concerns. *Journal of Cleaner Production, 236*, 117519. DOI: 10.1016/j.jclepro.2019.06.350

Kusumastuti, R., Silalahi, M., Sambodo, M. T., & Juwono, V. (2022). *Understanding rural context in the social innovation knowledge structure and its sector implementations*. Management Review Quarterly., DOI: 10.1007/s11301-022-00288-3

Lahouel, B. B., Zaied, Y. B., & Taleb, L. (2021). Éditorial. La finance s' éveille au réchauffement climatique. *Question (s) de management, 36*(6), 31-35.

Lauslahti, K., Mattila, J., & Seppala, T. (2018). Smart Contracts How Will BcT Affect Contractual Practices? SSRN *Electronic Journal, 68*. DOI: 10.2139/ssrn.3154043

Le-Anh, T., & Nguyen-To, T. (2020). Consumer purchasing behaviour of organic food in an emerging market. *International Journal of Consumer Studies, 44*(6), 563–573. DOI: 10.1111/ijcs.12588

Lee, J. W. (2020). Green finance and sustainable development goals: The case of China. Lee, Jung Wan (2020). Green Finance and Sustainable Development Goals: The Case of China. *The Journal of Asian Finance, Economics and Business, 7*(7), 577–586. DOI: 10.13106/jafeb.2020.vol7.no7.577

Lekhanya, L. M. (2018). The Digitalisation of Rural Entrepreneurship. In *Entrepreneurship - Trends and Challenges*. InTech., DOI: 10.5772/intechopen.75925

Le, V. L. T., Nguyen, T. H., & Pham, K. D. (2023). What drives Industry 4.0 technologies Adoption? Evidence from a SEM-neural network approach in the context of Vietnamese firms. *Sustainability (Basel)*, *15*(7), 5969. DOI: 10.3390/su15075969

Li, J., & Jaharuddin, N. S. (2020). Customer purchase intentions and actual purchase for organic food: A moderated mediation model of perceived value and trust. *Journal of Cleaner Production*, *242*, 118320. DOI: 10.1016/j.jclepro.2019.118320

Lin, F. R., Po, R. W., & Orellan, C. V. C. (2011). Mining purchasing decision rules from service encounter data of retail chain stores. *Information Systems and e-Business Management*, *9*(2), 193–221. DOI: 10.1007/s10257-010-0143-3

Liu, N., Qi, L., Huang, M., Chen, D., Yin, C., Zhang, Y., Wang, X., Yuan, G., Wang, R.-J., Yang, J., Peng, Y.-L., & Lu, X. (2022). Comparative secretome analysis of Magnaporthe oryzae identified proteins involved in virulence and cell wall integrity. *Genomics, Proteomics & Bioinformatics*, *20*(4), 728–746. DOI: 10.1016/j.gpb.2021.02.007

Liu, Y., Lei, L., & Buttner, E. H. (2020). Establishing the boundary conditions for female board directors' influence on firm performance through CSR. *Journal of Business Research*, *121*, 112–120. DOI: 10.1016/j.jbusres.2020.08.026

Li, X., Zhang, X., & Wang, Y. (2021). Cognitive legitimacy and perceived benefits in the adoption of innovative products. *Journal of Business Research*, *139*, 123–134. DOI: 10.1016/j.jbusres.2021.09.012

Li, Y., & Shan, B. (2025). Exploring the role of health consciousness and environmental awareness in purchase intentions for green-packaged organic foods: An extended TPB model. *Frontiers in Nutrition*, *12*, 1528016. Advance online publication. DOI: 10.3389/fnut.2025.1528016

Lopes, J. M., Gomes, S., Suchek, N., & Nogueira, S. (2024). The hidden reasons behind generation Z's green choices. *Discover Sustainability*, *5*(1), 1–17. DOI: 10.1007/s43621-024-00764-8

Lovell, H., & Powells, G. (2020). Smart grid knowledges and the state. *Area*, *52*(3), 583–590. DOI: 10.1111/area.12613

Lu, F., & Sohail, M. T. (2022). Exploring the effects of natural capital depletion and natural disasters on happiness and human wellbeing: A study in China. *Frontiers in Psychology*, *13*, 870623. DOI: 10.3389/fpsyg.2022.870623

MacDonald, T. J., Allen, D. W. E., & Potts, J. (2016). Blockchains and the boundaries of self-organized economies: Predictions for the future of banking. *New Economic Windows*, 279–296. DOI: 10.1007/978-3-319-42448-4_14

Madan, V., & Kour, M. (2023). Mobile Payment Usage: Systematic Literature Review. Emerging Trends and Innovations in Industries of the Developing World, 89-93.

Madan, V., & Kour, M. (2024, March). Fintech and Mobile Payments in Transition: An Analysis of Adoption Challenges. In *2024 IEEE International Conference on Interdisciplinary Approaches in Technology and Management for Social Innovation (IATMSI)* (Vol. 2, pp. 1-6). IEEE. DOI: 10.1109/IATMSI60426.2024.10503040

Mahoney, J. T. (1992). The choice of organizational form: Vertical financial ownership versus other methods of vertical integration. *Strategic Management Journal*, *13*(8), 559–584. DOI: 10.1002/smj.4250130802

Malaysian Investment Development Authority (MIDA). (2020). Food Industry in Malaysia. *Food Industries*, *13*, •••. http://www.mida.gov.my/home/administrator/system_files/modules/photo/uploads/20180903103354_Food Industry 2018_V4.pdf

Maloney, E. K., Lapinski, M. K., & Neuberger, L. (2013). Predicting Land Use Voting Behaviour: Expanding our Understanding of the Influence of Attitudes and Social Norms. *Journal of Applied Social Psychology, 43*(12), 2377–2390. DOI: 10.1111/jasp.12186

Masih, J., Singh, H., & Masih, C. (2025). Post-pandemic organic food trends: Sustainable eating explored through social media analysis. *Academy of Marketing Studies Journal, 29*(1), 1–14.

Mehdi, S. M., Rūtelionė, A., & Bhutto, M. Y. (2024). The Role of Environmental Values, Environmental Self-Identity, and Attitude in Generation Z's Purchase Intentions for Organic Food. *Environmental Research, Engineering and Management, 80*(2), 75–87. DOI: 10.5755/j01.erem.80.2.36649

Mfelam, J. R., Nasser, O. A., & Kadouamai, S. (2023). Coûts induits à la pratique de la finance verte dans les banques. *Revista del Instituto Internacional de Costos*, (22), 72–91.

Moilanen, J. H. (2015). The Wisdom of Tacit Knowing-in-Action and Mission Command. *Adult Learning, 26*(3), 101–108. DOI: 10.1177/1045159515583258

Mollick, E. (2014). The dynamics of crowdfunding: An exploratory study. *Journal of Business Venturing, 29*(1), 1–16. DOI: 10.1016/j.jbusvent.2013.06.005

Molloy, L., & Ronnie, L. (2021). Mindset shifts for the Fourth Industrial Revolution: Insights from the life insurance sector. *SA Journal of Human Resource Management, 19*, 13. DOI: 10.4102/sajhrm.v19i0.1543

Moran, P., & Ghoshal, S. (1996). Theories of economic organization: The case for realism and balance. *Academy of Management Review, 21*(1), 58–72.

Morinez, J., Smith, A., & Lee, K. (2007). Purchase intention and consumer behaviour. *JMR, Journal of Marketing Research, 44*(3), 567–579.

Morris, J., Morris, W., & Bowen, R. (2022). Implications of the digital divide on rural SME resilience. *Journal of Rural Studies*, *89*, 369–377. DOI: 10.1016/j.jrurstud.2022.01.005

Morrison, D. G. (1979). Purchase intentions and purchase behaviour. *Journal of Marketing*, *43*(2), 65–74. DOI: 10.1177/002224297904300207

Nakamoto, S. (2008). Bitcoin: A peer-to-peer electronic cash system.

Nethra, H. M., & Tamilmathi, D. (2025). A study on consumers' attitude towards purchase decision of organic food products with reference to Bengaluru City. *South Eastern European Journal of Public Health*, *XXVII*, 215–224. DOI: 10.70135/seejph.vi.5163

Nguyen, H., Nguyen, N., Nguyen, B., Lobo, A., & Vu, P. (2019). Organic Food Purchases in an Emerging Market: The Influence of Consumers' Personal Factors and Green Marketing Practices of Food Stores. *International Journal of Environmental Research and Public Health*, *16*(6), 1037–1053. DOI: 10.3390/ijerph16061037

Nguyen, P. M., & Vo, N. D. (2023). Exploring organic food purchase behaviours of gen z: An application of TPB and MOA model in a transition country. *Foundations of Management*, *15*(1), 35–50. DOI: 10.2478/fman-2023-0003

Nguyen, T. M., Park, J. H., & Choi, W. L. (2021). Factors Influencing Consumer Purchase Intention toward Organic Food Products: An Empirical Study in Vietnam Market. *Journal of Channel and Retailing*, *26*(1), 127–147. DOI: 10.17657/jcr.2021.01.31.6

Nittin, R. (2015). The impact of marketing strategies on purchase intention. *International Journal of Marketing Studies*, *7*(4), 45–58.

Nonaka, I., & Takeuchi, H. (1995). *The knowledge-creating company: How Japanese companies create the dynamics of innovation*. Oxford University Press. DOI: 10.1093/oso/9780195092691.001.0001

Noor, M. M., Hashim, N., & Jamin, R. M. (2020). Implications of ICT for development on enhancing rural entrepreneur program (rep) at telecentres in Malaysia. *International Journal of Business and Society*, *21*(2), 629–642. DOI: 10.33736/ijbs.3275.2020

Nur, M., Siddik, A., Sun, G., Yanjuan, C., & Kabiraj, S. (2014). Financial Inclusion through Mobile Banking: A Case of Bangladesh. *Journal of Applied Finance & Banking*, *4*(6), 1792–6599. www.btrc.gov.bd

OECD. (2017). *Investing in Climate, Investing in Growth.* OECD Publishing.

Onea, I. A. (2021). Framework for assessing innovation capacity and business efficiency in Romanian SMEs. *Proceedings of the International Conference on Business Excellence*, 15(1), 1083–1095. DOI: 10.2478/picbe-2021-0102

Ouma, S. A., Odongo, T. M., & Were, M. (2017). Mobile financial services and financial inclusion: Is it a boon for savings mobilization?. *Review of development finance*, *7*(1), 29-35.

Ouma, S. A., Odongo, T. M., & Were, M. (2017). Mobile financial services and financial inclusion: Is it a boon for savings mobilization? *Review of Development Finance*, *7*(1), 29–35. DOI: 10.1016/j.rdf.2017.01.001

Ozili, P. K. (2024). Digital Innovations for Increasing Financial Inclusion: CBDC, Cryptocurrency, Embedded finance, Artificial Intelligence, WaaS, Fintech, Bigtech, and DeFi. In *Impact of Artificial Intelligence on Society* (pp. 174-184). Chapman and Hall/CRC.

Ozili, P. K. (2020). Theories of financial inclusion. In *Uncertainty and challenges in contemporary economic behaviour* (pp. 89–115). Emerald Publishing Limited. DOI: 10.1108/978-1-80043-095-220201008

Pal, A., De', R., & Herath, T. (2020). The Role of Mobile Payment Technology in Sustainable and Human-Centric Development: Evidence from the Post-Demonetization Period in India. *Information Systems Frontiers*, *22*(3), 607–631. DOI: 10.1007/s10796-020-09982-7

Pang, S. M., Tan, B. C., & Lau, T. C. (2021). Antecedents of Consumers' Purchase Intention towards Organic Food: Integration of Theory of Planned Behaviour and Protection Motivation Theory. *Sustainability (Basel), 13*(9), 5218–5233. DOI: 10.3390/su13095218

Park, H. S. (2000). Relationships among attitudes and subjective norms: Testing the theory of reasoned action across cultures. *Communication Studies, 51*(2), 162–175. DOI: 10.1080/10510970009388516

Parra Moyano, J., & Ross, O. (2017). KYC Optimization Using Distributed Ledger Technology. *Business & Information Systems Engineering, 59*(6), 411–423. DOI: 10.1007/s12599-017-0504-2

Patel, H. R., Sharma, M., & Purohit, R. (2021). Factors Influencing Millennials' Purchase Intention of Organic Food. *International Journal of Future Generation Communication and Networking, 14*(1), 2032–2046.

Patel, H. R., Sharma, M., & Purohit, R. (2022). Role of Organic Certification and Trust in Organic Food Buying Intention: Attitude as a Mediator. *Ramanujan International Journal of Business and Research, 7*(2), 46–55. DOI: 10.51245/rijbr.v7i2.2022.324

Peters, G. W., & Panayi, E. (2016). Understanding modern banking ledgers through blockchain technologies: Future of transaction processing and smart contracts on the internet of money. *New Economic Windows*, 239–278. DOI: 10.1007/978-3-319-42448-4_13

Pew Research Centre. (2019). *Defining generations: Where Millennials end, and Generation Z begins.* https://www.pewresearch.org/short-reads/2019/01/17/where-millennials-end-and-generation-z-begins/

Plihon, D., & Rigot, S. (2022). Les intermédiaires financiers publics face au changement climatique. *Revue Économique (Paris), 73*(2), 243–266. DOI: 10.3917/reco.732.0243

Podsakoff, P. M., MacKenzie, S. B., Lee, J. Y., & Podsakoff, N. P. (2003). Common method biases in behavioral research: A critical review of the literature and recommended remedies. *The Journal of Applied Psychology, 88*(5), 879–903. DOI: 10.1037/0021-9010.88.5.879

Polanyi, M. (1966). *The Tacit Dimension*. Doubleday and Company.

Poovithira, P. (2024). Factors influencing intention of buying organic food products among generation Z in Malaysia. Master's thesis, University Utara Malaysia.

Prasetyo, P. E., & Setyadharma, A. (2022). Digitalization Technology for Sustainable Rural Entrepreneurship and Inequality. *Journal of Human Resource and Sustainability Studies*, *10*(03), 464–484. DOI: 10.4236/jhrss.2022.103028

Precedence Research. (2023). *Organic Food Market* (By Product: Fruits and vegetables, Dairy products, Meat, fish and poultry, Frozen foods, Others; By Distribution Channel: Online, Offline) - Global Industry Analysis, Size, Share, Growth, Trends, Regional Outlook, and Forecast 2023-2032. https://www.precedenceresearch.com/organic-food-market

Putritama, A. (2019). The Mobile Payment Fintech Continuance Usage Intention in Indonesia. *Journal of Economics*, *15*(2), 243–258. DOI: 10.21831/economia.v15i2.26403

Pyöriä, P., Ojala, S., Saari, T., & Järvinen, K. (2017). The Millennial Generation: A New Breed of Labour? *SAGE Open*, *7*(1), 1–14. DOI: 10.1177/2158244017697158

Radziwill, N. (2018). Blockchain Revolution: How the Technology Behind Bitcoin is Changing Money, Business, and the World. *The Quality Management Journal*, *25*(1), 64–65. DOI: 10.1080/10686967.2018.1404373

Rai, S., & Jambhulkar, S. (2018). An analytical study of green business practices in india with specific reference to selected indian companies. *International Journal of Management and Social Sciences*, *6*(09), 1–15.

Raj, B. (2020). *Role of FinTech in Accelerating Financial Inclusion in India Role of FinTech in Accelerating Financial Inclusion in India Paper presented at the 3 rd International Conference on Economics and Finance organised by the Nepal Rastra Bank at Kathmandu, Nepal. February.*

Reeves, M., & Deimler, M. (2011). Adaptability: The new competitive advantage. *Harvard Business Review*, *89*(7–8), 7. DOI: 10.1002/9781119204084.ch2

Rehman, S., Orij, R., & Khan, H. (2020). The search for alignment of board gender diversity, the adoption of environmental management systems, and the association with firm performance in Asian firms. *Corporate Social Responsibility and Environmental Management*, *27*(5), 2161–2175. DOI: 10.1002/csr.1955

Remie Mohd Johan, M., Azalanshah Md Syed, M., & Mohd Adnan, H. (2021). Mobile eateries SMEss: Occidentals & Malaysia chronicles. Journal of Tourism. *Hospitality & Culinary Arts*, *13*, 85–102.

Renub Research. (2025). *Malaysia Organic Food Market Outlook*. https://www.renub.com/malaysia-organic-food-market-p.php

Reserve Bank of India. (2024). Payment and settlement systems in India: Annual report.

Richardson, B. J. (2009). Keeping ethical investment ethical: Regulatory issues for investing for sustainability. *Journal of Business Ethics*, *87*(4), 555–572. DOI: 10.1007/s10551-008-9958-y

Robins, J. A. (1987). Organizational Economics : Notes on the Use of Transaction-Cost Theory in the Study of Organizations Author (s): James A. Robins Published by : Sage Publications, Inc. on behalf of the Johnson Graduate School of Management, Cornell University Stable. *Administrative Science Quarterly*, *32*(1), 68–86. DOI: 10.2307/2392743

Romero-Castro, N., López-Cabarcos, M. A., & Piñeiro-Chousa, J. (2023). Finance, technology, and values: A configurational approach to the analysis of rural entrepreneurship. *Technological Forecasting and Social Change*, *190*, 122444. Advance online publication. DOI: 10.1016/j.techfore.2023.122444

Rosen, R. H. (2000). *Global literacies: Lessons on business leadership and national cultures*. Simon and Schuster.

Roundy, P. T. (2020). The wisdom of ecosystems: A transactive memory theory of knowledge management in entrepreneurial ecosystems. *Knowledge and Process Management*, *27*(3), 234–247. DOI: 10.1002/kpm.1635

Ryszawska, B. (2016). Sustainability transition needs sustainable finance. *Copernican Journal of Finance & Accounting*, *5*(1), 185. DOI: 10.12775/CJFA.2016.011

Sachs, J. D., Schmidt-Traub, G., Kroll, C., Lafortune, G., Fuller, G., & Woelm, F. (2019). *Sustainable Development Report 2019*. Bertelsmann Stiftung and Sustainable Development Solutions Network.

Sadiku, M. N. O., Eze, K. G., Musa, S. M., & Perry, R. G. A, P. V., & View, P. (2018). Smart Contracts : A Primer Available online www.jsaer.com Journal of Scientific and Engineering Research, 2018, 5 (5): 538-541 Smart Contracts : A Primer. *Journal of Scientific and Engineering Research, 5*(June), 538–541. file:///C:/Users/USER/Downloads/JSAER2018-05-05-538-541.pdf

Sahay, R., von Allmen, U. E., Lahreche, A., Khera, P., Ogawa, S., Bazarbash, M., & Beaton, K. (2020). *The promise of fintech : financial inclusion in the post COVID-19 era* (Issue 20).

Saleki, R., Quoquab, F., & Mohammad, J. (2020). Factor affecting consumer's intention to purchase organic food: Empirical study from Malaysian context. *International Journal of Business Innovation and Research*, *23*(2), 183–204. DOI: 10.1504/IJBIR.2020.110096

Salim, M., Alam Khan, P., Abdul Jalil, N., Kaur Johl, S., Hasan Jafar, S., Irfan, F., & Khan, M. (2023). Fusion of Blockchain and Sustainable Development Goals: A Bibliometric Analysis for Future Trends. *KnE Social Sciences*, *2023*, 633–654. DOI: 10.18502/kss.v8i20.14629

Samuelson, P. A. (1954). The pure theory of public expenditure. *The Review of Economics and Statistics*, *36*(4), 387–389. DOI: 10.2307/1925895

Santos, F. M., & Eisenhardt, K. M. (2005). Organizational boundaries and theories of organization. *Organization Science*, *16*(5), 491–508. DOI: 10.1287/orsc.1050.0152

Sapovadia, V. (2018). Financial Inclusion, Digital Currency, and Mobile Technology. In *Handbook of Blockchain, Digital Finance, and Inclusion* (1st ed., Vol. 2). Elsevier Inc. DOI: 10.1016/B978-0-12-812282-2.00014-0

Sarstedt, M., Bengart, P., Shaltoni, A. M., & Lehmann, S. (2017). The use of sampling methods in advertising research: A gap between theory and practice. *International Journal of Advertising*, *37*(4), 1–14.

Schatsky, D., & Muraskin, C. (2015). Beyond bitcoin : Blockchain is coming to disrupt your industry. *Deloitte University Press*, 1–27.

Scholtens, B. (2017). Finance as a Driver of Corporate Social Responsibility. *Journal of Business Ethics*, *68*(1), 19–33. DOI: 10.1007/s10551-006-9037-1

Scranton, P., & Chandler, A. D. (1991). Scale and Scope: The Dynamics of Industrial Capitalism. *Technology and Culture*, *32*(4), 1102. DOI: 10.2307/3106164

Sekaran, U., & Bougie, R. (2013). *Research Methods for Business: A Skill-Building Approach* (6th ed.). Wiley.

Shadrick, S. B., & Lussier, J. W. (2010). Training Complex Cognitive Skills: A Theme-Based Approach to the Development of Battlefield Skills. In Development of Professional Expertise (pp. 286–311). Cambridge University Press. DOI: 10.1017/CBO9780511609817.016

Shahab, A., Shihua, Q., Rashid, A., Hasan, F. U., & Sohail, M. T. (2016). Evaluation of water quality for drinking and agricultural suitability in the lower indus plain in sindh province. Pakistan. *Polish Journal of Environmental Studies*, *25*(6), 2563–2574. DOI: 10.15244/pjoes/63777

Shahab, S., & Allam, Z. (2020). Reducing transaction costs of tradable permit schemes using Blockchain smart contracts. *Growth and Change*, *51*(1), 302–308. DOI: 10.1111/grow.12342

Shahira, N. (2023, May 8). Eksport produk halal Malaysia dijangka meningkat tahun ini – HDC. Buletin TV3. https://www.buletintv3.my/detik-niaga/eksport-produk-halal-malaysia-dijangka-meningkat-tahun-ini-hdc/

Shahriari, E., Torres, I. M., Zúñiga, M. A., & Yarlou, P. M. (2019). Values Driving Organic Food Purchase Intention: A Comparative Analysis between a Developing Eastern Country (Iran) and a Developed Western Country (US). *Journal of International Consumer Marketing*, *31*(4), 317–329. DOI: 10.1080/08961530.2018.1561345

Shelanski, H. A., & Klein, P. G. (1995). Empirical research in TCE: A review and assessment. *Journal of Law Economics and Organization*, *11*(2), 335–361. DOI: 10.1093/oxfordjournals.jleo.a036875

Shukla, S., Bisht, K., Tiwari, K., & Bashir, S. (2023). Comparative Study of the Global Data Economy. In *Data Economy in the Digital Age* (pp. 63–86). Springer Nature Singapore. DOI: 10.1007/978-981-99-7677-5_4

Singh, P., Verma, M., & Singh, R. (2024). Studies on Impact and Opinion of Organic Food Products of Human Life during [European Journal of Nutrition & Food Safety]. *COVID*, •••, 19.

Sinha, M., Majra, H., Hutchins, J., & Saxena, R. (2019). Mobile payments in India: The privacy factor. *International Journal of Bank Marketing*, *37*(1), 192–209. DOI: 10.1108/IJBM-05-2017-0099

Sohail, M. T., Xiuyuan, Y., Usman, A., Majeed, M. T., & Ullah, S. (2021). Renewable energy and non-renewable energy consumption: Assessing the asymmetric role of monetary policy uncertainty in energy consumption. *Environmental Science and Pollution Research International*, *28*(24), 31575–31584. DOI: 10.1007/s11356-021-12867-0

Somasundram, C., Razali, Z., & Santhirasegaram, V. (2016). A Review on Organic Food Production in Malaysia. *Horticulturae*, *2*(12), 1–5. DOI: 10.3390/horticulturae2030012

Sparkes, R. (2002). *Socially Responsible Investment: A Global Revolution*. John Wiley.

Stahl, N. A., & King, J. R. (2020). Understanding and Using Trustworthiness in Qualitative Research. *Journal of Developmental Education*, *44*(1), 26–28. DOI: 10.4135/9781483329574

Statista (2023). *Frequency of purchasing organic food among consumers in Malaysia as of September 2023*. https://www.statista.com/statistics/1010541/frequency-buying-organic-food-malaysia/

Stefanidis, A., Ioannidis, A., & Mourdoukoutas, P. (2007). Entrepreneurial networks in highly globalised industries: The case of the Greek shipping industry. *International Journal of Networking and Virtual Organisations*, *4*(2), 189–200. DOI: 10.1504/IJNVO.2007.013543

Stiglitz, J. E. (1999). Knowledge as a global public good. *Global public goods: International cooperation in the 21st century, 308*, 308-325.

Su, C.-H., Tsai, C.-H., Chen, M.-H., & Lv, W. Q. (2019). U.S. Sustainable Food Market Generation Z Consumer Segments. *Sustainability (Basel)*, *11*(13), 3607–3620. DOI: 10.3390/su11133607

Tang, W., & Zhu, J. (2020). Informality and rural industry: Rethinking the impacts of E-Commerce on rural development in China. *Journal of Rural Studies*, *75*, 20–29. DOI: 10.1016/j.jrurstud.2020.02.010

Tehseen, S., Ramayah, T., & Sajilan, S. (2017). Testing and Controlling for Common Method Variance: A Review of Available Methods. *Journal of Management Sciences*, *4*(2), 142–168. DOI: 10.20547/jms.2014.1704202

Teixeira, S. F., Barbosa, B., Cunha, H., & Oliveira, Z. (2022). Exploring the antecedents of organic food purchase intention: An extension of the theory of planned behaviour. *Sustainability (Basel)*, *14*(1), 242–254. DOI: 10.3390/su14010242

The Living Centre. (2025). *Organic Farming in Malaysia: A Growing Trend for Sustainable Living*. https://thelivingcentre.my/organic-farming-in-malaysia-a-growing-trend-for-sustainable-living/

Thomas, B. (2023). Exploring the facilitators of e-commerce adoption among rural entrepreneurs in Sabah. *Journal of BIMP-EAGA Regional Development*, *9*(1), 1–11. DOI: 10.51200/jbimpeagard.v9i1.4365

Tomaszewski, L. E., Zarestky, J., & Gonzalez, E. (2020). Planning Qualitative Research: Design and Decision Making for New Researchers. *International Journal of Qualitative Methods*, *19*, 1609406920967174. Advance online publication. DOI: 10.1177/1609406920967174

Trautman, L. J. (2016). Is Disruptive BcT the Future of Financial Services? *The Consumer Finance Law Quarterly Report, forthcomin*, 232–242. https://papers.ssrn.com/abstract=2786186

Treiblmaier, H. (2018). The impact of the blockchain on the supply chain: A theory-based research framework and a call for action. *Supply Chain Management*, *23*(6), 545–559. DOI: 10.1108/SCM-01-2018-0029

Tuitjer, G., & Küpper, P. (2022). Local and vertical networking as drivers of innovativeness and growth in rural businesses. *Journal of Rural Studies*, *95*, 412–422. DOI: 10.1016/j.jrurstud.2022.09.014

Ullah, H., Wang, Z., Mohsin, M., Jiang, W., & Abbas, H. (2022). Multidimensional perspective of green financial innovation between green intellectual capital on sustainable business: The case of Pakistan. *Environmental Science and Pollution Research International*, *29*(4), 5552–5568. DOI: 10.1007/s11356-021-15919-7

United Nations. (2015). "Transforming Our World: The 2030 Agenda for Sustainable Development." Assemblée Générale des Nations Unies. https://sdgs.un.org/2030agenda

Uyar, A., Kilic, M., Koseoglu, M. A., Kuzey, C., & Karaman, A. S. (2020). The link among board characteristics, corporate social responsibility performance, and financial performance: Evidence from the hospitality and tourism industry. *Tourism Management Perspectives*, *35*, 100714. DOI: 10.1016/j.tmp.2020.100714

Varian, H. R. (1992). *Microeconomic Analysis* (3rd ed.). Norton.

Vasudeva, G., & Teegen, H. (2011). Why do private firms invest in public goods? In *Cross-Sector Leadership for the Green Economy: Integrating Research and Practice on Sustainable Enterprise* (pp. 263–276). Palgrave Macmillan US. DOI: 10.1057/9781137015891_14

Vatiero, M. (2018). Smart Contracts and Transaction Costs. SSRN *Electronic Journal*. DOI: 10.2139/ssrn.3259958

Verhoeven, D., Musial, K., Hambusch, G., Ghannam, S., & Shashnov, M. (2022). Net effects: Examining strategies for women's inclusion and influence in ASX200 company boards. *Applied Network Science*, *7*(1), 48. DOI: 10.1007/s41109-022-00490-y

Waddock, S., & Graves, S. B. (1998). The corporate social performance–financial performance link. *Strategic Management Journal*, *18*(4), 303–319. DOI: 10.1002/(SICI)1097-0266(199704)18:4<303::AID-SMJ869>3.0.CO;2-G

Wahba, H., & Elsayed, K. (2015). The mediating effect of financial performance on the relationship between social responsibility and ownership structure. *Future Business Journal*, *1*(1-2), 1–12. DOI: 10.1016/j.fbj.2015.02.001

Wang, C., Deng, X., Álvarez-Otero, S., Sial, M. S., Comite, U., Cherian, J., & Oláh, J. (2021). Impact of women and independent directors on corporate social responsibility and financial performance: Empirical evidence from an emerging economy. *Sustainability (Basel)*, *13*(11), 6053. DOI: 10.3390/su13116053

Wang, Y., & Zhi, Q. (2016). The Role of Green Finance in Environmental Protection: Two Aspects of Market Mechanism and Policies. *Energy Procedia*, *104*, 311–316. DOI: 10.1016/j.egypro.2016.12.053

Wang, Z., & Sarkis, J. (2017). Corporate social responsibility governance, outcomes, and financial performance. *Journal of Cleaner Production*, *162*, 1607–1616. DOI: 10.1016/j.jclepro.2017.06.142

Wei, H., Zhang, Y., Xiu, P., Zhang, H., & Zhu, S. (2022). Index-based analysis of industrial structure and environmental efficiency based on sewage discharge assessment in China. *Alexandria Engineering Journal*, *61*(1), 493–500. DOI: 10.1016/j.aej.2021.06.006

Wen, C., Akram, R., Irfan, M., Iqbal, W., Dagar, V., Acevedo-Duqued, Á., & Saydaliev, H. B. (2022). The Asymmetric Nexus between Air Pollution and COVID-19: Evidence from a Non-linear Autoregressive Distributed Lag Model. *Environmental Research*, *209*, 112848. DOI: 10.1016/j.envres.2022.112848

Williamson, O. E. (1985). *The Economic Institutions of Capitalism: Firms, Markets, Relational Contracting*. https://papers.ssrn.com/abstract=1496720

Williamson, O. E. (1971). The vertical integration of production: Market failure considerations. *The American Economic Review*, *61*(2), 112–123.

Williamson, O. E. (1973). Markets and hierarchies, some elementary considerations. *The American Economic Review*, *63*(2), 316–325.

Williamson, O. E. (2002). The theory of the firm as governance structure: From choice to contract. *The Journal of Economic Perspectives*, *16*(3), 171–195. DOI: 10.1257/089533002760278776

Williamson, O.E. (1979). The Journal of Law and Economics-TCE. *The Journal of Law & Economics*, *22*(2), 233–261. DOI: 10.1086/466942

Williams, R. J. (2003). Women on corporate boards of directors and their influence on corporate philanthropy. *Journal of Business Ethics*, *42*(1), 1–10. DOI: 10.1023/A:1021626024014

Wolfert, S., van Wassenaer, L., van der Burg, S., Ryan, M., Klerkx, L., Rijswijk, K., ... & Beers, G. (2021). Navigating the Twilight Zone: Pathways towards digital transformation of food systems. Wageningen University & Research.

World Bank. (2023). Global Findex Database 2023: Financial inclusion and digital payments.

World Economic Forum. (2024). The future of financial services in emerging markets.

Wu, J. (2024). Role of green finance and carbon accounting in achieving sustainability. *Humanities & Social Sciences Communications*, *11*(1), 1–7. DOI: 10.1057/s41599-023-02492-2

Wuytens, N., Schepers, J., Vandekerkhof, P., & Voordeckers, W. (2022). Entrepreneurs Can Know More Than They Can Tell: Conceptualizing and Measuring Tacit Entrepreneurial Knowledge. *Frontiers in Psychology*, *13*, 892223. Advance online publication. DOI: 10.3389/fpsyg.2022.892223 PMID: 35747676

Xiao, A., Yang, S., & Iqbal, Q. (2018). Factors Affecting Purchase Intentions in Generation Y: An Empirical Evidence from Fast Food Industry in Malaysia. *Administrative Sciences*, *9*(4), 1–16. DOI: 10.3390/admsci9010004

Xie, J., Nozawa, W., & Managi, S. (2020). The role of women on boards in corporate environmental strategy and financial performance: A global outlook. *Corporate Social Responsibility and Environmental Management*, *27*(5), 2044–2059. DOI: 10.1002/csr.1945

Xu, J., Cui, Z., Wang, T., Wang, J., Yu, Z., & Li, C. (2023). Influence of Agricultural Technology Extension and Social Networks on Chinese Farmers' Adoption of Conservation Tillage Technology. *Land (Basel)*, *12*(6), 1215. DOI: 10.3390/land12061215

Yadav, R., & Pathak, G. S. (2016). Intention to purchase organic food among young consumers: Evidence from a developing nation. *Appetite*, *96*, 122–128. DOI: 10.1016/j.appet.2015.09.017

Yahaya, T. A. H., Kamarudin, D., & Hassan, N. S. M. (2019). *Marketing Strategy, Technological Innovation and Inventory Management Towards Malaysia's Food Industry Performance*. Cognitive-Crcs., DOI: 10.15405/epsbs.2019.08.53

Yale, T., Journal, L., & Williamson, O. (1984). Articles Corporate Governance. *Management*, *93*(7), 1197–1230.

Yao Lartey, P., Shi, J., Jaladi Santosh, R., Owusu Afriyie, S., Akolgo Gumah, I., Husein, M., & Binta Maci Bah, F. (2022). *Importance of Organizational Tacit Knowledge*. Barriers to Knowledge Sharing. In Recent Advances in Knowledge Management. IntechOpen., DOI: 10.5772/intechopen.101997

Yasara, A., Farooqa, T., Tabindaa, A. B., Sohailb, M. T., Mahfooza, Y., & Malika, A. (2019). Macrophytes as potential indicator of heavy metals in river water. *Desalination and Water Treatment*, *142*, 272–278. DOI: 10.5004/dwt.2019.23433

Yasin, N. H. M., Che Shalifullizam, N. I. F., & Tuan, S. A. (2025). T. N. Z., Yusoff, M. N. D., Zulkefli, N. S., Raja Omar, R. N., Rasdi. M. A., L. (2025). Consumer Purchase Intention of Organic Food: A Cross-Sectional Study Among Young Adults. *AIP Conference Proceedings*, *3271*, 050014. DOI: 10.1063/5.0260060

Yeoh, P. (2017). Regulatory issues in BcT. *Journal of Financial Regulation and Compliance*, *25*(2), 196–208. DOI: 10.1108/JFRC-08-2016-0068

Yermack, D. (2017). Corporate governance and blockchains. *Review of Finance*, *21*(1), 7–31. DOI: 10.1093/rof/rfw074

Yew, J. L. K. (2021). Family Firms, Enterprise Development and Tacit Knowledge Transformation: Small and Medium Enterprises (SMEs) Innovation in Malaysia. *Global Business Review*, 09721509211047648. Advance online publication. DOI: 10.1177/09721509211047648

Zahan, I., & Chuanmin, S. (2021). Towards a green economic policy framework in China: Role of green investment in fostering clean energy consumption and environmental sustainability. *Environmental Science and Pollution Research International*, *28*(32), 43618–43628. DOI: 10.1007/s11356-021-13041-2

Zahid, M., Rahman, H. U., Ali, W., Khan, M., Alharthi, M., Qureshi, M. I., & Jan, A. (2020). Boardroom gender diversity: Implications for corporate sustainability disclosures in Malaysia. *Journal of Cleaner Production*, *244*, 118683. DOI: 10.1016/j.jclepro.2019.118683

Zahra, S. A. (2021). The Resource-Based View, Resourcefulness, and Resource Management in Startup Firms: A Proposed Research Agenda. *Journal of Management*, *47*(7), 1841–1860. DOI: 10.1177/01492063211018505

Zainudin, F. (2018, April 18). Hidangan Malaysia tambat selera Jepun. Retrieved from https://www.bharian.com.my/authors/oleh-faiza-zainudin

Zakari, A., & Khan, I. (2022). The Introduction of Green Finance: A Curse or a Benefit to Environmental Sustainability? *Energy RESEARCH LETTERS*, *3*(3). Advance online publication. DOI: 10.46557/001c.29977

Zayed, M. F., Gaber, H. R., & el Essawi, N. (2022). Examining the Factors that Affect Consumers' Purchase Intention of Organic Food Products in a Developing Country. *Sustainability (Basel)*, *14*(10), 5868–5883. DOI: 10.3390/su14105868

Zhang, M., & Gao, L. (2022). Systems Dynanics-based Study on Contract and Tacit Knowledge Transfer. *Fuza Xitong Yu Fuzaxing Kexue*, *19*(1), 96–103. DOI: 10.13306/j.1672-3813.2022.01.013

Zhou, L., Huang, M., & Li, J. (2023). Psychological factors influencing purchase intention. *Journal of Business Research*, *56*(1), 78–89.

Zuraida, Z., Houqe, M. N., & Van Zijl, T. (2018). Value relevance of environmental, social and governance disclosure. In *Research Handbook of Finance and Sustainability* (pp. 458–483). Edward Elgar Publishing. DOI: 10.4337/9781786432636.00033

Related References

To continue our tradition of advancing information science and technology research, we have compiled a list of recommended IGI Global readings. These references will provide additional information and guidance to further enrich your knowledge and assist you with your own research and future publications.

Abdul Razak, R., & Mansor, N. A. (2021). Instagram Influencers in Social Media-Induced Tourism: Rethinking Tourist Trust Towards Tourism Destination. In M. Dinis, L. Bonixe, S. Lamy, & Z. Breda (Eds.), *Impact of New Media in Tourism* (pp. 135-144). IGI Global. https://doi.org/10.4018/978-1-7998-7095-1.ch009

Abir, T., & Khan, M. Y. (2022). Importance of ICT Advancement and Culture of Adaptation in the Tourism and Hospitality Industry for Developing Countries. In Ramos, C., Quinteiro, S., & Gonçalves, A. (Eds.), *ICT as Innovator Between Tourism and Culture* (pp. 30–41). IGI Global. https://doi.org/10.4018/978-1-7998-8165-0.ch003

Abir, T., & Khan, M. Y. (2022). Importance of ICT Advancement and Culture of Adaptation in the Tourism and Hospitality Industry for Developing Countries. In Ramos, C., Quinteiro, S., & Gonçalves, A. (Eds.), *ICT as Innovator Between Tourism and Culture* (pp. 30–41). IGI Global. https://doi.org/10.4018/978-1-7998-8165-0.ch003

Abtahi, M. S., Behboudi, L., & Hasanabad, H. M. (2017). Factors Affecting Internet Advertising Adoption in Ad Agencies. *International Journal of Innovation in the Digital Economy*, *8*(4), 18–29. DOI: 10.4018/IJIDE.2017100102

Afenyo-Agbe, E., & Mensah, I. (2022). Principles, Benefits, and Barriers to Community-Based Tourism: Implications for Management. In Mensah, I., & Afenyo-Agbe, E. (Eds.), *Prospects and Challenges of Community-Based Tourism and Changing Demographics* (pp. 1–29). IGI Global. DOI: 10.4018/978-1-7998-7335-8.ch001

Agbo, V. M. (2022). Distributive Justice Issues in Community-Based Tourism. In Mensah, I., & Afenyo-Agbe, E. (Eds.), *Prospects and Challenges of Community-Based Tourism and Changing Demographics* (pp. 107–129). IGI Global. https://doi.org/10.4018/978-1-7998-7335-8.ch005

Agrawal, S. (2017). The Impact of Emerging Technologies and Social Media on Different Business(es): Marketing and Management. In Rishi, O., & Sharma, A. (Eds.), *Maximizing Business Performance and Efficiency Through Intelligent Systems* (pp. 37–49). Hershey, PA: IGI Global. DOI: 10.4018/978-1-5225-2234-8.ch002

Ahmad, A., & Johari, S. (2022). Georgetown as a Gastronomy Tourism Destination: Visitor Awareness Towards Revisit Intention of Nasi Kandar Restaurant. In Valeri, M. (Ed.), *New Governance and Management in Touristic Destinations* (pp. 71–83). IGI Global. https://doi.org/10.4018/978-1-6684-3889-3.ch005

Alkhatib, G., & Bayouq, S. T. (2021). A TAM-Based Model of Technological Factors Affecting Use of E-Tourism. *International Journal of Tourism and Hospitality Management in the Digital Age*, *5*(2), 50–67. https://doi.org/10.4018/IJTHMDA.20210701.oa1

Altinay Ozdemir, M. (2021). Virtual Reality (VR) and Augmented Reality (AR) Technologies for Accessibility and Marketing in the Tourism Industry. In C. Eusébio, L. Teixeira, & M. Carneiro (Eds.), *ICT Tools and Applications for Accessible Tourism* (pp. 277-301). IGI Global. https://doi.org/10.4018/978-1-7998-6428-8.ch013

Anantharaman, R. N., Rajeswari, K. S., Angusamy, A., & Kuppusamy, J. (2017). Role of Self-Efficacy and Collective Efficacy as Moderators of Occupational Stress Among Software Development Professionals. *International Journal of Human Capital and Information Technology Professionals*, *8*(2), 45–58. DOI: 10.4018/IJHCITP.2017040103

Aninze, F., El-Gohary, H., & Hussain, J. (2018). The Role of Microfinance to Empower Women: The Case of Developing Countries. *International Journal of Customer Relationship Marketing and Management*, *9*(1), 54–78. DOI: 10.4018/IJCRMM.2018010104

Antosova, G., Sabogal-Salamanca, M., & Krizova, E. (2021). Human Capital in Tourism: A Practical Model of Endogenous and Exogenous Territorial Tourism Planning in Bahía Solano, Colombia. In Costa, V., Moura, A., & Mira, M. (Eds.), *Handbook of Research on Human Capital and People Management in the Tourism Industry* (pp. 282–302). IGI Global. https://doi.org/10.4018/978-1-7998-4318-4.ch014

Arsenijević, O. M., Orčić, D., & Kastratović, E. (2017). Development of an Optimization Tool for Intangibles in SMEs: A Case Study from Serbia with a Pilot Research in the Prestige by Milka Company. In Vemić, M. (Ed.), *Optimal Management Strategies in Small and Medium Enterprises* (pp. 320–347). Hershey, PA: IGI Global. DOI: 10.4018/978-1-5225-1949-2.ch015

Aryanto, V. D., Wismantoro, Y., & Widyatmoko, K. (2018). Implementing Eco-Innovation by Utilizing the Internet to Enhance Firm's Marketing Performance: Study of Green Batik Small and Medium Enterprises in Indonesia. *International Journal of E-Business Research, 14*(1), 21–36. DOI: 10.4018/IJEBR.2018010102

Asero, V., & Billi, S. (2022). New Perspective of Networking in the DMO Model. In Valeri, M. (Ed.), *New Governance and Management in Touristic Destinations* (pp. 105–118). IGI Global. https://doi.org/10.4018/978-1-6684-3889-3.ch007

Atiku, S. O., & Fields, Z. (2017). Multicultural Orientations for 21st Century Global Leadership. In Baporikar, N. (Ed.), *Management Education for Global Leadership* (pp. 28–51). Hershey, PA: IGI Global. DOI: 10.4018/978-1-5225-1013-0.ch002

Atiku, S. O., & Fields, Z. (2018). Organisational Learning Dimensions and Talent Retention Strategies for the Service Industries. In Baporikar, N. (Ed.), *Global Practices in Knowledge Management for Societal and Organizational Development* (pp. 358–381). Hershey, PA: IGI Global. DOI: 10.4018/978-1-5225-3009-1.ch017

Atsa'am, D. D., & Kuset Bodur, E. (2021). Pattern Mining on How Organizational Tenure Affects the Psychological Capital of Employees Within the Hospitality and Tourism Industry: Linking Employees' Organizational Tenure With PsyCap. *International Journal of Tourism and Hospitality Management in the Digital Age, 5*(2), 17–28. https://doi.org/10.4018/IJTHMDA.2021070102

Ávila, L., & Teixeira, L. (2018). The Main Concepts Behind the Dematerialization of Business Processes. In M. Khosrow-Pour, D.B.A. (Ed.), *Encyclopedia of Information Science and Technology, Fourth Edition* (pp. 888-898). Hershey, PA: IGI Global. https://doi.org/DOI: 10.4018/978-1-5225-2255-3.ch076

Ayorekire, J., Mugizi, F., Obua, J., & Ampaire, G. (2022). Community-Based Tourism and Local People's Perceptions Towards Conservation: The Case of Queen Elizabeth Conservation Area, Uganda. In Mensah, I., & Afenyo-Agbe, E. (Eds.), *Prospects and Challenges of Community-Based Tourism and Changing Demographics* (pp. 56–82). IGI Global. https://doi.org/10.4018/978-1-7998-7335-8.ch003

Baleiro, R. (2022). Tourist Literature and the Architecture of Travel in Olga Tokarczuk and Patti Smith. In R. Baleiro & R. Pereira (Eds.), *Global Perspectives on Literary Tourism and Film-Induced Tourism* (pp. 202-216). IGI Global. https://doi.org/10.4018/978-1-7998-8262-6.ch011

Barat, S. (2021). Looking at the Future of Medical Tourism in Asia. *International Journal of Tourism and Hospitality Management in the Digital Age*, *5*(1), 19–33. https://doi.org/10.4018/IJTHMDA.2021010102

Barbosa, C. A., Magalhães, M., & Nunes, M. R. (2021). Travel Instagramability: A Way of Choosing a Destination? In M. Dinis, L. Bonixe, S. Lamy, & Z. Breda (Eds.), *Impact of New Media in Tourism* (pp. 173-190). IGI Global. https://doi.org/10.4018/978-1-7998-7095-1.ch011

Bari, M. W., & Khan, Q. (2021). Pakistan as a Destination of Religious Tourism. In E. Alaverdov & M. Bari (Eds.), *Global Development of Religious Tourism* (pp. 1-10). IGI Global. https://doi.org/10.4018/978-1-7998-5792-1.ch001

Bartens, Y., Chunpir, H. I., Schulte, F., & Voß, S. (2017). Business/IT Alignment in Two-Sided Markets: A COBIT 5 Analysis for Media Streaming Business Models. In De Haes, S., & Van Grembergen, W. (Eds.), *Strategic IT Governance and Alignment in Business Settings* (pp. 82–111). Hershey, PA: IGI Global. DOI: 10.4018/978-1-5225-0861-8.ch004

Bashayreh, A. M. (2018). Organizational Culture and Organizational Performance. In Lee, W., & Sabetzadeh, F. (Eds.), *Contemporary Knowledge and Systems Science* (pp. 50–69). Hershey, PA: IGI Global. DOI: 10.4018/978-1-5225-5655-8.ch003

Bechthold, L., Lude, M., & Prügl, R. (2021). Crisis Favors the Prepared Firm: How Organizational Ambidexterity Relates to Perceptions of Organizational Resilience. In Zehrer, A., Glowka, G., Schwaiger, K., & Ranacher-Lackner, V. (Eds.), *Resiliency Models and Addressing Future Risks for Family Firms in the Tourism Industry* (pp. 178–205). IGI Global. https://doi.org/10.4018/978-1-7998-7352-5.ch008

Bedford, D. A. (2018). Sustainable Knowledge Management Strategies: Aligning Business Capabilities and Knowledge Management Goals. In Baporikar, N. (Ed.), *Global Practices in Knowledge Management for Societal and Organizational Development* (pp. 46–73). Hershey, PA: IGI Global. DOI: 10.4018/978-1-5225-3009-1.ch003

Bekjanov, D., & Matyusupov, B. (2021). Influence of Innovative Processes in the Competitiveness of Tourist Destination. In Soares, J. (Ed.), *Innovation and Entrepreneurial Opportunities in Community Tourism* (pp. 243–263). IGI Global. https://doi.org/10.4018/978-1-7998-4855-4.ch014

Bharwani, S., & Musunuri, D. (2018). Reflection as a Process From Theory to Practice. In M. Khosrow-Pour, D.B.A. (Ed.), *Encyclopedia of Information Science and Technology, Fourth Edition* (pp. 1529-1539). Hershey, PA: IGI Global. DOI: 10.4018/978-1-5225-2255-3.ch132

Bhatt, G. D., Wang, Z., & Rodger, J. A. (2017). Information Systems Capabilities and Their Effects on Competitive Advantages: A Study of Chinese Companies. *Information Resources Management Journal, 30*(3), 41–57. DOI: 10.4018/IRMJ.2017070103

Bhushan, M., & Yadav, A. (2017). Concept of Cloud Computing in ESB. In Bhadoria, R., Chaudhari, N., Tomar, G., & Singh, S. (Eds.), *Exploring Enterprise Service Bus in the Service-Oriented Architecture Paradigm* (pp. 116–127). Hershey, PA: IGI Global. DOI: 10.4018/978-1-5225-2157-0.ch008

Bhushan, S. (2017). System Dynamics Base-Model of Humanitarian Supply Chain (HSCM) in Disaster Prone Eco-Communities of India: A Discussion on Simulation and Scenario Results. *International Journal of System Dynamics Applications, 6*(3), 20–37. DOI: 10.4018/IJSDA.2017070102

Binder, D., & Miller, J. W. (2021). A Generations' Perspective on Employer Branding in Tourism. In Costa, V., Moura, A., & Mira, M. (Eds.), *Handbook of Research on Human Capital and People Management in the Tourism Industry* (pp. 152–174). IGI Global. https://doi.org/10.4018/978-1-7998-4318-4.ch008

Birch Freeman, A. A., Mensah, I., & Antwi, K. B. (2022). Smiling vs. Frowning Faces: Community Participation for Sustainable Tourism in Ghanaian Communities. In Mensah, I., & Afenyo-Agbe, E. (Eds.), *Prospects and Challenges of Community-Based Tourism and Changing Demographics* (pp. 83–106). IGI Global. https://doi.org/10.4018/978-1-7998-7335-8.ch004

Biswas, A., & De, A. K. (2017). On Development of a Fuzzy Stochastic Programming Model with Its Application to Business Management. In Trivedi, S., Dey, S., Kumar, A., & Panda, T. (Eds.), *Handbook of Research on Advanced Data Mining Techniques and Applications for Business Intelligence* (pp. 353–378). Hershey, PA: IGI Global. DOI: 10.4018/978-1-5225-2031-3.ch021

Boragnio, A., & Faracce Macia, C. (2021). "Taking Care of Yourself at Home": Use of E-Commerce About Food and Care During the COVID-19 Pandemic in the City of Buenos Aires. In Korstanje, M. (Ed.), *Socio-Economic Effects and Recovery Efforts for the Rental Industry: Post-COVID-19 Strategies* (pp. 45–71). IGI Global. https://doi.org/10.4018/978-1-7998-7287-0.ch003

Borges, V. D. (2021). Happiness: The Basis for Public Policy in Tourism. In Perinotto, A., Mayer, V., & Soares, J. (Eds.), *Rebuilding and Restructuring the Tourism Industry: Infusion of Happiness and Quality of Life* (pp. 1–25). IGI Global. https://doi.org/10.4018/978-1-7998-7239-9.ch001

Bücker, J., & Ernste, K. (2018). Use of Brand Heroes in Strategic Reputation Management: The Case of Bacardi, Adidas, and Daimler. In Erdemir, A. (Ed.), *Reputation Management Techniques in Public Relations* (pp. 126–150). Hershey, PA: IGI Global. DOI: 10.4018/978-1-5225-3619-2.ch007

Buluk Eşitti, B. (2021). COVID-19 and Alternative Tourism: New Destinations and New Tourism Products. In Demir, M., Dalgıç, A., & Ergen, F. (Eds.), *Handbook of Research on the Impacts and Implications of COVID-19 on the Tourism Industry* (pp. 786–805). IGI Global. https://doi.org/10.4018/978-1-7998-8231-2.ch038

Bureš, V. (2018). Industry 4.0 From the Systems Engineering Perspective: Alternative Holistic Framework Development. In Brunet-Thornton, R., & Martinez, F. (Eds.), *Analyzing the Impacts of Industry 4.0 in Modern Business Environments* (pp. 199–223). Hershey, PA: IGI Global. DOI: 10.4018/978-1-5225-3468-6.ch011

Buzady, Z. (2017). Resolving the Magic Cube of Effective Case Teaching: Benchmarking Case Teaching Practices in Emerging Markets – Insights from the Central European University Business School, Hungary. In Latusek, D. (Ed.), *Case Studies as a Teaching Tool in Management Education* (pp. 79–103). Hershey, PA: IGI Global. DOI: 10.4018/978-1-5225-0770-3.ch005

Camillo, A. (2021). *Legal Matters, Risk Management, and Risk Prevention: From Forming a Business to Legal Representation*. IGI Global. DOI: 10.4018/978-1-7998-4342-9.ch004

Căpusneanu, S., & Topor, D. I. (2018). Business Ethics and Cost Management in SMEs: Theories of Business Ethics and Cost Management Ethos. In Oncioiu, I. (Ed.), *Ethics and Decision-Making for Sustainable Business Practices* (pp. 109–127). Hershey, PA: IGI Global. DOI: 10.4018/978-1-5225-3773-1.ch007

Chan, R. L., Mo, P. L., & Moon, K. K. (2018). Strategic and Tactical Measures in Managing Enterprise Risks: A Study of the Textile and Apparel Industry. In Strang, K., Korstanje, M., & Vajjhala, N. (Eds.), *Research, Practices, and Innovations in Global Risk and Contingency Management* (pp. 1–19). Hershey, PA: IGI Global. DOI: 10.4018/978-1-5225-4754-9.ch001

Charlier, S. D., Burke-Smalley, L. A., & Fisher, S. L. (2018). Undergraduate Programs in the U.S: A Contextual and Content-Based Analysis. In Mendy, J. (Ed.), *Teaching Human Resources and Organizational Behavior at the College Level* (pp. 26–57). Hershey, PA: IGI Global. DOI: 10.4018/978-1-5225-2820-3.ch002

Chumillas, J., Güell, M., & Quer, P. (2022). The Use of ICT in Tourist and Educational Literary Routes: The Role of the Guide. In Ramos, C., Quinteiro, S., & Gonçalves, A. (Eds.), *ICT as Innovator Between Tourism and Culture* (pp. 15–29). IGI Global. https://doi.org/10.4018/978-1-7998-8165-0.ch002

Dahlberg, T., Kivijärvi, H., & Saarinen, T. (2017). IT Investment Consistency and Other Factors Influencing the Success of IT Performance. In De Haes, S., & Van Grembergen, W. (Eds.), *Strategic IT Governance and Alignment in Business Settings* (pp. 176–208). Hershey, PA: IGI Global. DOI: 10.4018/978-1-5225-0861-8.ch007

Damnjanović, A. M. (2017). Knowledge Management Optimization through IT and E-Business Utilization: A Qualitative Study on Serbian SMEs. In Vemić, M. (Ed.), *Optimal Management Strategies in Small and Medium Enterprises* (pp. 249–267). Hershey, PA: IGI Global. DOI: 10.4018/978-1-5225-1949-2.ch012

Daneshpour, H. (2017). Integrating Sustainable Development into Project Portfolio Management through Application of Open Innovation. In Vemić, M. (Ed.), *Optimal Management Strategies in Small and Medium Enterprises* (pp. 370–387). Hershey, PA: IGI Global. DOI: 10.4018/978-1-5225-1949-2.ch017

Daniel, A. D., & Reis de Castro, V. (2018). Entrepreneurship Education: How to Measure the Impact on Nascent Entrepreneurs. In Carrizo Moreira, A., Guilherme Leitão Dantas, J., & Manuel Valente, F. (Eds.), *Nascent Entrepreneurship and Successful New Venture Creation* (pp. 85–110). Hershey, PA: IGI Global. DOI: 10.4018/978-1-5225-2936-1.ch004

David, R., Swami, B. N., & Tangirala, S. (2018). Ethics Impact on Knowledge Management in Organizational Development: A Case Study. In Baporikar, N. (Ed.), *Global Practices in Knowledge Management for Societal and Organizational Development* (pp. 19–45). Hershey, PA: IGI Global. DOI: 10.4018/978-1-5225-3009-1.ch002

De Uña-Álvarez, E., & Villarino-Pérez, M. (2022). Fostering Ecocultural Resources, Identity, and Tourism in Inland Territories (Galicia, NW Spain). In G. Fernandes (Ed.), *Challenges and New Opportunities for Tourism in Inland Territories: Ecocultural Resources and Sustainable Initiatives* (pp. 1-16). IGI Global. https://doi.org/10.4018/978-1-7998-7339-6.ch001

Delias, P., & Lakiotaki, K. (2018). Discovering Process Horizontal Boundaries to Facilitate Process Comprehension. *International Journal of Operations Research and Information Systems*, *9*(2), 1–31. DOI: 10.4018/IJORIS.2018040101

Denholm, J., & Lee-Davies, L. (2018). Success Factors for Games in Business and Project Management. In *Enhancing Education and Training Initiatives Through Serious Games* (pp. 34–68). Hershey, PA: IGI Global. DOI: 10.4018/978-1-5225-3689-5.ch002

Deshpande, M. (2017). Best Practices in Management Institutions for Global Leadership: Policy Aspects. In Baporikar, N. (Ed.), *Management Education for Global Leadership* (pp. 1–27). Hershey, PA: IGI Global. DOI: 10.4018/978-1-5225-1013-0.ch001

Deshpande, M. (2018). Policy Perspectives for SMEs Knowledge Management. In Baporikar, N. (Ed.), *Knowledge Integration Strategies for Entrepreneurship and Sustainability* (pp. 23–46). Hershey, PA: IGI Global. DOI: 10.4018/978-1-5225-5115-7.ch002

Dezdar, S. (2017). ERP Implementation Projects in Asian Countries: A Comparative Study on Iran and China. *International Journal of Information Technology Project Management*, *8*(3), 52–68. DOI: 10.4018/IJITPM.2017070104

Domingos, D., Respício, A., & Martinho, R. (2017). Reliability of IoT-Aware BPMN Healthcare Processes. In Reis, C., & Maximiano, M. (Eds.), *Internet of Things and Advanced Application in Healthcare* (pp. 214–248). Hershey, PA: IGI Global. DOI: 10.4018/978-1-5225-1820-4.ch008

Dosumu, O., Hussain, J., & El-Gohary, H. (2017). An Exploratory Study of the Impact of Government Policies on the Development of Small and Medium Enterprises in Developing Countries: The Case of Nigeria. *International Journal of Customer Relationship Marketing and Management*, *8*(4), 51–62. DOI: 10.4018/IJCRMM.2017100104

Durst, S., Bruns, G., & Edvardsson, I. R. (2017). Retaining Knowledge in Smaller Building and Construction Firms. *International Journal of Knowledge and Systems Science*, *8*(3), 1–12. DOI: 10.4018/IJKSS.2017070101

Edvardsson, I. R., & Durst, S. (2017). Outsourcing, Knowledge, and Learning: A Critical Review. *International Journal of Knowledge-Based Organizations*, *7*(2), 13–26. DOI: 10.4018/IJKBO.2017040102

Edwards, J. S. (2018). Integrating Knowledge Management and Business Processes. In M. Khosrow-Pour, D.B.A. (Ed.), *Encyclopedia of Information Science and Technology, Fourth Edition* (pp. 5046-5055). Hershey, PA: IGI Global. DOI: 10.4018/978-1-5225-2255-3.ch437

Eichelberger, S., & Peters, M. (2021). Family Firm Management in Turbulent Times: Opportunities for Responsible Tourism. In Zehrer, A., Glowka, G., Schwaiger, K., & Ranacher-Lackner, V. (Eds.), *Resiliency Models and Addressing Future Risks for Family Firms in the Tourism Industry* (pp. 103–124). IGI Global. https://doi.org/10.4018/978-1-7998-7352-5.ch005

Eide, D., Hjalager, A., & Hansen, M. (2022). Innovative Certifications in Adventure Tourism: Attributes and Diffusion. In R. Augusto Costa, F. Brandão, Z. Breda, & C. Costa (Eds.), *Planning and Managing the Experience Economy in Tourism* (pp. 161-175). IGI Global. https://doi.org/10.4018/978-1-7998-8775-1.ch009

Ejiogu, A. O. (2018). Economics of Farm Management. In *Agricultural Finance and Opportunities for Investment and Expansion* (pp. 56–72). Hershey, PA: IGI Global. DOI: 10.4018/978-1-5225-3059-6.ch003

Ekanem, I., & Abiade, G. E. (2018). Factors Influencing the Use of E-Commerce by Small Enterprises in Nigeria. *International Journal of ICT Research in Africa and the Middle East*, *7*(1), 37–53. DOI: 10.4018/IJICTRAME.2018010103

Ekanem, I., & Alrossais, L. A. (2017). Succession Challenges Facing Family Businesses in Saudi Arabia. In Zgheib, P. (Ed.), *Entrepreneurship and Business Innovation in the Middle East* (pp. 122–146). Hershey, PA: IGI Global. DOI: 10.4018/978-1-5225-2066-5.ch007

El Faquih, L., & Fredj, M. (2017). Ontology-Based Framework for Quality in Configurable Process Models. *Journal of Electronic Commerce in Organizations*, *15*(2), 48–60. DOI: 10.4018/JECO.2017040104

Faisal, M. N., & Talib, F. (2017). Building Ambidextrous Supply Chains in SMEs: How to Tackle the Barriers? *International Journal of Information Systems and Supply Chain Management*, *10*(4), 80–100. DOI: 10.4018/IJISSCM.2017100105

Fernandes, T. M., Gomes, J., & Romão, M. (2017). Investments in E-Government: A Benefit Management Case Study. *International Journal of Electronic Government Research*, *13*(3), 1–17. DOI: 10.4018/IJEGR.2017070101

Figueira, L. M., Honrado, G. R., & Dionísio, M. S. (2021). Human Capital Management in the Tourism Industry in Portugal. In Costa, V., Moura, A., & Mira, M. (Eds.), *Handbook of Research on Human Capital and People Management in the Tourism Industry* (pp. 1–19). IGI Global. DOI: 10.4018/978-1-7998-4318-4.ch001

Gao, S. S., Oreal, S., & Zhang, J. (2018). Contemporary Financial Risk Management Perceptions and Practices of Small-Sized Chinese Businesses. In I. Management Association (Ed.), *Global Business Expansion: Concepts, Methodologies, Tools, and Applications* (pp. 917-931). Hershey, PA: IGI Global. DOI: 10.4018/978-1-5225-5481-3.ch041

Garg, R., & Berning, S. C. (2017). Indigenous Chinese Management Philosophies: Key Concepts and Relevance for Modern Chinese Firms. In Christiansen, B., & Koc, G. (Eds.), *Transcontinental Strategies for Industrial Development and Economic Growth* (pp. 43–57). Hershey, PA: IGI Global. DOI: 10.4018/978-1-5225-2160-0.ch003

Gencer, Y. G. (2017). Supply Chain Management in Retailing Business. In Akkucuk, U. (Ed.), *Ethics and Sustainability in Global Supply Chain Management* (pp. 197–210). Hershey, PA: IGI Global. DOI: 10.4018/978-1-5225-2036-8.ch011

Gera, R., Arora, S., & Malik, S. (2021). Emotional Labor in the Tourism Industry: Strategies, Antecedents, and Outcomes. In Costa, V., Moura, A., & Mira, M. (Eds.), *Handbook of Research on Human Capital and People Management in the Tourism Industry* (pp. 73–91). IGI Global. https://doi.org/10.4018/978-1-7998-4318-4.ch004

Giacosa, E. (2018). The Increasing of the Regional Development Thanks to the Luxury Business Innovation. In Carvalho, L. (Ed.), *Handbook of Research on Entrepreneurial Ecosystems and Social Dynamics in a Globalized World* (pp. 260–273). Hershey, PA: IGI Global. DOI: 10.4018/978-1-5225-3525-6.ch011

Glowka, G., Tusch, M., & Zehrer, A. (2021). The Risk Perception of Family Business Owner-Manager in the Tourism Industry: A Qualitative Comparison of the Intra-Firm Senior and Junior Generation. In Zehrer, A., Glowka, G., Schwaiger, K., & Ranacher-Lackner, V. (Eds.), *Resiliency Models and Addressing Future Risks for Family Firms in the Tourism Industry* (pp. 126–153). IGI Global. https://doi.org/10.4018/978-1-7998-7352-5.ch006

Glykas, M., & George, J. (2017). Quality and Process Management Systems in the UAE Maritime Industry. *International Journal of Productivity Management and Assessment Technologies*, *5*(1), 20–39. DOI: 10.4018/IJPMAT.2017010102

Glykas, M., Valiris, G., Kokkinaki, A., & Koutsoukou, Z. (2018). Banking Business Process Management Implementation. *International Journal of Productivity Management and Assessment Technologies*, *6*(1), 50–69. DOI: 10.4018/IJPMAT.2018010104

Gomes, J., & Romão, M. (2017). The Balanced Scorecard: Keeping Updated and Aligned with Today's Business Trends. *International Journal of Productivity Management and Assessment Technologies*, *5*(2), 1–15. DOI: 10.4018/IJPMAT.2017070101

Gomes, J., & Romão, M. (2017). Aligning Information Systems and Technology with Benefit Management and Balanced Scorecard. In De Haes, S., & Van Grembergen, W. (Eds.), *Strategic IT Governance and Alignment in Business Settings* (pp. 112–131). Hershey, PA: IGI Global. DOI: 10.4018/978-1-5225-0861-8.ch005

Goyal, A. (2021). Communicating and Building Destination Brands With New Media. In M. Dinis, L. Bonixe, S. Lamy, & Z. Breda (Eds.), *Impact of New Media in Tourism* (pp. 1-20). IGI Global. https://doi.org/10.4018/978-1-7998-7095-1.ch001

Grefen, P., & Turetken, O. (2017). Advanced Business Process Management in Networked E-Business Scenarios. *International Journal of E-Business Research*, *13*(4), 70–104. DOI: 10.4018/IJEBR.2017100105

Guasca, M., Van Broeck, A. M., & Vanneste, D. (2021). Tourism and the Social Reintegration of Colombian Ex-Combatants. In J. da Silva, Z. Breda, & F. Carbone (Eds.), *Role and Impact of Tourism in Peacebuilding and Conflict Transformation* (pp. 66-86). IGI Global. https://doi.org/10.4018/978-1-7998-5053-3.ch005

Haider, A., & Saetang, S. (2017). Strategic IT Alignment in Service Sector. In Rozenes, S., & Cohen, Y. (Eds.), *Handbook of Research on Strategic Alliances and Value Co-Creation in the Service Industry* (pp. 231–258). Hershey, PA: IGI Global. DOI: 10.4018/978-1-5225-2084-9.ch012

Hajilari, A. B., Ghadaksaz, M., & Fasghandis, G. S. (2017). Assessing Organizational Readiness for Implementing ERP System Using Fuzzy Expert System Approach. *International Journal of Enterprise Information Systems*, *13*(1), 67–85. DOI: 10.4018/IJEIS.2017010105

Haldorai, A., Ramu, A., & Murugan, S. (2018). Social Aware Cognitive Radio Networks: Effectiveness of Social Networks as a Strategic Tool for Organizational Business Management. In Bansal, H., Shrivastava, G., Nguyen, G., & Stanciu, L. (Eds.), *Social Network Analytics for Contemporary Business Organizations* (pp. 188–202). Hershey, PA: IGI Global. DOI: 10.4018/978-1-5225-5097-6.ch010

Hall, O. P.Jr. (2017). Social Media Driven Management Education. *International Journal of Knowledge-Based Organizations*, *7*(2), 43–59. DOI: 10.4018/IJKBO.2017040104

Hanifah, H., Halim, H. A., Ahmad, N. H., & Vafaei-Zadeh, A. (2017). Innovation Culture as a Mediator Between Specific Human Capital and Innovation Performance Among Bumiputera SMEs in Malaysia. In Ahmad, N., Ramayah, T., Halim, H., & Rahman, S. (Eds.), *Handbook of Research on Small and Medium Enterprises in Developing Countries* (pp. 261–279). Hershey, PA: IGI Global. DOI: 10.4018/978-1-5225-2165-5.ch012

Hartlieb, S., & Silvius, G. (2017). Handling Uncertainty in Project Management and Business Development: Similarities and Differences. In Raydugin, Y. (Ed.), *Handbook of Research on Leveraging Risk and Uncertainties for Effective Project Management* (pp. 337–362). Hershey, PA: IGI Global. DOI: 10.4018/978-1-5225-1790-0.ch016

Hass, K. B. (2017). Living on the Edge: Managing Project Complexity. In Raydugin, Y. (Ed.), *Handbook of Research on Leveraging Risk and Uncertainties for Effective Project Management* (pp. 177–201). Hershey, PA: IGI Global. DOI: 10.4018/978-1-5225-1790-0.ch009

Hawking, P., & Carmine Sellitto, C. (2017). Developing an Effective Strategy for Organizational Business Intelligence. In Tavana, M. (Ed.), *Enterprise Information Systems and the Digitalization of Business Functions* (pp. 222–237). Hershey, PA: IGI Global. DOI: 10.4018/978-1-5225-2382-6.ch010

Hawking, P., & Sellitto, C. (2017). A Fast-Moving Consumer Goods Company and Business Intelligence Strategy Development. *International Journal of Enterprise Information Systems*, *13*(2), 22–33. DOI: 10.4018/IJEIS.2017040102

Hawking, P., & Sellitto, C. (2017). Business Intelligence Strategy: Two Case Studies. *International Journal of Business Intelligence Research*, *8*(2), 17–30. DOI: 10.4018/IJBIR.2017070102

Hee, W. J., Jalleh, G., Lai, H., & Lin, C. (2017). E-Commerce and IT Projects: Evaluation and Management Issues in Australian and Taiwanese Hospitals. *International Journal of Public Health Management and Ethics*, *2*(1), 69–90. DOI: 10.4018/IJPHME.2017010104

Hernandez, A. A. (2018). Exploring the Factors to Green IT Adoption of SMEs in the Philippines. *Journal of Cases on Information Technology*, *20*(2), 49–66. DOI: 10.4018/JCIT.2018040104

Hollman, A., Bickford, S., & Hollman, T. (2017). Cyber InSecurity: A Post-Mortem Attempt to Assess Cyber Problems from IT and Business Management Perspectives. *Journal of Cases on Information Technology*, *19*(3), 42–70. DOI: 10.4018/JCIT.2017070104

Ibrahim, F., & Zainin, N. M. (2021). Exploring the Technological Impacts: The Case of Museums in Brunei Darussalam. *International Journal of Tourism and Hospitality Management in the Digital Age*, *5*(1), 1–18. https://doi.org/10.4018/IJTHMDA.2021010101

Igbinakhase, I. (2017). Responsible and Sustainable Management Practices in Developing and Developed Business Environments. In Fields, Z. (Ed.), *Collective Creativity for Responsible and Sustainable Business Practice* (pp. 180–207). Hershey, PA: IGI Global. DOI: 10.4018/978-1-5225-1823-5.ch010

Iwata, J. J., & Hoskins, R. G. (2017). Managing Indigenous Knowledge in Tanzania: A Business Perspective. In Jain, P., & Mnjama, N. (Eds.), *Managing Knowledge Resources and Records in Modern Organizations* (pp. 198–214). Hershey, PA: IGI Global. DOI: 10.4018/978-1-5225-1965-2.ch012

Jain, P. (2017). Ethical and Legal Issues in Knowledge Management Life-Cycle in Business. In Jain, P., & Mnjama, N. (Eds.), *Managing Knowledge Resources and Records in Modern Organizations* (pp. 82–101). Hershey, PA: IGI Global. DOI: 10.4018/978-1-5225-1965-2.ch006

James, S., & Hauli, E. (2017). Holistic Management Education at Tanzanian Rural Development Planning Institute. In Baporikar, N. (Ed.), *Management Education for Global Leadership* (pp. 112–136). Hershey, PA: IGI Global. DOI: 10.4018/978-1-5225-1013-0.ch006

Janošková, M., Csikósová, A., & Čulková, K. (2018). Measurement of Company Performance as Part of Its Strategic Management. In Leon, R. (Ed.), *Managerial Strategies for Business Sustainability During Turbulent Times* (pp. 309–335). Hershey, PA: IGI Global. DOI: 10.4018/978-1-5225-2716-9.ch017

Jean-Vasile, A., & Alecu, A. (2017). Theoretical and Practical Approaches in Understanding the Influences of Cost-Productivity-Profit Trinomial in Contemporary Enterprises. In Jean Vasile, A., & Nicolò, D. (Eds.), *Sustainable Entrepreneurship and Investments in the Green Economy* (pp. 28–62). Hershey, PA: IGI Global. DOI: 10.4018/978-1-5225-2075-7.ch002

Joia, L. A., & Correia, J. C. (2018). CIO Competencies From the IT Professional Perspective: Insights From Brazil. *Journal of Global Information Management*, *26*(2), 74–103. DOI: 10.4018/JGIM.2018040104

Juma, A., & Mzera, N. (2017). Knowledge Management and Records Management and Competitive Advantage in Business. In Jain, P., & Mnjama, N. (Eds.), *Managing Knowledge Resources and Records in Modern Organizations* (pp. 15–28). Hershey, PA: IGI Global. DOI: 10.4018/978-1-5225-1965-2.ch002

K., I., & A, V. (2018). Monitoring and Auditing in the Cloud. In K. Munir (Ed.), *Cloud Computing Technologies for Green Enterprises* (pp. 318-350). Hershey, PA: IGI Global. https://doi.org/DOI: 10.4018/978-1-5225-3038-1.ch013

Kabra, G., Ghosh, V., & Ramesh, A. (2018). Enterprise Integrated Business Process Management and Business Intelligence Framework for Business Process Sustainability. In Paul, A., Bhattacharyya, D., & Anand, S. (Eds.), *Green Initiatives for Business Sustainability and Value Creation* (pp. 228–238). Hershey, PA: IGI Global. DOI: 10.4018/978-1-5225-2662-9.ch010

Kaoud, M. (2017). Investigation of Customer Knowledge Management: A Case Study Research. *International Journal of Service Science, Management, Engineering, and Technology*, *8*(2), 12–22. DOI: 10.4018/IJSSMET.2017040102

Katuu, S. (2018). A Comparative Assessment of Enterprise Content Management Maturity Models. In Gwangwava, N., & Mutingi, M. (Eds.), *E-Manufacturing and E-Service Strategies in Contemporary Organizations* (pp. 93–118). Hershey, PA: IGI Global. DOI: 10.4018/978-1-5225-3628-4.ch005

Khan, M. Y., & Abir, T. (2022). The Role of Social Media Marketing in the Tourism and Hospitality Industry: A Conceptual Study on Bangladesh. In Ramos, C., Quinteiro, S., & Gonçalves, A. (Eds.), *ICT as Innovator Between Tourism and Culture* (pp. 213–229). IGI Global. https://doi.org/10.4018/978-1-7998-8165-0.ch013

Kinnunen, S., Ylä-Kujala, A., Marttonen-Arola, S., Kärri, T., & Baglee, D. (2018). Internet of Things in Asset Management: Insights from Industrial Professionals and Academia. *International Journal of Service Science, Management, Engineering, and Technology*, *9*(2), 104–119. DOI: 10.4018/IJSSMET.2018040105

Klein, A. Z., Sabino de Freitas, A., Machado, L., Freitas, J. C.Jr, Graziola, P. G.Jr, & Schlemmer, E. (2017). Virtual Worlds Applications for Management Education. In Tomei, L. (Ed.), *Exploring the New Era of Technology-Infused Education* (pp. 279–299). Hershey, PA: IGI Global. DOI: 10.4018/978-1-5225-1709-2.ch017

Kővári, E., Saleh, M., & Steinbachné Hajmásy, G. (2022). The Impact of Corporate Digital Responsibility (CDR) on Internal Stakeholders' Satisfaction in Hungarian Upscale Hotels. In Valeri, M. (Ed.), *New Governance and Management in Touristic Destinations* (pp. 35–51). IGI Global. https://doi.org/10.4018/978-1-6684-3889-3.ch003

Kożuch, B., & Jabłoński, A. (2017). Adopting the Concept of Business Models in Public Management. In Lewandowski, M., & Kożuch, B. (Eds.), *Public Sector Entrepreneurship and the Integration of Innovative Business Models* (pp. 10–46). Hershey, PA: IGI Global. DOI: 10.4018/978-1-5225-2215-7.ch002

Kumar, J., Adhikary, A., & Jha, A. (2017). Small Active Investors' Perceptions and Preferences Towards Tax Saving Mutual Fund Schemes in Eastern India: An Empirical Note. *International Journal of Asian Business and Information Management, 8*(2), 35–45. DOI: 10.4018/IJABIM.2017040103

Latusi, S., & Fissore, M. (2021). Pilgrimage Routes to Happiness: Comparing the Camino de Santiago and Via Francigena. In Perinotto, A., Mayer, V., & Soares, J. (Eds.), *Rebuilding and Restructuring the Tourism Industry: Infusion of Happiness and Quality of Life* (pp. 157–182). IGI Global. https://doi.org/10.4018/978-1-7998-7239-9.ch008

Lavassani, K. M., & Movahedi, B. (2017). Applications Driven Information Systems: Beyond Networks toward Business Ecosystems. *International Journal of Innovation in the Digital Economy, 8*(1), 61–75. DOI: 10.4018/IJIDE.2017010104

Lazzareschi, V. H., & Brito, M. S. (2017). Strategic Information Management: Proposal of Business Project Model. In Jamil, G., Soares, A., & Pessoa, C. (Eds.), *Handbook of Research on Information Management for Effective Logistics and Supply Chains* (pp. 59–88). Hershey, PA: IGI Global. DOI: 10.4018/978-1-5225-0973-8.ch004

Lechuga Sancho, M. P., & Martín Navarro, A. (2022). Evolution of the Literature on Social Responsibility in the Tourism Sector: A Systematic Literature Review. In Fernandes, G. (Ed.), *Challenges and New Opportunities for Tourism in Inland Territories: Ecocultural Resources and Sustainable Initiatives* (pp. 169–186). IGI Global. https://doi.org/10.4018/978-1-7998-7339-6.ch010

Lederer, M., Kurz, M., & Lazarov, P. (2017). Usage and Suitability of Methods for Strategic Business Process Initiatives: A Multi Case Study Research. *International Journal of Productivity Management and Assessment Technologies, 5*(1), 40–51. DOI: 10.4018/IJPMAT.2017010103

Lee, I. (2017). A Social Enterprise Business Model and a Case Study of Pacific Community Ventures (PCV). In Potocan, V., Üngan, M., & Nedelko, Z. (Eds.), *Handbook of Research on Managerial Solutions in Non-Profit Organizations* (pp. 182–204). Hershey, PA: IGI Global. DOI: 10.4018/978-1-5225-0731-4.ch009

Leon, L. A., Seal, K. C., Przasnyski, Z. H., & Wiedenman, I. (2017). Skills and Competencies Required for Jobs in Business Analytics: A Content Analysis of Job Advertisements Using Text Mining. *International Journal of Business Intelligence Research, 8*(1), 1–25. DOI: 10.4018/IJBIR.2017010101

Levy, C. L., & Elias, N. I. (2017). SOHO Users' Perceptions of Reliability and Continuity of Cloud-Based Services. In Moore, M. (Ed.), *Cybersecurity Breaches and Issues Surrounding Online Threat Protection* (pp. 248–287). Hershey, PA: IGI Global. DOI: 10.4018/978-1-5225-1941-6.ch011

Levy, M. (2018). Change Management Serving Knowledge Management and Organizational Development: Reflections and Review. In Baporikar, N. (Ed.), *Global Practices in Knowledge Management for Societal and Organizational Development* (pp. 256–270). Hershey, PA: IGI Global. DOI: 10.4018/978-1-5225-3009-1.ch012

Lewandowski, M. (2017). Public Organizations and Business Model Innovation: The Role of Public Service Design. In Lewandowski, M., & Kożuch, B. (Eds.), *Public Sector Entrepreneurship and the Integration of Innovative Business Models* (pp. 47–72). Hershey, PA: IGI Global. DOI: 10.4018/978-1-5225-2215-7.ch003

Lhannaoui, H., Kabbaj, M. I., & Bakkoury, Z. (2017). A Survey of Risk-Aware Business Process Modelling. *International Journal of Risk and Contingency Management, 6*(3), 14–26. DOI: 10.4018/IJRCM.2017070102

Li, J., Sun, W., Jiang, W., Yang, H., & Zhang, L. (2017). How the Nature of Exogenous Shocks and Crises Impact Company Performance?: The Effects of Industry Characteristics. *International Journal of Risk and Contingency Management, 6*(4), 40–55. DOI: 10.4018/IJRCM.2017100103

Lopez-Fernandez, M., Perez-Perez, M., Serrano-Bedia, A., & Cobo-Gonzalez, A. (2021). Small and Medium Tourism Enterprise Survival in Times of Crisis: "El Capricho de Gaudí. In Toubes, D., & Araújo-Vila, N. (Eds.), *Risk, Crisis, and Disaster Management in Small and Medium-Sized Tourism Enterprises* (pp. 103–129). IGI Global. DOI: 10.4018/978-1-7998-6996-2.ch005

Mahajan, A., Maidullah, S., & Hossain, M. R. (2022). Experience Toward Smart Tour Guide Apps in Travelling: An Analysis of Users' Reviews on Audio Odigos and Trip My Way. In R. Augusto Costa, F. Brandão, Z. Breda, & C. Costa (Eds.), *Planning and Managing the Experience Economy in Tourism* (pp. 255-273). IGI Global. https://doi.org/10.4018/978-1-7998-8775-1.ch014

Malega, P. (2017). Small and Medium Enterprises in the Slovak Republic: Status and Competitiveness of SMEs in the Global Markets and Possibilities of Optimization. In Vemić, M. (Ed.), *Optimal Management Strategies in Small and Medium Enterprises* (pp. 102–124). Hershey, PA: IGI Global. DOI: 10.4018/978-1-5225-1949-2.ch006

Malewska, K. M. (2017). Intuition in Decision-Making on the Example of a Non-Profit Organization. In Potocan, V., Üngan, M., & Nedelko, Z. (Eds.), *Handbook of Research on Managerial Solutions in Non-Profit Organizations* (pp. 378–399). Hershey, PA: IGI Global. DOI: 10.4018/978-1-5225-0731-4.ch018

Maroofi, F. (2017). Entrepreneurial Orientation and Organizational Learning Ability Analysis for Innovation and Firm Performance. In Baporikar, N. (Ed.), *Innovation and Shifting Perspectives in Management Education* (pp. 144–165). Hershey, PA: IGI Global. DOI: 10.4018/978-1-5225-1019-2.ch007

Marques, M., Moleiro, D., Brito, T. M., & Marques, T. (2021). Customer Relationship Management as an Important Relationship Marketing Tool: The Case of the Hospitality Industry in Estoril Coast. In M. Dinis, L. Bonixe, S. Lamy, & Z. Breda (Eds.), *Impact of New Media in Tourism* (pp. 39-56). IGI Global. https://doi.org/ DOI: 10.4018/978-1-7998-7095-1.ch003

Martins, P. V., & Zacarias, M. (2017). A Web-based Tool for Business Process Improvement. *International Journal of Web Portals*, *9*(2), 68–84. DOI: 10.4018/ IJWP.2017070104

Matthies, B., & Coners, A. (2017). Exploring the Conceptual Nature of e-Business Projects. *Journal of Electronic Commerce in Organizations*, *15*(3), 33–63. DOI: 10.4018/JECO.2017070103

Mayer, V. F., Fraga, C. C., & Silva, L. C. (2021). Contributions of Neurosciences to Studies of Well-Being in Tourism. In Perinotto, A., Mayer, V., & Soares, J. (Eds.), *Rebuilding and Restructuring the Tourism Industry: Infusion of Happiness and Quality of Life* (pp. 108–128). IGI Global. https://doi.org/10.4018/978-1-7998 -7239-9.ch006

McKee, J. (2018). Architecture as a Tool to Solve Business Planning Problems. In M. Khosrow-Pour, D.B.A. (Ed.), *Encyclopedia of Information Science and Technology, Fourth Edition* (pp. 573-586). Hershey, PA: IGI Global. DOI: 10.4018/978-1-5225-2255-3.ch050

McMurray, A. J., Cross, J., & Caponecchia, C. (2018). The Risk Management Profession in Australia: Business Continuity Plan Practices. In Bajgoric, N. (Ed.), *Always-On Enterprise Information Systems for Modern Organizations* (pp. 112–129). Hershey, PA: IGI Global. DOI: 10.4018/978-1-5225-3704-5.ch006

Meddah, I. H., & Belkadi, K. (2018). Mining Patterns Using Business Process Management. In Hamou, R. (Ed.), *Handbook of Research on Biomimicry in Information Retrieval and Knowledge Management* (pp. 78–89). Hershey, PA: IGI Global. DOI: 10.4018/978-1-5225-3004-6.ch005

Melian, A. G., & Camprubí, R. (2021). The Accessibility of Museum Websites: The Case of Barcelona. In Eusébio, C., Teixeira, L., & Carneiro, M. (Eds.), *ICT Tools and Applications for Accessible Tourism* (pp. 234–255). IGI Global. https://doi.org/10.4018/978-1-7998-6428-8.ch011

Mendes, L. (2017). TQM and Knowledge Management: An Integrated Approach Towards Tacit Knowledge Management. In Jaziri-Bouagina, D., & Jamil, G. (Eds.), *Handbook of Research on Tacit Knowledge Management for Organizational Success* (pp. 236–263). Hershey, PA: IGI Global. DOI: 10.4018/978-1-5225-2394-9.ch009

Menezes, V. D., & Cavagnaro, E. (2021). Communicating Sustainable Initiatives in the Hotel Industry: The Case of the Hotel Jakarta Amsterdam. In F. Brandão, Z. Breda, R. Costa, & C. Costa (Eds.), *Handbook of Research on the Role of Tourism in Achieving Sustainable Development Goals* (pp. 224-234). IGI Global. https://doi.org/10.4018/978-1-7998-5691-7.ch013

Menezes, V. D., & Cavagnaro, E. (2021). Communicating Sustainable Initiatives in the Hotel Industry: The Case of the Hotel Jakarta Amsterdam. In F. Brandão, Z. Breda, R. Costa, & C. Costa (Eds.), *Handbook of Research on the Role of Tourism in Achieving Sustainable Development Goals* (pp. 224-234). IGI Global. https://doi.org/10.4018/978-1-7998-5691-7.ch013

Mitas, O., Bastiaansen, M., & Boode, W. (2022). If You're Happy, I'm Happy: Emotion Contagion at a Tourist Information Center. In R. Augusto Costa, F. Brandão, Z. Breda, & C. Costa (Eds.), *Planning and Managing the Experience Economy in Tourism* (pp. 122-140). IGI Global. https://doi.org/10.4018/978-1-7998-8775-1.ch007

Mnjama, N. M. (2017). Preservation of Recorded Information in Public and Private Sector Organizations. In Jain, P., & Mnjama, N. (Eds.), *Managing Knowledge Resources and Records in Modern Organizations* (pp. 149–167). Hershey, PA: IGI Global. DOI: 10.4018/978-1-5225-1965-2.ch009

Mokoqama, M., & Fields, Z. (2017). Principles of Responsible Management Education (PRME): Call for Responsible Management Education. In Fields, Z. (Ed.), *Collective Creativity for Responsible and Sustainable Business Practice* (pp. 229–241). Hershey, PA: IGI Global. DOI: 10.4018/978-1-5225-1823-5.ch012

Monteiro, A., Lopes, S., & Carbone, F. (2021). Academic Mobility: Bridging Tourism and Peace Education. In J. da Silva, Z. Breda, & F. Carbone (Eds.), *Role and Impact of Tourism in Peacebuilding and Conflict Transformation* (pp. 275-301). IGI Global. https://doi.org/10.4018/978-1-7998-5053-3.ch016

Muniapan, B. (2017). Philosophy and Management: The Relevance of Vedanta in Management. In Ordóñez de Pablos, P. (Ed.), *Managerial Strategies and Solutions for Business Success in Asia* (pp. 124–139). Hershey, PA: IGI Global. DOI: 10.4018/978-1-5225-1886-0.ch007

Murad, S. E., & Dowaji, S. (2017). Using Value-Based Approach for Managing Cloud-Based Services. In Turuk, A., Sahoo, B., & Addya, S. (Eds.), *Resource Management and Efficiency in Cloud Computing Environments* (pp. 33–60). Hershey, PA: IGI Global. DOI: 10.4018/978-1-5225-1721-4.ch002

Mutahar, A. M., Daud, N. M., Thurasamy, R., Isaac, O., & Abdulsalam, R. (2018). The Mediating of Perceived Usefulness and Perceived Ease of Use: The Case of Mobile Banking in Yemen. *International Journal of Technology Diffusion*, *9*(2), 21–40. DOI: 10.4018/IJTD.2018040102

Naidoo, V. (2017). E-Learning and Management Education at African Universities. In Baporikar, N. (Ed.), *Management Education for Global Leadership* (pp. 181–201). Hershey, PA: IGI Global. DOI: 10.4018/978-1-5225-1013-0.ch009

Naidoo, V., & Igbinakhase, I. (2018). Opportunities and Challenges of Knowledge Retention in SMEs. In Baporikar, N. (Ed.), *Knowledge Integration Strategies for Entrepreneurship and Sustainability* (pp. 70–94). Hershey, PA: IGI Global. DOI: 10.4018/978-1-5225-5115-7.ch004

Naumov, N., & Costandachi, G. (2021). Creativity and Entrepreneurship: Gastronomic Tourism in Mexico. In Soares, J. (Ed.), *Innovation and Entrepreneurial Opportunities in Community Tourism* (pp. 90–108). IGI Global. https://doi.org/10.4018/978-1-7998-4855-4.ch006

Nayak, S., & Prabhu, N. (2017). Paradigm Shift in Management Education: Need for a Cross Functional Perspective. In Baporikar, N. (Ed.), *Management Education for Global Leadership* (pp. 241–255). Hershey, PA: IGI Global. DOI: 10.4018/978-1-5225-1013-0.ch012

Nedelko, Z., & Potocan, V. (2017). Management Solutions in Non-Profit Organizations: Case of Slovenia. In Potocan, V., Ünğan, M., & Nedelko, Z. (Eds.), *Handbook of Research on Managerial Solutions in Non-Profit Organizations* (pp. 1–22). Hershey, PA: IGI Global. DOI: 10.4018/978-1-5225-0731-4.ch001

Nedelko, Z., & Potocan, V. (2017). Priority of Management Tools Utilization among Managers: International Comparison. In Wang, V. (Ed.), *Encyclopedia of Strategic Leadership and Management* (pp. 1083–1094). Hershey, PA: IGI Global. DOI: 10.4018/978-1-5225-1049-9.ch075

Nedelko, Z., Raudeliūnienė, J., & Črešnar, R. (2018). Knowledge Dynamics in Supply Chain Management. In Baporikar, N. (Ed.), *Knowledge Integration Strategies for Entrepreneurship and Sustainability* (pp. 150–166). Hershey, PA: IGI Global. DOI: 10.4018/978-1-5225-5115-7.ch008

Nguyen, H. T., & Hipsher, S. A. (2018). Innovation and Creativity Used by Private Sector Firms in a Resources-Constrained Environment. In Hipsher, S. (Ed.), *Examining the Private Sector's Role in Wealth Creation and Poverty Reduction* (pp. 219–238). Hershey, PA: IGI Global. DOI: 10.4018/978-1-5225-3117-3.ch010

Obicci, P. A. (2017). Risk Sharing in a Partnership. In *Risk Management Strategies in Public-Private Partnerships* (pp. 115–152). Hershey, PA: IGI Global. DOI: 10.4018/978-1-5225-2503-5.ch004

Obidallah, W. J., & Raahemi, B. (2017). Managing Changes in Service Oriented Virtual Organizations: A Structural and Procedural Framework to Facilitate the Process of Change. *Journal of Electronic Commerce in Organizations, 15*(1), 59–83. DOI: 10.4018/JECO.2017010104

Ojo, O. (2017). Impact of Innovation on the Entrepreneurial Success in Selected Business Enterprises in South-West Nigeria. *International Journal of Innovation in the Digital Economy, 8*(2), 29–38. DOI: 10.4018/IJIDE.2017040103

Okdinawati, L., Simatupang, T. M., & Sunitiyoso, Y. (2017). Multi-Agent Reinforcement Learning for Value Co-Creation of Collaborative Transportation Management (CTM). *International Journal of Information Systems and Supply Chain Management, 10*(3), 84–95. DOI: 10.4018/IJISSCM.2017070105

Olivera, V. A., & Carrillo, I. M. (2021). Organizational Culture: A Key Element for the Development of Mexican Micro and Small Tourist Companies. In Soares, J. (Ed.), *Innovation and Entrepreneurial Opportunities in Community Tourism* (pp. 227–242). IGI Global. DOI: 10.4018/978-1-7998-4855-4.ch013

Ossorio, M. (2022). Corporate Museum Experiences in Enogastronomic Tourism. In R. Augusto Costa, F. Brandão, Z. Breda, & C. Costa (Eds.), *Planning and Managing the Experience Economy in Tourism* (pp. 107-121). IGI Global. https://doi.org/DOI: 10.4018/978-1-7998-8775-1.ch006

Ossorio, M. (2022). Enogastronomic Tourism in Times of Pandemic. In Fernandes, G. (Ed.), *Challenges and New Opportunities for Tourism in Inland Territories: Ecocultural Resources and Sustainable Initiatives* (pp. 241–255). IGI Global. https://doi.org/10.4018/978-1-7998-7339-6.ch014

Özekici, Y. K. (2022). ICT as an Acculturative Agent and Its Role in the Tourism Context: Introduction, Acculturation Theory, Progress of the Acculturation Theory in Extant Literature. In Ramos, C., Quinteiro, S., & Gonçalves, A. (Eds.), *ICT as Innovator Between Tourism and Culture* (pp. 42–66). IGI Global. https://doi.org/10.4018/978-1-7998-8165-0.ch004

Pal, K. (2018). Building High Quality Big Data-Based Applications in Supply Chains. In Kumar, A., & Saurav, S. (Eds.), *Supply Chain Management Strategies and Risk Assessment in Retail Environments* (pp. 1–24). Hershey, PA: IGI Global. DOI: 10.4018/978-1-5225-3056-5.ch001

Palos-Sanchez, P. R., & Correia, M. B. (2018). Perspectives of the Adoption of Cloud Computing in the Tourism Sector. In Rodrigues, J., Ramos, C., Cardoso, P., & Henriques, C. (Eds.), *Handbook of Research on Technological Developments for Cultural Heritage and eTourism Applications* (pp. 377–400). Hershey, PA: IGI Global. DOI: 10.4018/978-1-5225-2927-9.ch018

Papadopoulou, G. (2021). Promoting Gender Equality and Women Empowerment in the Tourism Sector. In F. Brandão, Z. Breda, R. Costa, & C. Costa (Eds.), *Handbook of Research on the Role of Tourism in Achieving Sustainable Development Goals* (pp. 152-174). IGI Global. https://doi.org/DOI: 10.4018/978-1-7998-5691-7.ch009

Papp-Váry, Á. F., & Tóth, T. Z. (2022). Analysis of Budapest as a Film Tourism Destination. In R. Baleiro & R. Pereira (Eds.), *Global Perspectives on Literary Tourism and Film-Induced Tourism* (pp. 257-279). IGI Global. https://doi.org/10.4018/978-1-7998-8262-6.ch014

Patiño, B. E. (2017). New Generation Management by Convergence and Individual Identity: A Systemic and Human-Oriented Approach. In Baporikar, N. (Ed.), *Innovation and Shifting Perspectives in Management Education* (pp. 119–143). Hershey, PA: IGI Global. DOI: 10.4018/978-1-5225-1019-2.ch006

Patro, C. S. (2021). Digital Tourism: Influence of E-Marketing Technology. In M. Dinis, L. Bonixe, S. Lamy, & Z. Breda (Eds.), *Impact of New Media in Tourism* (pp. 234-254). IGI Global. https://doi.org/10.4018/978-1-7998-7095-1.ch014

Pawliczek, A., & Rössler, M. (2017). Knowledge of Management Tools and Systems in SMEs: Knowledge Transfer in Management. In Bencsik, A. (Ed.), *Knowledge Management Initiatives and Strategies in Small and Medium Enterprises* (pp. 180–203). Hershey, PA: IGI Global. DOI: 10.4018/978-1-5225-1642-2.ch009

Pejic-Bach, M., Omazic, M. A., Aleksic, A., & Zoroja, J. (2018). Knowledge-Based Decision Making: A Multi-Case Analysis. In Leon, R. (Ed.), *Managerial Strategies for Business Sustainability During Turbulent Times* (pp. 160–184). Hershey, PA: IGI Global. DOI: 10.4018/978-1-5225-2716-9.ch009

Perano, M., Hysa, X., & Calabrese, M. (2018). Strategic Planning, Cultural Context, and Business Continuity Management: Business Cases in the City of Shkoder. In Presenza, A., & Sheehan, L. (Eds.), *Geopolitics and Strategic Management in the Global Economy* (pp. 57–77). Hershey, PA: IGI Global. DOI: 10.4018/978-1-5225-2673-5.ch004

Pereira, R., Mira da Silva, M., & Lapão, L. V. (2017). IT Governance Maturity Patterns in Portuguese Healthcare. In De Haes, S., & Van Grembergen, W. (Eds.), *Strategic IT Governance and Alignment in Business Settings* (pp. 24–52). Hershey, PA: IGI Global. DOI: 10.4018/978-1-5225-0861-8.ch002

Pérez-Uribe, R. I., Torres, D. A., Jurado, S. P., & Prada, D. M. (2018). Cloud Tools for the Development of Project Management in SMEs. In Perez-Uribe, R., Salcedo-Perez, C., & Ocampo-Guzman, D. (Eds.), *Handbook of Research on Intrapreneurship and Organizational Sustainability in SMEs* (pp. 95–120). Hershey, PA: IGI Global. DOI: 10.4018/978-1-5225-3543-0.ch005

Petrisor, I., & Cozmiuc, D. (2017). Global Supply Chain Management Organization at Siemens in the Advent of Industry 4.0. In Saglietto, L., & Cezanne, C. (Eds.), *Global Intermediation and Logistics Service Providers* (pp. 123–142). Hershey, PA: IGI Global. DOI: 10.4018/978-1-5225-2133-4.ch007

Pierce, J. M., Velliaris, D. M., & Edwards, J. (2017). A Living Case Study: A Journey Not a Destination. In Silton, N. (Ed.), *Exploring the Benefits of Creativity in Education, Media, and the Arts* (pp. 158–178). Hershey, PA: IGI Global. DOI: 10.4018/978-1-5225-0504-4.ch008

Pipia, S., & Pipia, S. (2021). Challenges of Religious Tourism in the Conflict Region: An Example of Jerusalem. In E. Alaverdov & M. Bari (Eds.), *Global Development of Religious Tourism* (pp. 135-148). IGI Global. https://doi.org/10.4018/978-1-7998-5792-1.ch009

Poulaki, P., Kritikos, A., Vasilakis, N., & Valeri, M. (2022). The Contribution of Female Creativity to the Development of Gastronomic Tourism in Greece: The Case of the Island of Naxos in the South Aegean Region. In Valeri, M. (Ed.), *New Governance and Management in Touristic Destinations* (pp. 246–258). IGI Global. https://doi.org/10.4018/978-1-6684-3889-3.ch015

Radosavljevic, M., & Andjelkovic, A. (2017). Multi-Criteria Decision Making Approach for Choosing Business Process for the Improvement: Upgrading of the Six Sigma Methodology. In Stanković, J., Delias, P., Marinković, S., & Rochhia, S. (Eds.), *Tools and Techniques for Economic Decision Analysis* (pp. 225–247). Hershey, PA: IGI Global. DOI: 10.4018/978-1-5225-0959-2.ch011

Radovic, V. M. (2017). Corporate Sustainability and Responsibility and Disaster Risk Reduction: A Serbian Overview. In Camilleri, M. (Ed.), *CSR 2.0 and the New Era of Corporate Citizenship* (pp. 147–164). Hershey, PA: IGI Global. DOI: 10.4018/978-1-5225-1842-6.ch008

Raghunath, K. M., Devi, S. L., & Patro, C. S. (2018). Impact of Risk Assessment Models on Risk Factors: A Holistic Outlook. In Strang, K., Korstanje, M., & Vajjhala, N. (Eds.), *Research, Practices, and Innovations in Global Risk and Contingency Management* (pp. 134–153). Hershey, PA: IGI Global. DOI: 10.4018/978-1-5225-4754-9.ch008

Raman, A., & Goyal, D. P. (2017). Extending IMPLEMENT Framework for Enterprise Information Systems Implementation to Information System Innovation. In Tavana, M. (Ed.), *Enterprise Information Systems and the Digitalization of Business Functions* (pp. 137–177). Hershey, PA: IGI Global. DOI: 10.4018/978-1-5225-2382-6.ch007

Rao, Y., & Zhang, Y. (2017). The Construction and Development of Academic Library Digital Special Subject Databases. In Ruan, L., Zhu, Q., & Ye, Y. (Eds.), *Academic Library Development and Administration in China* (pp. 163–183). Hershey, PA: IGI Global. DOI: 10.4018/978-1-5225-0550-1.ch010

Ravasan, A. Z., Mohammadi, M. M., & Hamidi, H. (2018). An Investigation Into the Critical Success Factors of Implementing Information Technology Service Management Frameworks. In Jakobs, K. (Ed.), *Corporate and Global Standardization Initiatives in Contemporary Society* (pp. 200–218). Hershey, PA: IGI Global. DOI: 10.4018/978-1-5225-5320-5.ch009

Rezaie, S., Mirabedini, S. J., & Abtahi, A. (2018). Designing a Model for Implementation of Business Intelligence in the Banking Industry. *International Journal of Enterprise Information Systems, 14*(1), 77–103. DOI: 10.4018/IJEIS.2018010105

Richards, V., Matthews, N., Williams, O. J., & Khan, Z. (2021). The Challenges of Accessible Tourism Information Systems for Tourists With Vision Impairment: Sensory Communications Beyond the Screen. In Eusébio, C., Teixeira, L., & Carneiro, M. (Eds.), *ICT Tools and Applications for Accessible Tourism* (pp. 26–54). IGI Global. https://doi.org/10.4018/978-1-7998-6428-8.ch002

Rodrigues de Souza Neto, V., & Marques, O. (2021). Rural Tourism Fostering Welfare Through Sustainable Development: A Conceptual Approach. In Perinotto, A., Mayer, V., & Soares, J. (Eds.), *Rebuilding and Restructuring the Tourism Industry: Infusion of Happiness and Quality of Life* (pp. 38–57). IGI Global. https://doi.org/10.4018/978-1-7998-7239-9.ch003

Romano, L., Grimaldi, R., & Colasuonno, F. S. (2017). Demand Management as a Success Factor in Project Portfolio Management. In Romano, L. (Ed.), *Project Portfolio Management Strategies for Effective Organizational Operations* (pp. 202–219). Hershey, PA: IGI Global. DOI: 10.4018/978-1-5225-2151-8.ch008

Rubio-Escuderos, L., & García-Andreu, H. (2021). Competitiveness Factors of Accessible Tourism E-Travel Agencies. In Eusébio, C., Teixeira, L., & Carneiro, M. (Eds.), *ICT Tools and Applications for Accessible Tourism* (pp. 196–217). IGI Global. https://doi.org/10.4018/978-1-7998-6428-8.ch009

Rucci, A. C., Porto, N., Darcy, S., & Becka, L. (2021). Smart and Accessible Cities?: Not Always – The Case for Accessible Tourism Initiatives in Buenos Aries and Sydney. In Eusébio, C., Teixeira, L., & Carneiro, M. (Eds.), *ICT Tools and Applications for Accessible Tourism* (pp. 115–145). IGI Global. https://doi.org/10.4018/978-1-7998-6428-8.ch006

Ruhi, U. (2018). Towards an Interdisciplinary Socio-Technical Definition of Virtual Communities. In M. Khosrow-Pour, D.B.A. (Ed.), *Encyclopedia of Information Science and Technology, Fourth Edition* (pp. 4278-4295). Hershey, PA: IGI Global. DOI: 10.4018/978-1-5225-2255-3.ch371

Ryan, L., Catena, M., Ros, P., & Stephens, S. (2021). Designing Entrepreneurial Ecosystems to Support Resource Management in the Tourism Industry. In Costa, V., Moura, A., & Mira, M. (Eds.), *Handbook of Research on Human Capital and People Management in the Tourism Industry* (pp. 265–281). IGI Global. https://doi.org/10.4018/978-1-7998-4318-4.ch013

Sabuncu, I. (2021). Understanding Tourist Perceptions and Expectations During Pandemic Through Social Media Big Data. In Demir, M., Dalgıç, A., & Ergen, F. (Eds.), *Handbook of Research on the Impacts and Implications of COVID-19 on the Tourism Industry* (pp. 330–350). IGI Global. https://doi.org/10.4018/978-1-7998-8231-2.ch016

Safari, M. R., & Jiang, Q. (2018). The Theory and Practice of IT Governance Maturity and Strategies Alignment: Evidence From Banking Industry. *Journal of Global Information Management*, *26*(2), 127–146. DOI: 10.4018/JGIM.2018040106

Sahoo, J., Pati, B., & Mohanty, B. (2017). Knowledge Management as an Academic Discipline: An Assessment. In Gunjal, B. (Ed.), *Managing Knowledge and Scholarly Assets in Academic Libraries* (pp. 99–126). Hershey, PA: IGI Global. DOI: 10.4018/978-1-5225-1741-2.ch005

Saini, D. (2017). Relevance of Teaching Values and Ethics in Management Education. In Baporikar, N. (Ed.), *Management Education for Global Leadership* (pp. 90–111). Hershey, PA: IGI Global. DOI: 10.4018/978-1-5225-1013-0.ch005

Sambhanthan, A. (2017). Assessing and Benchmarking Sustainability in Organisations: An Integrated Conceptual Model. *International Journal of Systems and Service-Oriented Engineering*, *7*(4), 22–43. DOI: 10.4018/IJSSOE.2017100102

Sambhanthan, A., & Potdar, V. (2017). A Study of the Parameters Impacting Sustainability in Information Technology Organizations. *International Journal of Knowledge-Based Organizations*, *7*(3), 27–39. DOI: 10.4018/IJKBO.2017070103

Sánchez-Fernández, M. D., & Manríquez, M. R. (2018). The Entrepreneurial Spirit Based on Social Values: The Digital Generation. In Isaias, P., & Carvalho, L. (Eds.), *User Innovation and the Entrepreneurship Phenomenon in the Digital Economy* (pp. 173–193). Hershey, PA: IGI Global. DOI: 10.4018/978-1-5225-2826-5.ch009

Sanchez-Ruiz, L., & Blanco, B. (2017). Process Management for SMEs: Barriers, Enablers, and Benefits. In Vemić, M. (Ed.), *Optimal Management Strategies in Small and Medium Enterprises* (pp. 293–319). Hershey, PA: IGI Global. DOI: 10.4018/978-1-5225-1949-2.ch014

Sanz, L. F., Gómez-Pérez, J., & Castillo-Martinez, A. (2018). Analysis of the European ICT Competence Frameworks. In Ahuja, V., & Rathore, S. (Eds.), *Multidisciplinary Perspectives on Human Capital and Information Technology Professionals* (pp. 225–245). Hershey, PA: IGI Global. DOI: 10.4018/978-1-5225-5297-0.ch012

Sarvepalli, A., & Godin, J. (2017). Business Process Management in the Classroom. *Journal of Cases on Information Technology, 19*(2), 17–28. DOI: 10.4018/JCIT.2017040102

Saxena, G. G., & Saxena, A. (2021). Host Community Role in Medical Tourism Development. In Singh, M., & Kumaran, S. (Eds.), *Growth of the Medical Tourism Industry and Its Impact on Society: Emerging Research and Opportunities* (pp. 105–127). IGI Global. https://doi.org/10.4018/978-1-7998-3427-4.ch006

Saygili, E. E., Ozturkoglu, Y., & Kocakulah, M. C. (2017). End Users' Perceptions of Critical Success Factors in ERP Applications. *International Journal of Enterprise Information Systems, 13*(4), 58–75. DOI: 10.4018/IJEIS.2017100104

Saygili, E. E., & Saygili, A. T. (2017). Contemporary Issues in Enterprise Information Systems: A Critical Review of CSFs in ERP Implementations. In Tavana, M. (Ed.), *Enterprise Information Systems and the Digitalization of Business Functions* (pp. 120–136). Hershey, PA: IGI Global. DOI: 10.4018/978-1-5225-2382-6.ch006

Schwaiger, K. M., & Zehrer, A. (2021). The COVID-19 Pandemic and Organizational Resilience in Hospitality Family Firms: A Qualitative Approach. In Zehrer, A., Glowka, G., Schwaiger, K., & Ranacher-Lackner, V. (Eds.), *Resiliency Models and Addressing Future Risks for Family Firms in the Tourism Industry* (pp. 32–49). IGI Global. https://doi.org/10.4018/978-1-7998-7352-5.ch002

Scott, N., & Campos, A. C. (2022). Cognitive Science of Tourism Experiences. In R. Augusto Costa, F. Brandão, Z. Breda, & C. Costa (Eds.), *Planning and Managing the Experience Economy in Tourism* (pp. 1-21). IGI Global. https://doi.org/DOI: 10.4018/978-1-7998-8775-1.ch001

Seidenstricker, S., & Antonino, A. (2018). Business Model Innovation-Oriented Technology Management for Emergent Technologies. In M. Khosrow-Pour, D.B.A. (Ed.), *Encyclopedia of Information Science and Technology, Fourth Edition* (pp. 4560-4569). Hershey, PA: IGI Global. DOI: 10.4018/978-1-5225-2255-3.ch396

Selvi, M. S. (2021). Changes in Tourism Sales and Marketing Post COVID-19. In Demir, M., Dalgıç, A., & Ergen, F. (Eds.), *Handbook of Research on the Impacts and Implications of COVID-19 on the Tourism Industry* (pp. 437–460). IGI Global. DOI: 10.4018/978-1-7998-8231-2.ch021

Senaratne, S., & Gunarathne, A. D. (2017). Excellence Perspective for Management Education from a Global Accountants' Hub in Asia. In Baporikar, N. (Ed.), *Management Education for Global Leadership* (pp. 158–180). Hershey, PA: IGI Global. DOI: 10.4018/978-1-5225-1013-0.ch008

Sensuse, D. I., & Cahyaningsih, E. (2018). Knowledge Management Models: A Summative Review. *International Journal of Information Systems in the Service Sector, 10*(1), 71–100. DOI: 10.4018/IJISSS.2018010105

Seth, M., Goyal, D., & Kiran, R. (2017). Diminution of Impediments in Implementation of Supply Chain Management Information System for Enhancing its Effectiveness in Indian Automobile Industry. *Journal of Global Information Management, 25*(3), 1–20. DOI: 10.4018/JGIM.2017070101

Seyal, A. H., & Rahman, M. N. (2017). Investigating Impact of Inter-Organizational Factors in Measuring ERP Systems Success: Bruneian Perspectives. In Tavana, M. (Ed.), *Enterprise Information Systems and the Digitalization of Business Functions* (pp. 178–204). Hershey, PA: IGI Global. DOI: 10.4018/978-1-5225-2382-6.ch008

Shaqrah, A. A. (2018). Analyzing Business Intelligence Systems Based on 7s Model of McKinsey. *International Journal of Business Intelligence Research, 9*(1), 53–63. DOI: 10.4018/IJBIR.2018010104

Sharma, A. J. (2017). Enhancing Sustainability through Experiential Learning in Management Education. In Baporikar, N. (Ed.), *Management Education for Global Leadership* (pp. 256–274). Hershey, PA: IGI Global. DOI: 10.4018/978-1-5225-1013-0.ch013

Shetty, K. P. (2017). Responsible Global Leadership: Ethical Challenges in Management Education. In Baporikar, N. (Ed.), *Innovation and Shifting Perspectives in Management Education* (pp. 194–223). Hershey, PA: IGI Global. DOI: 10.4018/978-1-5225-1019-2.ch009

Sinthupundaja, J., & Kohda, Y. (2017). Effects of Corporate Social Responsibility and Creating Shared Value on Sustainability. *International Journal of Sustainable Entrepreneurship and Corporate Social Responsibility, 2*(1), 27–38. DOI: 10.4018/IJSECSR.2017010103

Škarica, I., & Hrgović, A. V. (2018). Implementation of Total Quality Management Principles in Public Health Institutes in the Republic of Croatia. *International Journal of Productivity Management and Assessment Technologies, 6*(1), 1–16. DOI: 10.4018/IJPMAT.2018010101

Skokic, V. (2021). How Small Hotel Owners Practice Resilience: Longitudinal Study Among Small Family Hotels in Croatia. In Zehrer, A., Glowka, G., Schwaiger, K., & Ranacher-Lackner, V. (Eds.), *Resiliency Models and Addressing Future Risks for Family Firms in the Tourism Industry* (pp. 50–73). IGI Global. DOI: 10.4018/978-1-7998-7352-5.ch003

Smuts, H., Kotzé, P., Van der Merwe, A., & Loock, M. (2017). Framework for Managing Shared Knowledge in an Information Systems Outsourcing Context. *International Journal of Knowledge Management, 13*(4), 1–30. DOI: 10.4018/IJKM.2017100101

Sousa, M. J., Cruz, R., Dias, I., & Caracol, C. (2017). Information Management Systems in the Supply Chain. In Jamil, G., Soares, A., & Pessoa, C. (Eds.), *Handbook of Research on Information Management for Effective Logistics and Supply Chains* (pp. 469–485). Hershey, PA: IGI Global. DOI: 10.4018/978-1-5225-0973-8.ch025

Spremic, M., Turulja, L., & Bajgoric, N. (2018). Two Approaches in Assessing Business Continuity Management Attitudes in the Organizational Context. In Bajgoric, N. (Ed.), *Always-On Enterprise Information Systems for Modern Organizations* (pp. 159–183). Hershey, PA: IGI Global. DOI: 10.4018/978-1-5225-3704-5.ch008

Steenkamp, A. L. (2018). Some Insights in Computer Science and Information Technology. In *Examining the Changing Role of Supervision in Doctoral Research Projects: Emerging Research and Opportunities* (pp. 113–133). Hershey, PA: IGI Global. DOI: 10.4018/978-1-5225-2610-0.ch005

Stipanović, C., Rudan, E., & Zubović, V. (2022). Reaching the New Tourist Through Creativity: Sustainable Development Challenges in Croatian Coastal Towns. In Valeri, M. (Ed.), *New Governance and Management in Touristic Destinations* (pp. 231–245). IGI Global. https://doi.org/10.4018/978-1-6684-3889-3.ch014

Tabach, A., & Croteau, A. (2017). Configurations of Information Technology Governance Practices and Business Unit Performance. *International Journal of IT/Business Alignment and Governance, 8*(2), 1–27. DOI: 10.4018/IJITBAG.2017070101

Talaue, G. M., & Iqbal, T. (2017). Assessment of e-Business Mode of Selected Private Universities in the Philippines and Pakistan. *International Journal of Online Marketing, 7*(4), 63–77. DOI: 10.4018/IJOM.2017100105

Tam, G. C. (2017). Project Manager Sustainability Competence. In *Managerial Strategies and Green Solutions for Project Sustainability* (pp. 178–207). Hershey, PA: IGI Global. DOI: 10.4018/978-1-5225-2371-0.ch008

Tambo, T. (2018). Fashion Retail Innovation: About Context, Antecedents, and Outcome in Technological Change Projects. In I. Management Association (Ed.), *Fashion and Textiles: Breakthroughs in Research and Practice* (pp. 233-260). Hershey, PA: IGI Global. https://doi.org/DOI: 10.4018/978-1-5225-3432-7.ch010

Tantau, A. D., & Frăţilă, L. C. (2018). Information and Management System for Renewable Energy Business. In *Entrepreneurship and Business Development in the Renewable Energy Sector* (pp. 200–244). Hershey, PA: IGI Global. DOI: 10.4018/978-1-5225-3625-3.ch006

Teixeira, N., Pardal, P. N., & Rafael, B. G. (2018). Internationalization, Financial Performance, and Organizational Challenges: A Success Case in Portugal. In Carvalho, L. (Ed.), *Handbook of Research on Entrepreneurial Ecosystems and Social Dynamics in a Globalized World* (pp. 379–423). Hershey, PA: IGI Global. DOI: 10.4018/978-1-5225-3525-6.ch017

Teixeira, P., Teixeira, L., Eusébio, C., Silva, S., & Teixeira, A. (2021). The Impact of ICTs on Accessible Tourism: Evidence Based on a Systematic Literature Review. In Eusébio, C., Teixeira, L., & Carneiro, M. (Eds.), *ICT Tools and Applications for Accessible Tourism* (pp. 1–25). IGI Global. DOI: 10.4018/978-1-7998-6428-8.ch001

Trad, A., & Kalpić, D. (2018). The Business Transformation Framework, Agile Project and Change Management. In M. Khosrow-Pour, D.B.A. (Ed.), *Encyclopedia of Information Science and Technology, Fourth Edition* (pp. 620-635). Hershey, PA: IGI Global. https://doi.org/DOI: 10.4018/978-1-5225-2255-3.ch054

Trad, A., & Kalpić, D. (2018). The Business Transformation and Enterprise Architecture Framework: The Financial Engineering E-Risk Management and E-Law Integration. In Sergi, B., Fidanoski, F., Ziolo, M., & Naumovski, V. (Eds.), *Regaining Global Stability After the Financial Crisis* (pp. 46–65). Hershey, PA: IGI Global. DOI: 10.4018/978-1-5225-4026-7.ch003

Trengereid, V. (2022). Conditions of Network Engagement: The Quest for a Common Good. In R. Augusto Costa, F. Brandão, Z. Breda, & C. Costa (Eds.), *Planning and Managing the Experience Economy in Tourism* (pp. 69-84). IGI Global. https://doi.org/10.4018/978-1-7998-8775-1.ch004

Turulja, L., & Bajgoric, N. (2018). Business Continuity and Information Systems: A Systematic Literature Review. In Bajgoric, N. (Ed.), *Always-On Enterprise Information Systems for Modern Organizations* (pp. 60–87). Hershey, PA: IGI Global. DOI: 10.4018/978-1-5225-3704-5.ch004

Vargas-Hernández, J. G. (2017). Professional Integrity in Business Management Education. In Baporikar, N. (Ed.), *Management Education for Global Leadership* (pp. 70–89). Hershey, PA: IGI Global. DOI: 10.4018/978-1-5225-1013-0.ch004

Varnacı Uzun, F. (2021). The Destination Preferences of Foreign Tourists During the COVID-19 Pandemic and Attitudes Towards: Marmaris, Turkey. In Demir, M., Dalgıç, A., & Ergen, F. (Eds.), *Handbook of Research on the Impacts and Implications of COVID-19 on the Tourism Industry* (pp. 285–306). IGI Global. https://doi.org/10.4018/978-1-7998-8231-2.ch014

Vasista, T. G., & AlAbdullatif, A. M. (2017). Role of Electronic Customer Relationship Management in Demand Chain Management: A Predictive Analytic Approach. *International Journal of Information Systems and Supply Chain Management, 10*(1), 53–67. DOI: 10.4018/IJISSCM.2017010104

Vieru, D., & Bourdeau, S. (2017). Survival in the Digital Era: A Digital Competence-Based Multi-Case Study in the Canadian SME Clothing Industry. *International Journal of Social and Organizational Dynamics in IT, 6*(1), 17–34. DOI: 10.4018/IJSODIT.2017010102

Vijayan, G., & Kamarulzaman, N. H. (2017). An Introduction to Sustainable Supply Chain Management and Business Implications. In Khan, M., Hussain, M., & Ajmal, M. (Eds.), *Green Supply Chain Management for Sustainable Business Practice* (pp. 27–50). Hershey, PA: IGI Global. DOI: 10.4018/978-1-5225-0635-5.ch002

Vlachvei, A., & Notta, O. (2017). Firm Competitiveness: Theories, Evidence, and Measurement. In Vlachvei, A., Notta, O., Karantininis, K., & Tsounis, N. (Eds.), *Factors Affecting Firm Competitiveness and Performance in the Modern Business World* (pp. 1–42). Hershey, PA: IGI Global. DOI: 10.4018/978-1-5225-0843-4.ch001

Wang, C., Schofield, M., Li, X., & Ou, X. (2017). Do Chinese Students in Public and Private Higher Education Institutes Perform at Different Level in One of the Leadership Skills: Critical Thinking?: An Exploratory Comparison. In Wang, V. (Ed.), *Encyclopedia of Strategic Leadership and Management* (pp. 160–181). Hershey, PA: IGI Global. DOI: 10.4018/978-1-5225-1049-9.ch013

Wang, J. (2017). Multi-Agent based Production Management Decision System Modelling for the Textile Enterprise. *Journal of Global Information Management, 25*(4), 1–15. DOI: 10.4018/JGIM.2017100101

Wiedemann, A., & Gewald, H. (2017). Examining Cross-Domain Alignment: The Correlation of Business Strategy, IT Management, and IT Business Value. *International Journal of IT/Business Alignment and Governance, 8*(1), 17–31. DOI: 10.4018/IJITBAG.2017010102

Wolf, R., & Thiel, M. (2018). Advancing Global Business Ethics in China: Reducing Poverty Through Human and Social Welfare. In Hipsher, S. (Ed.), *Examining the Private Sector's Role in Wealth Creation and Poverty Reduction* (pp. 67–84). Hershey, PA: IGI Global. DOI: 10.4018/978-1-5225-3117-3.ch004

Yablonsky, S. (2018). Innovation Platforms: Data and Analytics Platforms. In *Multi-Sided Platforms (MSPs) and Sharing Strategies in the Digital Economy: Emerging Research and Opportunities* (pp. 72–95). Hershey, PA: IGI Global. DOI: 10.4018/978-1-5225-5457-8.ch003

Yaşar, B. (2021). The Impact of COVID-19 on Volatility of Tourism Stocks: Evidence From BIST Tourism Index. In Demir, M., Dalgıç, A., & Ergen, F. (Eds.), *Handbook of Research on the Impacts and Implications of COVID-19 on the Tourism Industry* (pp. 23–44). IGI Global. https://doi.org/10.4018/978-1-7998-8231-2.ch002

Yusoff, A., Ahmad, N. H., & Halim, H. A. (2017). Agropreneurship among Gen Y in Malaysia: The Role of Academic Institutions. In Ahmad, N., Ramayah, T., Halim, H., & Rahman, S. (Eds.), *Handbook of Research on Small and Medium Enterprises in Developing Countries* (pp. 23–47). Hershey, PA: IGI Global. DOI: 10.4018/978-1-5225-2165-5.ch002

Zacher, D., & Pechlaner, H. (2021). Resilience as an Opportunity Approach: Challenges and Perspectives for Private Sector Participation on a Community Level. In Zehrer, A., Glowka, G., Schwaiger, K., & Ranacher-Lackner, V. (Eds.), *Resiliency Models and Addressing Future Risks for Family Firms in the Tourism Industry* (pp. 75–102). IGI Global. https://doi.org/10.4018/978-1-7998-7352-5.ch004

Zanin, F., Comuzzi, E., & Costantini, A. (2018). The Effect of Business Strategy and Stock Market Listing on the Use of Risk Assessment Tools. In *Management Control Systems in Complex Settings: Emerging Research and Opportunities* (pp. 145–168). Hershey, PA: IGI Global. DOI: 10.4018/978-1-5225-3987-2.ch007

Zgheib, P. W. (2017). Corporate Innovation and Intrapreneurship in the Middle East. In Zgheib, P. (Ed.), *Entrepreneurship and Business Innovation in the Middle East* (pp. 37–56). Hershey, PA: IGI Global. DOI: 10.4018/978-1-5225-2066-5.ch003

About the Contributors

Parvez Alam Khan is a Lecturer at University Technology PETRONAS with four years of industry and five years of research experience He completed his PhD in Management from University Technology PETRONAS, Malaysia. His research has been featured in leading journals, including Business Strategy and the Environment, Cogent Business & Management, Environmental Science and Pollution Research, and Journal of Risk and Financial Management. Dr Parvez also edited a book with IGI Global and Taylors and Francis. His research interests include sustainable innovation, green innovation, social innovation, sustainable development goals (SDGs), and corporate governance. He teaches courses on accounting, sustainability, sustainable finance, corporate governance, and strategic management.

Satirenjit Kaur Johl is currently working as Associate Professor at the Universiti Teknologi PETRONAS (UTP), Malaysia. She has been in the academic, research and consultancy field since 1992. She obtained her doctorate degree in business studies for the University Of Nottingham, UK. She supervises master's and PhD students in the areas of entrepreneurship, corporate governance, and strategic management. She received awards from International bodies for best dissertation, awarded by British Aerospace & Loughborough University, UK. She has also received the Hariram Jayaram Special and Gold Award at the 23rd International Invention Innovation & Technology Exhibition

Mohd Salim currently serves as an Assistant Professor at the School of Business, Woxsen University, Hyderabad, India. He brings over 3

years of corporate experience from Wipro Pvt. Ltd., where he worked as a Financial Analyst specializing in Bloomberg's U.S. municipal processes. With a strong academic foundation, Dr. Salim has five years of research experience and two years of teaching experience. He holds a Ph.D. in Commerce from Aligarh Muslim University (AMU), India. His research interests span Entrepreneurship, Emerging Technologies, Blockchain, Climate Change, Sustainable Development, Green Financing, Corporate Governance, and ESG (Environmental, Social, and Governance).

Lawrence Arokiasamy is an Associate Professor of Management and Humanities, at Universiti Teknologi Petronas, Malaysia. He earned his bachelor's degree in Business Administration from the University of Malaya, Malaysia in 1999 and a Master of Science in Human Resource Development from University Putra Malaysia in 2003. Then, he obtained his Ph.D. from University Putra Malaysia in 2011. He involves actively in research encompasses the areas of applied and basic research on academician's career development and cyber entrepreneurship among business students in private higher education. He has more than 65 papers accepted/published in national and international journal articles including those ranked by Thomson Reuters (ISI) (8 articles) and indexed in SCOPUS/ERA (30 articles), conference, or seminar proceedings and international papers. He has appointed as a Penal for MQA Assessor by MQA. He was also awarded the Fundamental Research Grant Scheme (FRGS) from the Ministry of Higher Education (MOHE) Malaysia (2010). He was appointed as a paper reviewer for the World Applied Sciences Journal (Scopus indexed). He has also been appointed as an external examiner for Ph.D. VIVA for selected public and private universities in Malaysia and Oversea. He is on the Editorial Board for the American Research Institute for Policy Development for the Journal of Human Resource Management and Labor Studies.

Nasir Abdul Jalil is currently Senior Lecturer and Program Leader for the Master of Business Analytics (MsBA) at the Department of Business Analytics, Sunway University Business School, Sunway University, Malaysia, and currently teaching Business Statistics, Business Analytics & Information Technology, and Database Systems. Dr. Nasir Abdul Jalil has highly industrial experience in sales and marketing analytics and manages corporate accounts as a sales manager with 18 years of extensive knowledge in customer relations and sales team management and demonstrated a strong client focus coupled with outstanding business acumen. Possesses highly developed analytical and communication skills complemented with excellent negotiation abilities in achieving organizational goals.

***

Mohammad Ammar Ahsan, is pursuing Ph.D. in the field of Banking and Finance, specifically FinTech (Financial Technology) at Department of Commerce from Aligarh Muslim University, Aligarh, India. Mr. Ammar has successfully completed his graduation as Bachelor of Commerce (Honors) and Masters of Business Administration in Financial Management from Aligarh Muslim University, itself. Mr. Ammar is a naive researcher in banking & financial efficiency and green innovation domain. He has published few papers in this domain and many more studies are still under review with various Scopus indexed journals. He has participated and attended several international conferences, workshops and seminars in last couple of years. In addition, Mr. Ammar has more than five years of corporate work experiences in India, with couple of multi-national corporations where he worked as finance and accounts analyst.

Mei Ling Goh is a lecturer at the Faculty of Business, Multimedia University. He holds a master's degree in Industrial Economics from the National University of Malaysia. In addition to his teaching responsibilities, he engages in research, with a focus on consumer behaviour and sustainability-related issues. His research work has been published in several peer-reviewed journals, including Global Business and Management Research, International Journal of Supply Chain Management, International Journal of Industrial Management, Journal of International Business, Economics and Entrepreneurship, and International Journal of Business and Technology Management.

Rajinder Kaur is an Assistant Professor at University School of Business, Chandigarh University, Mohali, Punjab. She has done PhD in

Finance and Accounting from Department of Commerce, Punjabi University, Patiala. She holds MCom and B.com degree. She is UGC NET-JRF qualified in commerce field. Her industry and academic experience extends to 7 years. Her research interest comprises of investment management, volatility in Financial Markets, Derivatives and Event Study. She is author of numerous articles published in national and international journals.

Manjit Kour is working as Professor at University Business School at Chandigarh University. She holds a PhD in Business Management from IK Gujral Punjab Technical University, India. She has a good research record with several research papers published in reputed journals. She is an editorial board member and reviewer of many reputed journals including Scopus and ABDC-indexed journals. Her areas of interest include sustainability, green practices, Fintech, online marketing trends and business ethics.

Ridzuan Masri is currently an Associate Professor in the School of Management and Business. His area of research is in the area of Ethics, Islamic and Contemporary Management and Strategic Management.

Siti Haryani is a principal lecturer in the Faculty of Business, Department of Business graduate studies, Nilai University.

Nur Zulaikha is currently a Lecturer in the School of Management and Business in MILA University

Swati Sharma is working as assistant professor in university school of business, Chandigarh University. She has done master in philosophy in Human resource, master's in business management with dual specialization in human resource management and finance and pursuing PHD in human resource. She has published many research paper, articles and book chapters in renowned journals and books. She has 6 years of core experience as academician in renowned universities and institutes.

Shamaela Tabassum is a research scholar in the Department of Commerce at Aligarh Muslim University (AMU), currently pursuing a

Ph.D. in Human Resource Management (HRM) . In addition to her primary focus on HRM, she has a strong interest in finance and entrepreneurship. Ms. Shamaela has published two research papers in SCOPUS-indexed journals, with several other papers under review. She has been awarded the prestigious Maulana Azad National Fellowship. She is a commerce graduate and also holds an MBA in Financial Management from AMU. Additionally, she has participated in various workshops, seminars, and conferences at both national and international levels. Her active involvement in these events has enabled her to stay updated with the latest developments in her field and network with leading experts and scholars.

Yip Yen Yen obtained her PhD from the School of Management, Universiti Sains Malaysia (USM). She is a member of Malaysian Institute of Accountants (MIA) and as well as CPA Australia. She serves the examiner for professional examination of CTIM (Chartered Tax Institute of Malaysia) since 2019. In 2018, Dr. Yip was appointed as the Deputy Head of Accounting unit for Faculty of Business, MMU Melaka. Currently, she teaches both post-graduate and undergraduate accounting subjects which consist of Accounting for Managers, ICAEW strategic credit paper in Taxation such as Tax Compliance, Business Planning Taxation etc. Dr. Yip was the the paper reviewer of Capital Markets Review. Her research works were published in the scopus-indexed journals. In 2019, her research paper was being selected as the Best Paper in 10th Global Conference on Business and Social Sciences 2019.

Index

www.ingramcontent.com/pod-product-compliance
Lightning Source LLC
LaVergne TN
LVHW081523300926
849161LV00006B/1275